EXPLORING PRACTICAL PHILOSOPHY: FROM ACTION TO VALUES

The broad label 'practical philosophy' brings together such topics as ethics and metaethics as well as philosophy of law, society, art and religion. In practical philosophy, theory of value and action is basic, and woven into our understanding of all practical and ethical reasoning.

New essays from leading international philosophers illustrate that substantial results in the subdisciplines of practical philosophy require insights into its core issues: the nature of actions, persons, values and reasons. This anthology is published in honour of Ingmar Persson on his fiftieth birthday.

Contributors: Roger Crisp; Fred Feldman; Göran Hermerén; Derek Parfit; Wlodek Rabinowicz; Michael Smith; Paul Snowdon; Galen Strawson; Larry S. Temkin; Torbjörn Tännsjö; Michael J. Zimmerman

T0347292

Exploring Practical Philosophy: From Action to Values

Edited by

DAN EGONSSON, JONAS JOSEFSSON,
BJÖRN PETERSSON, AND
TONI RØNNOW-RASMUSSEN
Lund University, Sweden

Routledge
Taylor & Francis Group

LONDON AND NEW YORK

First published 2001 by Ashgate Publishing

Reissued 2018 by Routledge
2 Park Square, Milton Park, Abingdon, Oxon OX14 4RN
711 Third Avenue, New York, NY 10017, USA

Routledge is an imprint of the Taylor & Francis Group, an informa business

Publisher's Note
The publisher has gone to great lengths to ensure the quality of this reprint
but points out that some imperfections in the original copies may be apparent.

Disclaimer
The publisher has made every effort to trace copyright holders and welcomes
correspondence from those they have been unable to contact.

A Library of Congress record exists under LC control number: 2001041271

ISBN 13: 978-1-138-63401-5 (hbk)
ISBN 13: 978-0-415-79155-7 (pbk)
ISBN 13: 978-1-315-21223-4 (ebk)

Contents

Preface

How can philosophy, an activity characterised by a high level of abstraction and generality, be practical? 'Practical philosophy' stems from *praxis* (Greek: action, deed) and is traditionally used to cover all those philosophical aspects of human life that concern acting, individually and socially. Its aim is to understand general truths about human behaviour and the evaluative implications thereof. Practical philosophy includes such basic areas as theory of value and action, topics that are woven into our understanding of practical reasoning and ethics. The nature of values and actions are crucial to theories in philosophy of law, society, art and religion.

This is a festschrift for Ingmar Persson on his fiftieth birthday. Since the early eighties, Ingmar Persson has been an important advocate for practical philosophy. He has published thought-provoking articles on applied ethics in the Scandinavian press, and is known in the international philosophical community for his penetrating contributions to all of the themes in this anthology. As with this selection of essays, Ingmar Persson's own work illustrates that substantial results in the sub-disciplines of practical philosophy require insights into the nature of actions, persons, values and reasons.

Ingmar Persson began his philosophical work with an elaborate analysis of individual reasons for acting in *Reasons and Reason-governed Actions*. It is therefore natural to open this collection of essays with Paul Snowdon's discussion of action-theoretical concepts. Derek Parfit examines the connection between some action-theoretical concepts and individual practical rationality by forcefully criticising desire-based views of practical reason. Personal identity is a central concept in both Fred Feldman's contribution on the status of dead people, and Roger Crisp's on a potential identity problem raised by genetic therapy. In 'Hume on Himself', Galen Strawson argues that David Hume is less ontologically ungenerous about subjects of experience than many have thought, and pairs this exegetical point with a defence of continuous, non-compound and short-lived human selves. In Larry S. Temkin's paper, practical reasoning is discussed in the light of three common decision-theoretical assumptions. He shows that they may be hard to uphold coherently.

With Michael Smith's essay, focus is turned from individual rationality to the basis of moral commitments. Smith proceeds from Ingmar Persson's criticism of Richard Hare's role reversal argument for utilitarianism, and develops an analogous criticism of a closely related popular argument for rational altruism. Michael J. Zimmerman discusses which entities can be bearers of value. He gives a straight defence of states as the proper value-bearers and, as a consequence, also questions the distinction between 'final' and 'intrinsic' value. The problems dealt with by Wlodek Rabinowicz range from decision theory and moral philosophy to political philosophy. He shows that the so-called priority view must allow for the possibility that a prospect may be better for everyone involved without being better overall. 'Virtue Ethics' by Torbjörn Tännsjö is a refutation of a classical and recently revived position in normative ethics.

The title of the concluding paper alludes to Ingmar Persson's article 'Sensational Beauty'. Göran Hermerén's 'Fractal and Fragile Beauty' questions the idea that fractal theory enhances our understanding of the nature and value of art.

The editors would like first and foremost to thank the authors for generous co-operation. Lena Halldenius and Caj Strandberg kindly helped with proofreading. Sarah Lloyd at Ashgate Publishing gave her support to the project from our first contact and has been very helpful. Dennis Brice efficiently checked the language in the contributions from Sweden. Thanks also to Johan Laserna for the type-setting. The book is published with financial support from Stiftelsen Erik & Gurli Hultengrens fond för filosofi, Anders Karitz stiftelse and Fornanderska stiftelsen.

All four editors are deeply indebted to Ingmar Persson for enjoyable debates and guidance in our own philosophical efforts. This collection confirms what we strongly suspected – that many of the philosophers we most admire share our respect for Ingmar. We all hope you will enjoy reading this book Ingmar!

Lund 2001

Dan, Jonas, Björn and Toni

Acting, Trying and Rewiring

Paul Snowdon

The aim of this paper is to formulate, and give a partial criticism of, one line of support for a certain philosophical theory of bodily action (that might be called the Trying Theory) and in the course of these criticisms to outline an interesting type of bodily action (rewiring cases) reflection upon which may reveal something about action. Neither task gets much beyond the preliminary stages.[1]

1. Introduction

Philosophers who write about what is standardly called 'action' tend to assume that we have a concept of action that picks out, or applies to, a distinctive, but varied, class of events, occurrences or happenings. An initial fix on what is meant here by action can be achieved by citing examples of what, supposedly, are clearly *not* actions – for example, a fire burning, your heart beating, your fainting – and, in contrast, what supposedly are clearly actions – for example, normal cases of playing the piano, scratching an itch, raising your arm or speaking. It is further natural to assume that creatures that share the capacity to perform such actions share an important, special and fundamental property. We can mark this by saying that they are agents and they share the capacity for agency. I think that these are reasonable assumptions, and they constitute part of the framework of the present paper. It is not, however, assumed here that the English expression 'action' normally or always is restricted in its application to events of this type. It is also certainly not assumed that agency is such a special phenomenon that it defies a naturalistic explanation. One task, then, for philosophy is to analyse this general concept. But philosophers can also advance theories about the phenomenon that the concept of action applies to that go beyond what conceptual analysis reveals. They can advance general and substantial theories of action in a way that philosophers have advanced general and substantial theories of perception. The topic of the present paper is a particular philosophical theory of bodily action, or at least, it amounts to a part of a philosophical theory of bodily action (see section 5, comment (1)). In discussing it I shall leave undecided whether the theory is to be understood as a suggested conceptual analysis or whether it purports to go beyond purely conceptual analysis. I shall, basically, attempt to determine whether it applies to all possible cases that I am inclined to count as bodily actions, relying on what seems to me reasonable and coherent judgements about possible cases of action.

If something needed to be said about the general notion of *action*, a little also needs to be said about the notion of *bodily* actions. It might be suggested that bodily actions are actions the performance of which require the agent's body to be in some condition. On this understanding it is probable that all human actions whatsoever are bodily. If, as a rather general and fairly uncontentious physicalism says, there is no more to an agent than his or her body, then anything that an agent does will require his or her body to be in certain conditions. So, if the notion of bodily action is intended to pick out a sub-class of actions, it is better to say: an action description D picks out a bodily action if it is *a priori* that the application of D to an agent entails that the agent's body is in some condition. This criterion is fulfilled by such descriptions as 'raising one's arm' and 'winking', but not by (1) action descriptions which might be described as mental, such as imagining being in Lund, and not by (2) action descriptions which capture what the agent has done in terms of consequences or upshots outside the body, such as 'opening the door' and 'amusing the audience'. This definition may be somewhat rough at the edges, but it allows us to fix the subject matter of the present discussion. Can we say anything informative about what is involved in performing such bodily actions?

2. Some potted recent history

The traditional philosophical conception of bodily actions is, of course, that they involve a psychological or mental element that causes the required bodily movement or condition. The psychological element was supposed to be a volition, by which was meant, I take it, a conscious envisaging, with a distinctive volitional quality of what was to happen (or some aspect of it). Proponents of this picture disagreed over the precise content of the envisaging (was it the action itself or the bodily movement?) and also over the status of the volitional episode (was it an exercise of agency itself or not?). The theory also incorporates a distinctive explanation for the knowledge that agents have of their own attempted performances. It was supposed that the agent knows what he or she is aiming at by attending to, and reading it off from, the content of the volition. This volitional theory was severely criticised in early post-war philosophy of mind, at some length by Ryle, and also by Wittgenstein and others, and under their influence it ceased to be accepted.[2]

The next phase in post-war philosophy of action consisted of attempts to analyse action-related notions, such as intention or acting for a reason, without employing the notion of causal links within the body, a notion which was, of course, central to the abhorred volitional theory. This general constraint was taken to be one endorsed by Wittgenstein. Pursuing the philosophy of action subject to this constraint was always something of a challenge (though, I do not mean by this that it was mistaken), and in the early 1960s, under the influence particularly of Davidson (and others), but also as part of the quite general reappearance of the notion of causation in analyses in the philosophy of mind, causal links were redeployed in the analysis of action, but not at exactly the point it occupied in the traditional theories. The causal relata, according to the new approach, were, rather, on the one side, those psychological states which were taken to constitute reasons for an agent to perform an act (normally thought of as a desire plus a belief), and, on the other side, sometimes the action, or, alternatively, sometimes the bodily movement. These were not clearly distinguished. There were, of course, disagreements amongst those who work within this framework, over, for example, how intentions fit into the picture. However, one distinctive feature of this model is that what reasons, and perhaps intentions, cause is not a further psychologically characterisable occurrence which is an element in, or the start of, the action and which itself causes the bodily movement, but rather the movement itself. We might put it this way: this approach (in contrast to the volitional one) does not think that the action of raising one's arm is anything other than the arm's movement. There is a second possible contrast. The volitional theory standardly views the action as, at least, starting with the volition. Now, the volition is simply a distinctive mental occurrence, and there is no obvious reason to suppose that such an occurrence must arise from any particular psychological antecedents. This means that the volitional theory need not be committed to the claim that actions must be done for a reason. In contrast, according to the standard Davidsonian framework, if a movement qualifies as an action, it must arise from a complex psychological state which amount to a *reason* for performing it. This implies that any action must be performed for a reason, and it is not at all clear that this implication should be accepted. However, in favour of the Davidsonian framework is first that it satisfies the sense that a significant role must be played by internal causation in the account of bodily action, and second, that it accords with the criticisms of volitions advanced by Ryle and Wittgenstein.

In the middle of the 1970s, though, a theory of bodily action emerged which has a similar structure to the traditional theory of bodily action, but which differs from it in its characterisation of the initiating psychological or mental element. According to the new theory the psychological element is best described as a *trying*. It claims that, in bodily action, the required bodily movement or condition is caused by a trying (or a striving) on the part of the agent. This theory abandons the conception of the psychological element in bodily action as a conscious envisaging with a distinctive subjective quality and with it the linked epistemology of first-person action knowledge. How one is aware of one's tryings remains to be explained. Well known proponents of this theory are Brian O'Shaughnessy, Jennifer Hornsby, and Colin McGinn.[3]

3. The Trying Theory

I want, in this paper to expound and explore the theory by concentrating on some elements in Jennifer Hornsby's presentation of it in her book *Actions*. Although these may not represent her current views they remain very interesting. One statement she gives of the theory is this:

> Is there any type of event instances of which can be shown to occur before muscles contract, and instances of which can be shown to be actions?
>
> I shall answer these questions 'Yes'... Every action is an event of trying or attempting to act, and every attempt that is an action precedes and causes a contraction, of muscles and a movement of the body.[4]

Hornsby is claiming that whenever an agent performs a bodily action, for example moves his or her arm, there is a bodily movement, the arm's rising, preceded and caused by a trying of the agent. This thesis is what I shall call the *Trying Theory*. I want to separate this claim from some others with which Hornsby associates it and also to some extent, to limit the pretensions of the theory. Before doing that, however, I shall sketch the line of thought that is meant to support this claim. There are, currently, two main lines of support for it, one offered by Hornsby, the other by O'Shaughnessy. This paper is concerned with that proposed by Hornsby. The basic difference between the arguments is that the present argument rests on the claim, derived from Davidson, that any action must be intentional under a description, whereas O'Shaughnessy's argument does not rest on this claim, which O'Shaughnessy rejects.[5]

4. Hornsby's argument

In outline, the argument for the theory relies on two premises. The first premise is this:

(1) whenever anyone performs a bodily action he or she can be described as trying to do something.

I call this the Universality of Trying claim (UT). Note that UT merely claims that there is a trying whenever there is a bodily action. It does not say anything else about the relation of the action and the trying, nor about the relation of the trying and the bodily movement. It does not claim that the trying is prior to the movement, or that they are causally related. Despite not claiming too much, UT has not been accepted by everyone. The most famous opponent is usually taken to be Wittgenstein. He says: 'when I raise my arm I do not usually try to raise it.' He adds: 'At all costs I will get to that house'. But if there is no difficulty about it – can I try at all costs to get to the house?'[6] It should perhaps be pointed out that Wittgenstein does not literally deny UT, for UT does not claim that for any bodily action that an agent performs he or she will try to do that sort of action, which is, at most, what Wittgenstein denies. However, I do think that Wittgenstein's remark is very much against the spirit of UT, and that it is right to take him as an opponent.

The second premise characterises the relation between trying and movement in cases where an action involves trying and movement. It claims this:

(2) in cases (of bodily action) where there is a trying and a movement, the trying precedes and causes the bodily movement.

This is perhaps in need of a better statement, but for the moment I shall leave it as it stands. I call it the Causal Claim (CC).

If both UT and CC are true then it seems to follow that the Trying Theory is correct.

The strategy that I wish to explore in this paper is, first, to query the ground offered for UT, thereby leaving the Trying Theory unsupported, and, second, to argue, by counter example, that UT is actually false, which implies the falsity of the Trying Theory. What then are the reasons for accepting UT and CC? The argument for UT is both illuminating and powerful. It relies on two ideas. The first is something like Davidson's elucidation of action; Davidson's slogan is that an event is an action by an agent if it is intentional under a description. The heart of the proposal is that where someone performs an action he or she does something intentionally.[7] This claim links the notion of an action with that of intention. The second idea is that where one does something intentionally one can be described as trying to do that thing. The heart of this proposal is that intentional action and trying are linked. The ground for this is that it is intuitively plausible to describe someone who is intentionally doing something as trying to do it. The recognition that they are intentionally doing it just *seems* linked with the appropriateness of speaking of trying. Thus, if I see someone who is talking to another person in what seems to be an insulting manner, I can ask: is he trying to insult him/her? And it seems that the answer must be 'yes' if I learn that he is intentionally insulting him/her. Finally, it is added that the opposition to supposing the agent is trying derives, most likely, from mistakenly thinking that something like a doubt or denial about success which marks the occasions when we tend to *speak* of trying are conditions for the *truth* of talking about trying.

The ingenious argument for CC derives from what we should say of unexpected failure. Suppose you are paralysed in your arm, but do not realise it. You are asked to raise your arm and, expecting no difficulty, you try, and are surprised at your failure. Now this trying is independent of an outer bodily movement, since you are paralysed, and yet it must occur somewhere – presumably inside the body. However, this trying was not special in nature – the agent after all, anticipated no difficulty, and so, as it is said, did not try in a special way; thus, the trying present on this occasion is, surely, similarly located to the trying that is present in cases of normal success. So, there the trying is also inner, and independent of bodily movement. But if the trying is inner and a component in moving your arm, there seems no alternative to supposing that it precedes and causes the arm movement.

5. Some initial comments

I wish to begin with a series of comments on the Trying Theory, to clarify its nature and scope, before criticising one aspect of the argument for it.

(1) The Trying Theory belongs to that general class of philosophical theories of psychological states or occurrences that can be classified as decompositional. Such theories take an occurrence that does not present itself to the subject as complex, and decomposes it into a sequence of causally linked stages. Another example of a decompositional theory would be causal theories of perception (or vision). Now, about such theories it is important to be clear what it is they are giving a theory of. In the case of perception, for example, the decompostion is, usually, into experience plus a distinct causal origin. It does not, therefore, offer a theory of experience, taking that notion for granted but rather, recommends thinking of perception as a sort of distinctively caused experience. Similarly, the Trying Theory, at least as it stands, is not a theory of the nature of action, since it simply thinks of tryings as actions. It is rather a decomposition of bodily action into a distinct (inner) action of trying along with a suitable effect. It gives no general account of action that is of that very general type of occurrence. Rather, it describes what we do and what happens when we physically act. It would therefore be a misnomer to call it a theory of action.

(2) As Hornsby states and develops the theory, she embeds it in a Davidsonian theory of the nature of actions as events, and, in particular, his view that when an agent performs an action A by performing an action B, action A is identical to

action B. This thesis is sometimes called ASIT – Action Sequence Identity Thesis. This leads Hornsby to say, in the light of the conclusion that all bodily movements involve tryings (which are actions) that all bodily actions are identical with tryings, and must share the properties of tryings. I prefer to detach, as far as possible, issues in the theory of action from issues in the metaphysics of events. This is because the metaphysics of events is so obscure that extreme caution must be exercised in discussing it. We can, I believe, register whatever level of correctness the Trying Theory has within any account of action identity. Although I propose to detach the Trying Theory from ASIT, I do not mean, thereby, to put into the Trying Theory anything *inconsistent* with ASIT.

(3) In the statement that I quoted earlier from Hornsby's expression of the theory, it said that 'every attempt that is an action precedes and causes a contraction$_1$ of muscles.' This is, however, not a statement we should accept if it is intended as a necessary truth about bodily action. There surely *could* be non-muscular intermediaries between, say, nerve impulses and surface movements; muscles are simply a certain sort of animal tissue, and there could be prosthetic devices that play their role. If there were, they would *enable* people to perform actions. The reference to muscle contractions in the general characterisation of bodily action is mistaken.

(4) My next comment concerns what, in Hornsby's *Actions*, was one of the main conclusions she drew from the Trying Theory. Her view is that tryings are *internal* events, that is, internal to the body. Since she accepts that the actions we do by trying are identical with the tryings (in accordance with ASIT) *and* that all bodily actions are done by trying (the Trying Theory) she concludes that all bodily actions are 'internal events'. She also says 'actions themselves lie within the body'.

Now, this thesis has been felt to be paradoxical; but we can ask whether it follows from Hornsby's arguments. I want to suggest that it may not follow. We can distinguish two interpretations of the words 'internal' and 'lying within the body'. The first is 'completely internal' – meaning – it is within the body and does not reach the surface. The second is 'partially internal' – meaning – something which starts internally, and does not *have to* reach the surface. Now, it seems to me that the reasons for CC gives a reason to hold that some tryings start and remain inside the body, and that successful tryings start in the same way, that is, they are at least partially internal. However, no particular reason is given in the discussion for placing a limit on the outward extent of the trying. Why cannot we treat the movement outwards of successful action *as* the movement outwards of the trying? All I am suggesting is that no reason is given to deny this. Further, it is not a totally inappropriate way of speaking. It would treat the trying as akin to a message; the message has been sent, down the wire, and we can trace its journey. The attempt is like the message.

This does not end discussion of the implications of the Trying Theory – but the stress placed by Hornsby on the internal nature of trying may not be obligatory.[8]

(5) The strategy I shall adopt is to query UT and I shall not reject CC. This is because I find the argument for CC plausible. However, it has to be acknowledged that it is not obvious that CC is correct. The reason is that the argument for CC is structurally parallel to a much disputed argument in the philosophy of perception, about which it is, I think, reasonable to be suspicious. The common structure of argument is as follows. There are two premises, the first of which claims that the psychological state in question has a certain property in a special case, and the second of which claims that it is reasonable to 'spread' the characterisation across the whole psychological class. The particularly questionable aspect to such arguments is the spreading step. Why must we treat all the cases of the state alike? Those opposed to this uniform treatment in the case of experience have offered what are known as disjunctive theories as an alternative. It is not obvious that a disjunctive theory of trying cannot be devised.

On this issue I wish to make three observations. (1) The evidence assembled to support CC does not entail that it is true. We can allow that all intentional action involves trying, and that some tryings are internal, and that when they are internal the agent is not, as one might say, aiming to try in a special way, but hold that the tryings in successful action are not internal. Despite the agent not thinking anything is special about the trying when it is internal maybe in fact there is. (2) At this point, though, something that was said in section 1 is relevant. We need not understand CC as an *a priori* conceptual truth, but as simply a truth. We can therefore add to the assembled evidence the undeniable fact that bodily movement does arise from muscle contractions, which themselves arise from internally generated nerve impulses, all of which seem to be amongst the things that agents can be credited with doing. It then becomes much harder to deny that in all cases of bodily action there are tryings by the agent which precede the final bodily movement. Bodily actions in fact always seem to involve actional achievements before the movement on the surface. (3) If you accept CC then it is natural to think of ordinary agents as consisting, in part, of a central unit in which, in some sense, decisions about actions occur, followed by what should be described as attempts to execute them. There will, then, be a point where execution starts. Now, in actual cases this point is well before the surface movements that eventually result, which is, of course, what leaves room for tryings that precede the movement. But perhaps we can imagine a creature where the first point of execution is the surface bodily change. In such a case, if the creature cannot produce such a surface change it cannot try. If this makes sense it brings out two things. First, in recognising that *we* (i.e., human agents) can try without a bodily movement occurring, we are relying on what is broadly an empirical discovery. Second, the Trying Theory should probably not be counted as a conceptual truth.

6. Criticisms of UT, the reliance on Davidson

The argument for UT that Hornsby advances rests on something like Davidson's characterisation of action; actions are events which are intentional under a description.[9] What does this famous slogan commit Davidson to? The natural way to understand it is this: agent A has performed an action if and only if there is some description, D, which applies to a bodily movement of A's body, and which can figure in a true sentence of the form: A intentionally D'ed.

Now the central question is whether Davidson's elucidation represents a necessary condition for action; for if it is not then the reason for linking action to trying, via the link between intentionally doing something and trying, would lapse. However, I want first to raise a question about the sufficiency of Davidson's account.

Davidson's theory is *close* to saying that if there is an intentional so and so-ing by A then there is an action by A. But this is questionable. There can be intentional *refrainings*. I can see a fight and quite deliberately and intentionally refrain from intervening. Refraining from intervening and letting something continue are not *actions*: they are, rather, refrainings from action. Another example is this; I am, in a completely relaxed state, rolling down the side of a hill. I see that I shall collide with a Swedish film starlet who is sitting at the bottom. I do not do anything to alter my path and allow the collision to occur. I intentionally allowed the collision with the starlet to occur. How can we *intentionally* or deliberately refrain or allow? It seems to me that when we deliberate about what to do, one option is – do *nothing*. If one endorses that, after deliberation and knowingly, then it can be said one deliberately and intentionally refrains.

Now, if these claims are correct, they may not strictly amount to a counter example to Davidson's account, for it may be that there is no *event*, in Davidson's sense, which is intentional under a description, and hence, his theory is not committed to counting the case one of action. However, the moral is that one must be cautious about thinking that the idea of a description's intentionally applying to oneself captures the essence of *action*.

There are, however, two other arguments which I wish to present in criticism of Davidson's account.

The first, which I shall expound in a somewhat brief way, derives from O'Shaughnessy. He claims that there are what he calls sub-intentional bodily actions. They are *actions* which are *not* intentional under any descriptions. The argument for this thesis is by example: there are examples of movements about which it seems to be plausible to say (1) that they are actions of the subject in question, and (2) the agent can be completely unaware that he is doing these things, or things of the sort, and be totally surprised to be *told* they are doing them, and which, therefore, must be counted as not intentional. The example that O'Shaughnessy uses is the fairly constant but slight movements we make with our tongues, touching parts of our mouths, as we, for example, sit and listen to someone speaking.

I find both of O'Shaughnessy's claims about the example plausible, though I do see that it is possible to challenge them. I want to *add* two points, both perhaps equally disputable, which may add some strength to the claim that there are such cases.

If we are inclined to believe in sub-intentional actions, and look at human beings, with a preparedness on our part to employ the concept, it seems to invite *extensive* application. It is a mistake to suppose that it covers only rare and recherche movements. Thus, consider a human being who is giving a talk. His goal is to talk to an audience in a clear and coherent and perhaps persuasive way. He will concentrate on and monitor his performance in relation to that purpose or goal. But such a person will, it seems, be doing all sorts of other things, which have no rational connection with the primary purpose; for example, he might flick his hair, smile slightly, incline this way and that, lightly brush his hand against his knee and so on. These actions (or apparent actions), having *no* link with the goal, are not monitored, are not done with a purpose. If asked to say *what* he is doing the subject would talk of speaking, and would be able to say *why* he was doing that. He would not mention all these other things, and would think of no good *reason* or *purpose* for doing them. It appears, I think, that human beings are constantly doing things – but not intentionally. Sub-intentional actions are very *common*. This provides an explanation why puppets are such unnatural mimics of human beings; their controller can make them do only a few things – and so they do not resemble ordinary ceaselessly active human beings.

There is another consideration, which I call the *Relaxation Argument*. It would seem that the opposite of being active, doing things, is, in normal states of awakeness, being *relaxed*. Thus, if a doctor instructs you to *relax* your arm, you are being asked to *do* nothing with it. Now, this gives us a *clue* as to how active we are in normal circumstances; namely, we hardly ever relax significant parts of our bodies; which is to say, therefore, that we are *doing* things with them. In fact, relaxation takes an *effort*! Since, then, we do *not* count those areas of our bodies to which we are paying no attention and which are not figuring in purposive action at all, as *relaxed*, we must be doing things with them, but sub-intentionally.

Now, I am suggesting that these supplementary remarks strengthen O'Shaughnessy's case for the existence of sub-intentional actions. I am aware that they might be resisted. I want, though, rather than considering possible objections to them, to present a third objection to Davidson's account.

Davidson's slogan requires for action that there is some description of the bodily movement under which it is intentional. This, however, seems to face a problem given the possibility of what might be called *rewiring* cases. We can imagine the following; the afferent nerves that normally control the left arm are redirected to control the right arm. The subject does not know. He is told to raise his left arm; we can assume that he will try to do so, but will find, to his amazement, that his right arm is rising. He is, as it turns out, raising his right arm. He raised it by trying to raise his left arm. It seems clear to me that the agent performed an action of moving his or her arm, but under what description is it intentional? His right arm was raised by him – but that part of his body was not the topic of any intention on his part. Do we then have a movement which was an action but which was not intentional under any description?

We do not, as yet, have a pure counterexample to Davidson, because the right arm movement falls under the description 'arm movement' and perhaps the agent did intentionally move an arm. Now there are two issues raised here. One is a question about when the agent can count as intentionally doing something. The reason why finding a counterexample to Davidson might seem hard is that where the agent tries to do something but succeeds, because of rewiring, in doing something completely unexpected, there will be a description of what they intended (of a vague sort) which the result, in virtue of being a movement of their body, will fall under; perhaps moving the body. And, it might seem that this will mean that in such cases they will intentionally do something that the bodily movement can be described as. However, one may doubt that the mere fact that they intended to do an F and actually did an F means that they F-ed intentionally. The reason is that the F-ing that occurred was so different from the F-ing that was intended, that it was not performed intentionally. Here is an example. I aim to kill Tom by shooting him. I aim the revolver and fire but miss him completely. However, the noise of the gun causes Bill to die of a heart attack. I aimed to kill a man, and did kill a man, but it cannot be said that I killed a man intentionally.

But the second question is whether we can imagine rewiring cases where there is *no* overlap between what was tried and what occurred. For example, maybe the result of the rewiring is that the agent moves his left leg when trying to hold his right arm still. The description 'moving a limb' need not be in common between what is tried and what the agent did. An ever more extreme, and possibly disputable, example, would be this: some new afferent nerve is constructed from the thinking centre to the left arm; so when thinking about action my arm goes up; I do raise my arm, by thinking about action. Isn't then raising my arm something I do but it is not intentional under any description?

It seems to me reasonable to conclude that Davidson's theory which links intentionality and action is probably wrong and that in consequence UT is without support.

7. Trying and intentionally acting

There is a second criticism of the argument for UT. It is assumed, in the argument, that if someone can be described as F-ing intentionally then he or she can
be described as trying to F. This assumption was what linked Davidson's slogan
to trying. This assumption is not, however, true. One counter example is the case
of trying itself. When I try to do something it is, surely, right to say that I intentionally tried. How could it not be true? However, I did not try to try. A second
type of counter example is this: suppose I do something knowing that I am taking
a serious risk of injury. It could be said that I intentionally took a risk, but it
would be odd to claim that I tried to take a risk. These examples indicate that the
link between doing something intentionally and trying to do it is looser than the
argument assumes. However, having registered this criticism I shall not analyse
it further.

8. One response considered

The argument of the previous sections attempted, primarily by criticising Davidson's
account of action, to undermine the support provided for UT. There are two
strategies for responding to this criticism. The first is to defend, in some way,
Davidson's claim. The second would be to argue that there is another link between action and intention, but not exactly the one alleged to hold by Davidson,
which can, however, sustain the argument for UT.

An example of the first sort of response, which I wish to discuss, can be ex-
tracted from section 2.2 of chapter 3 of Jennifer Hornsby's book. It suggests that
we do not really need to consider the counter examples to Davidson's theory
given above. We can concede, or at least leave open, that there is some notion of
agency or action to which the theory does not apply. However, our business as
philosophers of action, is to advance theories about what might be called significant categories. Davidson's condition does define such a category, that of agents
who are acting with purposes and intentions, whose behaviour, therefore, admits
of a distinct type of explanation. So we are entitled to ignore supposed cases of
bodily action where the agent is not intentionally moving his or her body.

On this response I wish to make three comments. (1) Although it is perfectly
legitimate to stipulate that the Trying Theory is to be restricted to intentional
actions, that does not correspond to how the theory is usually and initially presented. The impression is very strongly given that a proposal like Davidson's that
links action and intention is an informative characterisation of the class of events
which fall under the pre-philosophical concept of 'action'. So, I believe that this
response is out of line with the usual conception of the status of this theory.

(2) Even if the stipulation is made, there, of course, remains the quite genuine question as to what can be said about the intuitive and non-Davidsonian concept or notion of action. Part of that question is what relation that notion has to the notion of intention. These are interesting questions, and the present stipulation does not define them out of existence. (3) There is no reason as yet to assume that if we do drop Davidson's account we shall not arrive at an equally, indeed maybe more, theoretically important category.

I am inclined, therefore, to pursue an account of action which does not accept Davidson's analysis.

9. Criticism of UT: counter examples

Let us suppose, then, that UT is unsupported. Are there grounds for rejecting it? I want to offer *four* criticisms of UT.

(1) We already have one type of case which arguably is contrary to UT, namely O'Shaughnessy's sub-intentional actions. As well as seeming correct to say that we do not do those things intentionally it also seems plausible to say that we do not actually *try* to do them. How can we be *trying* to do them if we are completely unaware that we are doing so, and we have no purpose that such attempts further. In fact, in such cases, if I was asked – 'Why are you trying to move your tongue about?' I would say – 'I wasn't trying to'.

It needs to be pointed out that O'Shaughnessy himself does argue that such cases involve trying or striving; and he has some arguments that deserve consideration, but intuitively the conclusion is implausible. So we might hold that sub-intentional actions are performed without trying. We do not do them *by* trying to do them.

(2) I want to offer rewiring cases as counter examples too. Consider this case, which I call the *Incompetent Rewiring case*. A surgeon rewires you. He reconnects the afferent nerves which previously led to your left hand to something else. Unfortunately, he is incompetent and looses track of what he has wired it to. How can he find out? He can say to the subject; 'You've been rewired but I can't say *how*. To find out what I've done, do what you previously did to move your left hand. It won't move your left hand, I can assure you of that, but do *that* and see what is moved.' We might then find that the subject moves his right hand.

Now, how should we describe what the agent is trying? We can argue that the agent cannot really be trying to move his or her left hand when he acts, for he knows that he cannot do so in the way he was acting. Obviously, he is not trying to do something else – since he has no idea what to expect. Why should he be trying to do anything? I think that we should say that he does what he took previously to be the thing to do when trying to move his left hand. However, in this case by doing that (whatever it is) he is not *trying* to do anything: but, of course, he is *doing* something, viz. moving his right hand.

If so, it cannot be said that the essential psychological description of what is involved in initiating bodily movement is a trying. That title, or description, it seems, is conferred on an action, or its initiation, so long as it is embedded within suitable beliefs and purposes the agent has; but it is not essential to what fundamentally the agent initially does.

There is, unfortunately, a mistaken step in this argument. The rewiring case shows, I think, that an agent can perform a bodily action without trying to move his or her body. However, it is not a case of bodily action without trying, for the agent was trying to do that which he previously did when he tried to move his left arm.[10]

A little argument, though, may take us slightly further than the rewiring example itself does. If it is accepted that the agent actually does the same thing when, before the operation, he tries to raise his left hand, and when, after the operation, he tries to do what previously he did when trying to raise his left hand, it has to be accepted that what he did is not essentially one of those tryings rather than the other. It is not essentially any particular sort of trying. But what makes it one of those tryings rather than the other? The answer seems to be that it is determined by what prompted it. Thus, in the original case it was prompted by the aim of raising the left hand, whereas in the post-operative case it was prompted by the aim of doing what had previously been done when raising the left hand. If we assume that the status of what was done as a trying was determined by what prompted it we have to wonder why the self same action could not have occurred unprompted in any way which constitutes it a trying. This is, of course, merely a question, and the rewiring case does not answer it. However, a supporter of UT owes us some substantial reason for thinking that the earliest stages of action cannot occur without those psychological promptings which confer on it its status as a trying. If we are thinking in this causal, genetic way, there seems no clear reason to suppose there cannot be actions without this sort of prompting.

(3) This conclusion can be reinforced by a different and rather more fanciful type of rewiring case. It is natural to think of agency along these lines: something typically engenders a plan or goal in the agent. We can thus say that at t the agent adopts the goal of doing G at t+n. Then, at t+n the agent begins to do something. Let us say that he or she does D. (This will be something inside the body.) Now, in the earlier rewiring cases the causal upshot of D is altered by rewiring. However, it seems that in principle we could reconfigure the brain of the agent so that having formed the plan to do G at t+n what the agent is disposed to do, when the time comes, is D* instead. I am assuming that the causal disposition to do D in pursuit of G-ing is dependent on something in the brain. Alter that without informing the agent and he or she will find themselves doing something quite

different when aiming to do G. I call this a Pre-actional Rewiring Case. Now, let us suppose that previously the agent would have done D* when trying to do H. How should we describe the resulting case? It seems to me that the agent tried to do G by doing that which he or she had previously done when trying to H. This description, which seems natural to me, supports the claim that a doing which is a trying to F counts as such because of the psychological context in which it occurs. What then is to stop the agent from doing the thing in question outside the psychological context which confers upon it the title of a trying to do so and so?

(4) I want to add to this a little reflection that fits and confirms it. We are, surely, not born knowing what we can do. We must learn what our actional capacities are. But how do we do this? It would seem that we must simply do things, noting what they are. But these doings cannot be initiated by *tryings* since what leads to what, is as yet unknown. The primitive exercise of agency on the basis of which we learn these things cannot involve tryings.

10. Conclusion

In the light of these examples we should regard UT as questionable. The description of the initiating stages of bodily actions as *tryings* does not capture their essential psychological nature. Such a description is only appropriate once the occurrence is embedded in *beliefs* (and goals) that are, however, external to the essence of what is done. A proper analysis of trying would articulate what the appropriate beliefs and goals are and I do not wish to attempt that. But pushing this further, we should consider saying that the inner, initiating stages of bodily movements when there are actions do not essentially or basically have psychological or mental descriptions at all. The mistake common to trying theorists and volitionalists is to think they do.[11]

Notes

[1]   About this theory and such examples I have not had the benefit of Ingmar's wisdom. I have, however, had the benefit of it about many other things, and this paper is my tribute to Ingmar for that wisdom and his friendship.

[2]   See Ryle 1949, chapter 3, and Wittgenstein 1953, sections 611–628.

[3]   See O'Shaughnessy 1974, and 1980, esp chapter 9–13, Hornsby 1980, chapter 3, Hornsby 1995, and McGinn 1982.

[4]   Hornsby (1980) p. 33.

[5]   For O'Shaughnessy's argument see O'Shaughnessy 1980, chapter 11.

[6]   Wittgenstein, (1953) *Philosophical Investigations* (London: Blackwell) sections 622 and 623. The answer to Wittgenstein's question in 623 is that one can try at all costs to do

something if there is no difficulty. This is how one would describe the attempt of someone who believed there was a difficulty even if there was not.

[7]   See Davidson 1980 p. 46.

[8]   This comment puts in a rather informal way the point made in Smith 1983.

[9]   See Davidson 1980 p. 46.

[10] I am grateful to Edward Harcourt and Alan Thomas for bringing this point out.

[11] This paper has been delivered to audiences in Canterbury, Oxford and Umeå. I am grateful to Bill Child, Philippa Foot, Edward Harcourt, Jennifer Hornsby, Alan Thomas, Helen Steward, Roland Stout, Peter Strawson and others, for their comments.

References

Davidson, Donald (1980), *Actions and Other Events* (Oxford: Oxford University Press).

Hornsby, Jennifer (1980), *Actions* (London: Routledge & Kegan Paul).

Hornsby, Jennifer (1995), Reasons for Trying, *Journal of Philosophical Research* XX, 525–539.

McGinn, Colin (1982), *The Character of Mind* (Oxford: Oxford University Press).

O'Shaughnessy, Brian (1974), Trying (as the Mental Pineal Gland), *Journal of Philosophy* LXXI, 365–392.

O'Shaughnessy, Brian (1980), *The Will: A Dual Aspect Theory* Vol 2 (Cambridge: Cambridge University Press).

Ryle, Gilbert (1949), *The Concept of Mind* (London: Hutchinson).

Smith, Michael (1983), Actions, Attempts and Internal Events, *Analysis* 43: 142–146.

Wittgenstein, Ludwig (1953), *Philosophical Investigations* (Oxford: Blackwells).

Rationality and Reasons

Derek Parfit

When Ingmar and I discuss metaphysics or morality, our views are seldom far apart. But on the subjects of this paper, rationality and reasons, we deeply disagree. I had intended this paper to include some discussion of Ingmar's views about these subjects. But, when I reread some of the relevant parts of Ingmar's published and unpublished work, it soon became clear that his arguments are much too subtle and wide-ranging for a brief discussion. So I shall say only that I don't yet have what seem to me good answers to some of Ingmar's arguments. He is one of the people whom I would most like to convince. But perhaps, when I try to answer his arguments, he will convince me.

I shall discuss two questions:

> What do we have most reason to want, and do?
> What is it most rational for us to want, and do?

These questions differ in only one way. While reasons are provided by the facts, the rationality of our desires and acts depends instead on our beliefs. When we know the relevant facts, these questions have the same answers. But if we are ignorant, or have false beliefs, it can be rational to want, or do, what we have no reason to want, or do. Thus, if I believe falsely that my hotel is on fire, it may be rational for me to jump into the canal. But I have no reason to jump. I merely think I do. And, if some dangerous treatment would save your life, but you don't know that fact, it would be irrational for you to take this treatment, but that is what you have most reason to do.[1]

These claims are about *normative* reasons. When we have such a reason, and we act for that reason, it becomes our *motivating* or *explanatory* reason. But we can have either kind of reason without having the other. Thus, if I jump into the canal, my motivating reason was provided by my false belief; but I had no normative reason to jump. And, if I failed to notice that the canal was frozen, I had a normative reason not to jump which because it was unknown to me, could not motivate me.

There are many kinds of normative reason, such as reasons for believing, for caring, and for acting. Reasons are provided by facts, such as the fact that someone's finger-prints are on some gun, or that calling an ambulance might save someone's life. If we are asked what reasons are, it is hard to give a helpful answer. Facts give us reasons, we might say, when they count in favour of our having some belief or desire, or acting in some way. But 'counts in favour of' means 'is a reason for'. Like some other fundamental concepts, such as those of *reality*, *necessity*, and *time*, the concept of a reason cannot be explained in other terms.

1

According to *desire-based* theories, practical reasons are all provided by our desires, or aims. According to *value-based* theories, these reasons are provided by facts about what is relevantly good, or worth achieving. This distinction roughly coincides with the distinction that some writers draw between theories that appeal to *internal* or *external* reasons.

Desire-based theories appeal to facts of two kinds. According to theories of *instrumental* rationality, we have a reason to do something just in case

(A) doing this thing might help to fulfil one of our present desires.

According to theories of *deliberative* rationality, we have such a reason just in case

(B) if we knew the relevant facts, and went through some process of deliberation, we would be motivated to do this thing.

Facts are relevant if our knowledge of them might affect our motivation. We are motivated to do something if we are, to some degree, inclined or disposed to do it. (A) and (B) we can call the *motivational facts*.

According to many desire-based theories, when we have some reason for acting, this fact is the same as one or both of the motivational facts. These theories are *reductive*, or naturalist. But desire-based theories could also take non-reductive forms. On such theories, we cannot have some reason for acting unless our act might fulfil one of our desires, or is something that, after informed deliberation, we would be motivated to do. But the fact that we have some reason, though it depends on such a causal or psychological fact, is irreducibly normative.

I believe that we should reject all forms of reductive naturalism. But I shall not try to defend that belief here.[2] I also believe that, even when they take non-reductive forms, desire-based theories are mistaken. On the kind of value-based theory that I accept, no reasons are provided by desires.[3]

Desire-based theories are now the ones that are most widely accepted. In economics and the other social sciences, rationality is often defined in a desire-based way. If so many people believe that *all* reasons are provided by desires, how could it be true that, as value-based theories claim, *no* reasons are so provided? How could all these people be so mistaken?

One answer is that, in most cases, these two kinds of theory partly agree. Even on value-based theories, we usually have some reason to fulfil our desires. That is in part because, in most cases, what we want is in some way worth achieving. But, though these theories agree that we have some reason to fulfil these desires, they make conflicting claims about what these reasons are. On desire-based theories, our reasons to fulfil these desires are provided by these desires. On value-based theories, these reasons are provided, not by the fact that we have these desires, but by the facts that give us reasons to have them. If some aim is worth achieving, we have a reason both to have this aim and to try to achieve it. Since our reason for acting is the same as our reason for having the desire on which we act, this desire is not itself part of this reason. And we would have this reason even if we didn't have this desire.

Even on value-based theories, there are certain other reasons that we *wouldn't* have if we didn't have certain desires. But though these reasons *depend* on our desires, they too are not *provided* by these desires. They are provided by other facts that depend on our having these desires. When we have some desire, for example, that may make it true that this desire's fulfilment would give us pleasure, or that its non-fulfilment would be distressing, or distracting. In such cases, it would be these other facts, and not the fact that we had these desires, that gave us reasons to fulfil them.

Since these theories disagree about what our reasons are for fulfilling our desires, they may also disagree about how strong these reasons are. Thus, on most desire-based theories, the strength of these reasons depends on the strength of our desires. On value-based theories, their strength depends instead on how good, or worth achieving, the fulfilment of our desires would be. Since we often prefer what would be less worth achieving, these theories often disagree about what we have most reason to do, or ought rationally to do.

The deepest disagreement comes, not over our reasons for acting, but over our reasons for having our desires, or aims. If we consider only reasons for acting, desire-based theories may seem to cover most of the truth. But the most important practical reasons are not merely, or mainly, reasons for acting. They are also reasons for having the desires on which we act. These are reasons which desire-based theories cannot recognize, or explain.

Within the group of value-based theories, we have a further choice. There are two views about what it is for something to be good, in the sense that is relevant to choice. On one view, suggested by G.E. Moore, if some thing – such as some event – would have certain natural properties, these give it the non-natural property of being good, and its being good may then give us reasons to want or to try to achieve this thing. On a second view, goodness is not itself a reason-giving property, but is the property of having such properties. Something's being good is the same as its having certain natural properties that would, in certain contexts, give us reasons to want this thing. Scanlon calls this the *buck-passing* view.[4]

When we consider instrumental goodness, this view seems clearly better. Thus some drug is good if it is safe and effective, and it is these properties that give us reasons to prefer this drug to those that are unsafe or ineffective. Our reasons to prefer this drug are not provided by some distinct property of goodness. The same may be true of intrinsic goodness. On a Moorean view, if one of two ordeals would be more painful, that fact would give this ordeal the property of being worse, and its being worse would give us a reason to prefer the other ordeal. On the buck-passing view, this ordeal's being worse is not a separate reason-giving property. It is the property of having some natural reason-giving property – in this case, that of being more painful.

If this second view is true, as I am inclined to believe, value-based theories needn't even use the concepts *good*, *bad*, or *value*. That may seem to undo my distinction between value-based and desire-based theories. But that distinction remains as deep. On desire-based theories, our reasons to try to achieve some aim are provided by our desire to achieve it, and we cannot have non-derivative reasons to have such desires. On value-based theories, we do have such reasons. These reasons are provided by various natural features of the objects of our desires, and it is from these reasons that all other reasons derive their force. That statement of this disagreement makes no use of the concepts *good* or *value*. When some object has such reason-giving features, we can call it good, but that is merely an abbreviation: a way of implying that it has such features.

These remarks can be misunderstood. When I say that value-based theories need not appeal to a non-natural property of goodness, I do not mean that such theories need not appeal to any non-natural properties or truths. Truths about reasons are, I believe, irreducibly normative, and hence non-natural. My point is only that such theories need not include, among these normative truths, truths about what is good or bad.

2

In considering these theories, we can first distinguish two kinds of desire. Our desires are *intrinsic* when we want things for their own sake, *instrumental* when we want them only as a means to something else. The relation between ends and means is most often causal, though it can take other forms. Thus, when a king's second son wanted to become the legitimate heir to his father's throne, his elder brother's death constituted rather than caused his achievement of that aim.

We often have long chains of instrumental desires, but such chains all end with some intrinsic desire. Thus, we may want medical treatment, not for its own sake, but only to restore our health, and we may want that, not for its own sake, but only so that we can finish some great work of art, and we may want that, not for its own sake, but only to achieve posthumous fame. This desire may in turn be instrumental, since we may want such fame only to confound our critics, or to increase the income of our heirs. But, if we want posthumous fame for its own sake, this intrinsic desire would end this particular chain.

Many people have believed that, at the end of all such chains, there is some intrinsic desire for pleasure, or the avoidance of pain. That is clearly false. Of those who hold this view, some confuse it with the view that we always get pleasure from the thought of our desire's fulfilment, or pain from the thought of its non-fulfilment. This view is also, though less obviously, false. And, even if it were true, it would not show that what we really want is such pleasure, or the avoidance of such pain. Thus, if we want posthumous fame, we may get pleasure, while we are alive, from thinking about how later generations will remember us. But that would not show that we want such fame for the sake of the pleasure that its contemplation brings. On the contrary, as Butler argued, such pleasure would be likely to depend on our wanting fame for its own sake. In the same way, to enjoy many games, we must have an independent desire to win.

Besides having intrinsic desires for things other than our own pleasure, we may not even want pleasure for its own sake. Consider some power-hungry businessman or politician, whom we find one afternoon basking in the sun. When we ask for his motive, he replies 'Enjoyment'. Given our knowledge of this man's character, that reply may be baffling. This man never does anything because he enjoys it. He then explains that his doctor warned that, unless he learnt to relax, his health would suffer, thereby hindering his pursuit of wealth and power. Our bafflement disappears. This man wants to enjoy himself, not for its own sake, but only because such enjoyment would have effects that he wants.

Turn now to our reasons for having desires. All desires have *objects*, which are *what* we want. Though I shall talk of our wanting some thing, that thing is usually not an object in the ordinary sense, but some event, process, or state of affairs. Even when we want some ordinary object – such as some book, or bottle of wine – what we want is, more accurately, the state or process of owning, using, consuming, or having some other relation to this thing.

Of our reasons to have some desire, some are provided by facts about this desire's object. These reasons we can call *object-given*. We can have such reasons to want some thing either for its own sake, or for the sake of its effects. If the former, these reasons are intrinsic; if the latter, they are instrumental. If we have such reasons to have some desire, this desire is *supported* by reason, and if we have such reasons *not* to have it, it is *contrary* to reason. Other reasons to want something are provided by facts, not about what we want, but about our *having* this desire. These reasons we can call *state-given*. Such reasons can also be either intrinsic or instrumental.

On value-based theories, these four kinds of reason can be shown as follows:

	intrinsic	*instrumental*
object-given	What we want would be in itself relevantly good, or worth achieving	This thing would have good effects
state-given	Our wanting this thing would be in itself good	Our wanting this thing would have good effects

We might have all four kinds of reason to have the same desire. Thus, if you are suffering, we might have all these reasons to want your suffering to end. What we want would be in itself good, and it may have the good effect of allowing you to enjoy life again. Our wanting your suffering to end may be in itself good, and it may have good effects, such as your being comforted by our sympathy.

Value-based theories, I have said, disagree about what is *relevantly* good, or worth achieving. One value-based theory is that form of consequentialism that takes moral reasons to be rationally overriding. On this view, what we have most reason to want is that history go in the way that would be, impartially, best. According to most other value-based theories, we are not rationally required to be impartial. On these theories, what is most worth achieving is the well-being of certain people, such as ourselves and those we love. As that remark implies, our reasons to want some thing may be claimed to depend, in part, on our relation to this thing. Such reasons are still, in my sense, object-given. On some theories, certain things are worth achieving in ways that do not depend on their contribution to anyone's well-being. Nor is it only outcomes that can be claimed to be worth achieving. It may be worth acting in some way, not to promote but only to respect some value. That may be true, for example, of acts that obey some deontological constraint, or of expressive acts, such as those that show loyalty to some dead friend. Respecting such values, in these ways, may be something that is worth achieving.

Though value-based theories disagree in all these ways, there are many claims that all such theories would accept. We have a reason, for example, to want to avoid pain; and, if one of two ordeals would be more painful, that gives us a reason to prefer the other.

These claims may seem too obvious to be worth making. Who could possibly deny that we have such reasons? But such claims have been either denied or ignored by many great philosophers, and in most recent accounts of rationality.

Desire-based theories, moreover, *must* deny these claims. On these theories, our diagram becomes:

	intrinsic	*instrumental*
object-given	We want this thing	This thing would have effects that we want
state-given	We want to want this thing	Our wanting this thing would have effects that we want

Three of these kinds of fact can be intelligibly claimed to give us reasons. Thus, if we want you to enjoy life again, and that would be one effect of the ending of your suffering, these facts can be claimed to give us an instrumental object-given reason to want your suffering to end. And we can be claimed to have both kinds of state-given reason, since we may want to have such sympathetic desires, and we may also want you to be comforted by our sympathy.

Desire-based theories cannot, however, recognize intrinsic object-given reasons. On such theories, all reasons to have some desire must be provided by some desire. And this must be some *other* desire. We can have a reason to want some thing to happen if its happening would have effects that we want, or we want to have this desire, or we want the effects of having it. But we cannot have any reason, given by facts about some thing, to want this thing for its own sake. Such a reason would have to be provided by our wanting this thing. But the fact that we *had* this desire could not give us a *reason* to have it. So we cannot have intrinsic reasons, given by the nature of your suffering, to want that suffering to end.

Similar remarks apply even to our own suffering. If one of two ordeals would be more painful, this fact, I have claimed, gives us an intrinsic reason to prefer the other. But desire-based theories cannot recognize this reason. If we prefer to postpone some ordeal, despite knowing that this would make it more painful, this preference, according to these theories, cannot be contrary to reason.

It may be objected that, if one of two ordeals would be more painful, we would have, during this ordeal, stronger desires not to be suffering this pain. That might be claimed to give us desire-based reasons to prefer the less painful ordeal. But this objection misunderstands what desire-based theories claim. On these theories, reasons are provided only by our *present* desires: either what we actually want, or what, if we had deliberated on the facts, we would now want.

Consider, for example, some smoker, who does not care about her further future, and whose indifference would survive informed deliberation. According to desire-based theories, this person has no reason to stop smoking. It is true that, if she later got lung cancer, she would then have many strong desires that her fatal illness would frustrate. But these predictable future desires do not, on desire-based theories, give her *now* any reason to stop smoking. If we appeal to such future desires, claiming that they give this person such a reason, we are appealing to a value-based theory. We are claiming that, even though this person doesn't now care about her further future, and would not be brought to care by informed deliberation, she has reasons to care, and ought rationally to care. These reasons are provided by facts about her own future well-being. It is irrelevant that, in describing the facts that give her these reasons, we appeal in part to the predictable frustration of her future desires.

Return now to a case in which we prefer the more painful of two ordeals. Suppose that, to avoid some mild pain that would start now, we choose agony tomorrow. On value-based theories, we have a strong object-given reason not to make that choice. This reason is provided by the intrinsic difference between mild pain and agony. But, on desire-based theories, we have no such reason. According to these theories, all reasons are provided by our actual or counterfactual present desires. The difference between mild pain and agony cannot itself provide a reason, since this difference is not a fact about our present desires.

Consider next intrinsic *state*-given reasons. If we want to have some desire, that might be claimed to give us a reason to have it. But state-given reasons to *have* some desire are better regarded as object-given reasons to *want* to have it, and to try to have it. And, when so regarded, state-given desire-based reasons disappear. Our wanting to have some desire cannot give us a reason to want to have it. So, on desire-based theories, we cannot have either kind of intrinsic reason.

Such theories can still claim that we have both kinds of instrumental reason. If some thing would have effects that we want, or we want the effects of wanting this thing, these facts can be claimed to give us reasons to want, or to want to want, this thing. How important are such reasons?

According to value-based theories, we have an instrumental reason to want some thing if this thing would be a means to something else, and we have a reason to want that other thing. As that claim implies, every instrumental reason depends upon some other reason. This other reason may itself be instrumental, depending upon some third reason. Such instrumental reasons may form a long chain. But, at the end of any such chain, there must be one or more intrinsic object-given reasons. It is from such intrinsic reasons that all instrumental reasons get their force.

Desire-based theorists must reject these claims. According to them, instrumental reasons get their force, not from some intrinsic reason, but from some intrinsic desire. And on such theories, as we have seen, we cannot have reasons to have such desires. So all reasons get their force from some desire that, on these theories, we have no reason to have. Our having such desires cannot itself, I am arguing, give us any reasons. If that is true, desire-based theories are built on sand.

It is worth noting how, when Hume described such a chain of instrumental reasons, he forgot his own theory. Hume wrote:

> Ask a man *why he uses exercises*; he will answer *because he desires to keep his health*. If you then enquire *why he desires health*, he will readily reply *because sickness is painful*. If you push your enquiries further and desire a reason *why he hates pain*, it is impossible he can ever give any. *This is an ultimate end*, and is never referred to any other object ... beyond this it is an absurdity to ask for a reason. It is impossible there can be a progress *in infinitum*; and that one thing can always be a reason why another is desired. Something must be desirable on its own account ...

For 'desirable' Hume should have written 'desired'. Something is desirable if it has features that give us reasons to want this thing. Hume denied that there could be such reasons.

3

We can now reintroduce another question. Besides asking what we have reasons to want, we can ask whether and how our desires can be rational or irrational.

These questions differ, I have claimed, in only one way. While reasons are provided by the facts, the rationality of our desires depends instead on our non-normative beliefs. (Why I say 'non-normative' I shall explain later.) When we know the relevant facts, these questions have the same answers. But if we are ignorant, or have false beliefs, it can be rational to want what we have no reason to want, and vice versa.

We are rational insofar as we respond to reasons, or apparent reasons. We have some *apparent* reason when we have some belief whose truth would give us that reason. As these claims imply, our desires are rational if they depend upon beliefs whose truth would give us reasons to have these desires. If these reasons are object-given, so is the rationality of these desires. Such desires might be called *objectively rational*. But, since that phrase might be misunderstood, we can talk of the *object-given rationality* of these desires.

The most important object-given reasons are intrinsic reasons: reasons to want some thing for its own sake, given by facts about this thing. When we have beliefs whose truth would give us such reasons, this desire would be *intrinsically rational*. Our desires are contrary to reason when we have such reasons *not* to have these desires, and these reasons outweigh any reasons we may have to have them. If we have beliefs whose truth would make some desire clearly and strongly contrary to reason, such a desire would be *intrinsically irrational*. I add the words 'clearly and strongly' because, like the charge 'wicked', the charge 'irrational' is at one extreme. If we have beliefs whose truth would make some desire less obviously or only weakly contrary to reason, such a desire may not deserve to be called irrational, though it would be open to rational criticism.

There are, we have seen, many desires to which these claims do not apply. The largest single class are hedonic desires: the likings or dislikings of our own present conscious states that make these states pleasant, painful, or unpleasant. We could not have intrinsic object-given reasons for or against having these dislikes, nor could they be rational or irrational. If some people like sensations that other people hate, neither group are making evaluative mistakes. Other non-rational desires include such instinctive urges as those involved in thirst, hunger, or a non-belief-dependent desire to sleep.

Most other kinds of desire can be intrinsically rational, or irrational. As before, our examples can be *meta-hedonic* desires: the desires we have about our own future pleasure or pain. If one of two ordeals would be more painful, this fact gives us a reason to prefer the other. Unless we have some contrary apparent reason, it would be intrinsically irrational to prefer, for its own sake, the more painful of two ordeals.

Such a preference would be most irrational if we preferred the more painful ordeal because it would be more painful. That preference may never have been had. When people prefer the more painful of two ordeals, that is nearly always because they believe that this ordeal would have some other feature. They may, for example, regard this ordeal as punishment that they deserve, or as a way of strengthening their will, or their powers of endurance. That might be enough to make their preferences rational.

Another kind of case involves our attitudes to time. We may prefer the worse of two ordeals because of a difference in *when* this ordeal would come. One example is my imagined man who has *Future Tuesday Indifference*.[5] This man cares about his own future suffering, except when it will come on any future Tuesday. His attitude does not, I supposed, depend on any false beliefs. Pain on Tuesdays will, he knows, be just as painful, and be just as much *his* pain; and he regards Tuesday as merely a conventional calendar division. Even so, given the choice, he would prefer agony next Tuesday to mild pain on any other day of the week. That some ordeal would be much more painful is a strong reason *not* to prefer it; that it would be on a Tuesday is *no* reason to prefer it. So this man's preference is irrational.

Return next to an attitude that we nearly all have: caring more about what is near. Suppose that, because you have this bias, you want some ordeal to be briefly postponed, at the foreseen cost of being much worse. Rather than having one hour of mild pain starting now, you prefer one hour of agony tomorrow. This preference is also, though more weakly, contrary to reason. Unlike the fact that some ordeal would be on a future Tuesday, if some ordeal would be further from the present, this fact might be claimed to give us some reason to care about it less. But, on any plausible version of this view, postponement by only one day would be heavily outweighed by the difference between mild pain and agony. So this preference is also, though more weakly, irrational.

These claims may again seem too obvious to be worth making. Who could possibly deny that such preferences are irrational? But such claims are denied, or ignored, by many writers. When these writers discuss the rationality of our desires or preferences, they appeal to certain other claims. Some appeal to the *effects* of our desires. Others appeal to facts about the *origin* of our desires, or to whether our desires would survive informed deliberation. On a third criterion, our desires are irrational if they are *inconsistent*. These criteria make no reference to the objects of our desires, or *what* we want. According to these writers, if our desires have no bad effects, or they arose in certain ways, or they would survive certain tests, or they are consistent with each other, one or more of these facts is enough to make these desires rational. Such desires are rational *whatever* their objects.

These views are, I believe, seriously mistaken. Their main failing is to ignore intrinsic object-given reasons, and intrinsic rationality. There are also reasons to reject most of the criteria to which these views appeal.

4

Consider first the view that our desires are rational if they have good effects. This claim conflates object-given and state-given reasons. If we believe that our having some desire would have good effects, what that belief makes rational is not this desire itself, but our wanting and trying to have it. Irrational desires may have good effects. Thus, if I knew that I shall be tortured tomorrow, it might be better for me if I wanted to be tortured, since I would then happily look forward to what lies ahead. But this would not make my desire rational. It is irrational to want, for its own sake, to be tortured. The good effects of such a desire might make it rational for me, if I could, to cause myself to have it. But that would be a case of rational irrationality.

Consider next views that appeal to the origin of our desires. According to some writers, our desires are rational if they were formed through autonomous deliberation, and they are irrational if they were formed in certain other ways, such as through indoctrination, hypnosis, or self-deception. On a similar set of views, the rationality of our desires depends, not on how we came to have them, but on what would cause us to lose them, or on whether they would survive certain tests. On Brandt's view, for example, our desires are rational if they would survive cognitive psychotherapy.[6]

Suppose that, though we have formed some desire in one of these favoured ways, we want what we have no reason to want, and have strong reason not to want. We prefer agony tomorrow to mild pain today, or our horror of eating or gaining weight makes us want to starve ourselves to death, or we have some other obsessive desire, whose fulfilment would, we know, have only bad effects. In such cases, our desire's origin would not make either it, or us, rational. If anything, the reverse is true. If we were caused to have some irrational desire by some form of external interference, such as hypnosis or brain surgery, our way of acquiring this desire would not show us to be irrational. If instead we developed this desire in the way that these criteria favour, such as through calm reflection on the facts, that *would* show us to be irrational. On Brandt's view, for our desires to be rational, it may be enough for us to be incurably insane. That cannot be right.

Of those who appeal to facts about the origin of our desires, most, like Brandt, give most attention to the relation between our desires and our beliefs. According to some writers, our desires are irrational when they depend on false beliefs. Thus Hume wrote that, though desires cannot be 'contrary to reason', they can be, in a loose sense, 'called unreasonable' when they are 'founded on false suppositions'.

This claim is obviously mistaken. False beliefs can be rational; and, if some desire depends on a rational belief, the falsity of this belief does not make this desire irrational. Thus, if we believe rationally but falsely that some medicine would restore our health, it is not irrational for us to want to take this medicine. When our desires rest on false beliefs, desire-based theorists should at most claim that these desires do not give us reasons for acting.

Hume may have meant that our desires can be called irrational when and because they depend on irrational beliefs. This claim, which many writers make, is another though less obvious mistake.

This mistake is clearest when we apply this claim to our instrumental desires. Suppose that I want to smoke because I want to protect my health, and I have the irrational belief that smoking will achieve this aim. I have that belief because my neighbour smoked until the age of 100, and I take that fact to outweigh all of the well-known evidence that smoking kills. To simplify the example, we can also suppose that I don't enjoy smoking. I want to smoke only because I believe that smoking will protect my health. Does the irrationality of my belief make my desire to smoke irrational?

Not in any useful sense. Given my belief that smoking will achieve my aim, my desire to smoke is rational. Suppose instead that I wanted to smoke because I had the rational belief that smoking would damage my health. On the view that we are now considering, since my desire to smoke would here depend on a rational belief, this desire would be rational. That is clearly false. If I had the rational belief that smoking would damage my health, that would make it rational for me, not to want to smoke, but to want *not* to smoke. So, in these two cases, my desire to smoke is rational only when it depends on an *irrational* belief.

If this conclusion seems paradoxical, that is because we are conflating two questions. The rationality of most of our beliefs depends on whether, in having these beliefs, we are responding to apparent reasons for having them. We have such apparent reasons if the evidence available to us makes it sufficiently likely that these beliefs are true. The rationality of our desires depends, not on the rationality of our beliefs, but on whether, in having these desires, we are responding to apparent reasons for having these desires. We have such apparent reasons if we have beliefs whose truth would make what we want worth achieving, either in itself or in its effects. We might respond well to either set of reasons, while responding badly to the other. Thus, if I want to smoke because I believe that smoking will protect my health, I am responding badly to my reasons for believing, but responding well to my reasons for desiring. If instead I want to smoke because I believe that smoking will damage my health, I am responding well to my reasons for believing, but responding badly to my reasons for desiring.

As these remarks imply, for instrumental desires to be rational, we must believe that what we want may help us to achieve some aim. It is irrelevant whether this belief is rational. Thus, in these examples, it is rational for me to want to smoke when and because I have the irrational belief that smoking would achieve my aim of protecting my health, and irrational to want to smoke when and because I have the rational belief that smoking would frustrate my aim.

Turn now to intrinsic desires. Many writers again claim that these desires are rational when they depend on true beliefs, or, more plausibly, on rational beliefs.

Return to my imagined man who prefers agony next Tuesday to mild pain on any other day next week. This man's preference depends, I supposed, only on true and rational beliefs. He understands the difference between mild pain and agony, he knows that future Tuesdays will be as much part of his life, and he regards Tuesday as merely a conventional calendar division. On the views that we are now considering, since this man prefers the agony because he has these true and rational beliefs, his preference is rational. Suppose instead that he had this preference because he had the false and irrational belief that the agony on Tuesday would be in some way unreal. On these views, that would make his preference irrational. As before, the reverse is true. This man's preference would be rational only if it depended on some such irrational belief.

What makes our desires rational is not, we have seen, the rationality of the beliefs on which they depend. It is the *content* of these beliefs. In the case of instrumental desires, that content is easily described. These desires are rational when, and because, we have these desires because we believe that what we want might help us to achieve some aim. Desire-based theories can be easily revised, so that they make this claim.

For our intrinsic desires to be rational, they must depend on certain other kinds of belief. The content of these beliefs cannot be so easily described. Such desires are rational when we believe that what we want has certain features, and these are features that would give us reasons to want this thing, for its own sake. Value-based theories disagree about some of these features. For example some claim, while others deny, that knowledge, rationality, or fame are, in themselves, worth achieving. Some Stoics and Christians have even claimed, though only as the implication of certain other beliefs, that pain is not, in itself, worth avoiding.

Desire-based theories, as we have seen, cannot make such claims. On these theories, intrinsic desires cannot be irrational, since there cannot be desire-based reasons to want something for its own sake. As Hume would have said, it is not contrary to reason to prefer agony next Tuesday to mild pain on any other day.

I have rejected the common view that our desires are rational when and because they depend on true or rational beliefs. Often, I have said, the opposite is true. Our desires are rational when they depend on beliefs whose truth would give us reasons to have these desires. It is irrelevant whether these beliefs are either false or irrational. Remember next that, in making these claims, I have been discussing only non-normative beliefs. When we turn to normative beliefs, we should make different claims.

Suppose that my imagined man believes that agony is in itself worth achieving, or believes that we have no reason to avoid agony on future Tuesdays. These are beliefs whose truth would give him a reason to prefer the agony on Tuesday. Similarly, if this man believes that this preference is rational, that is a belief whose truth would make his preference rational. But, even if his preference depends on these beliefs, that does not make it rational. When our desires depend on such normative beliefs, these desires *are* rational only when, and because, these beliefs are rational. If these normative beliefs are false or irrational, like the belief that agony is worth achieving, or that future Tuesdays do not matter, it is irrelevant whether these are beliefs whose truth would make these desires rational. The view that I have rejected, when considering other beliefs, here gets things right.

This difference is not surprising. We are rational when and insofar as we respond to reasons, or apparent reasons. When our desires depend on non-normative beliefs, there are two quite different sets of reasons, or apparent reasons, to which we are responding, or failing to respond. One set are reasons for or against having some non-normative belief, such as the belief that some experience would be painful. The other set are reasons for or against having some desire, such as the desire to avoid this experience. Since these reasons are quite different, and are reasons for quite different responses, the rationality of these desires should not be claimed to depend on the rationality of these beliefs.

When our desires depend on normative beliefs, and in the way just sketched, these remarks do not apply. Some writers suggest that, when we want to achieve some aim because we believe it to be worth achieving, this desire cannot really be distinguished from this belief. That seems an exaggeration. We can indeed reject Hume's claim that no belief can motivate without the help of some independent desire: some desire that is not itself produced by this belief. Hume said nothing that supports that claim. But there is still a difference between believing that some aim is worth achieving and wanting to achieve it, even when this desire consists in our being motivated by this belief.

There is, however, another ground for claiming that the rationality of such desires, or of our being motivated by such normative beliefs, depends on the rationality of these beliefs. Our reasons to have these beliefs are very closely related to our reasons to have these desires. In the simplest cases, that relation is this. We have some desire because we believe that some fact gives us a reason to have it, and we have this belief because this fact does give us such a reason.

That may suggest that, in having this desire and this belief, we are responding to the same reason. That is not so. Practical and epistemic reasons are always quite different. But, in this kind of case, these reasons partly overlap. Suppose that, because I am in a burning building, I know that

(A) Jumping is my only way to save my life.

This fact gives me a reason to jump. I also have a reason to *believe* that I have this reason. But this second reason, though it depends on the truth of (A), is not provided by this truth. It is provided by the fact that

(B) Since jumping would save my life, I have a reason to jump.

My reason to jump, being practical, is provided by the good effects of jumping. My reason to *believe* that I should jump, being epistemic, is not provided by the good effects of jumping. It is provided by the fact that, since jumping would have these good effects, it is obviously *true* that I should jump. (This is one of the kinds of belief for which we don't need evidence, or theoretical support.)

Similar remarks apply to our intrinsic desires. Suppose we want to avoid some experience because we know that it would be painful. We may have this desire because we believe that we have a reason to have it, since pain has features that make it worth avoiding. But, while our reason to want to avoid this experience is provided by the fact that this experience would be painful, our reason to believe that we have this reason is provided by the different fact *that* this fact gives us this reason.

Though these are different facts, one includes the other. And that provides a sense in which, when we have some desire because we believe that we have some reason to have it, both our desire and our belief are, though in different ways, responses to the same practical reason. Our desire is a response to our awareness of this reason, and our belief that we have this reason, or our awareness of it, is a response to the fact that we have it.

Since such desires and beliefs are so closely related, being in these different ways responses to the same practical reason, or reason-giving fact, such desires are rational when and because the normative beliefs on which they depend are rational.

To put the point in another way, there is an overlap here between practical and theoretical rationality. Practical rationality involves, not only responding to our reasons for caring and acting, but also responding to our epistemic reasons for having beliefs about these practical reasons. This other part of practical rationality, which we can call practical reasoning, is a special case of theoretical reasoning: since it is theoretical reasoning about practical reasons.

Several writers, we can note in passing, reject this last claim. Thus Korsgaard criticises realists for believing that when we ask 'practical normative questions ... there is something ... that we are trying to find out', and that our relation to reasons is one of knowing truths about them.[7] Our relation to practical reasons, we should agree, isn't only one of knowing truths about them. To be practically rational, it isn't enough to respond to our epistemic reasons for believing that we have certain practical reasons, since we should also respond to these practical reasons in our desires and acts. But, when we ask what we have most reason to do, or ought rationally to do, there is, I believe, something that we are trying to find out. If there was nothing to find out, because there were no truths about what we had reason to want or to do, this would be another way in which our belief in normative reasons would be an illusion.

I have explained why, on my view, when our desires depend on certain normative beliefs, the rationality of these desires depends on the rationality of these beliefs. Let us now briefly consider a different view. According to some writers, the rationality of these desires depends only on their coherence with the normative beliefs on which they depend. In his *What We Owe to Each Other*, Scanlon makes a qualified version of this claim. Scanlon suggests that, though there are other grounds on which our desires can be open to rational criticism, our desires should not be called irrational unless they are inconsistent with our own normative beliefs.

Consider two versions of my imagined man. In one version, this man prefers agony next Tuesday to mild pain on any other day next week, and this preference is brute, since it does not depend on any normative beliefs. This man, we can suppose, accepts Hume's view that no desires or preferences could be either supported by or contrary to reason. In the second version of this case, this man prefers the agony on Tuesday because he believes that he has reasons to have this preference, and he therefore believes that this preference is rational. He believes that agony is in itself a good state to be in, or he believes that future Tuesdays do not matter. On Scanlon's view, in both these cases, this man's preference is not irrational. Suppose next that this man outdoes Hume, since he believes that no belief could be contrary to reason. Or suppose he believes that he has reasons to believe that agony is in itself good, or that future Tuesdays do not matter. On Scanlon's view, this man's beliefs may not be irrational either.

Suppose next that, when we learn that some ordeal has been postponed from this afternoon to next year, we are mildly relieved, though we believe that we have no reason to be relieved, since mere distance from the present has no rational significance. On Scanlon's view, our relief is irrational. It is irrational for us to prefer that an ordeal be postponed, even when that makes it no worse. But, when my imagined man prefers agony next Tuesday to mild pain on any other day, his preference is not irrational. I would make the opposite claims. On my view, this man's preference is very irrational, as are his normative beliefs; but, when we are relieved that our ordeal has been postponed, we are at most open only to weak rational criticism.

Scanlon's view, I should now explain, does not really differ from mine. His proposal is that we should restrict the charge 'irrational' so that it expresses only one kind of rational criticism: the criticism that we deserve when our beliefs, desires or acts fail to respond to our own judgments about our reasons for having these beliefs or desires, or for acting in these ways. In such cases, we are failing even in our own terms, since it is inconsistent to believe that we have certain reasons but to fail to respond to these reasons.

This kind of inconsistency is, I agree, one distinctive kind of rational failing. But it seems misleading to restrict the charge 'irrational' to these cases. That suggests that this kind of failing is what deserves the strongest rational criticism. As my examples show, and Scanlon agrees, that is not so. When we are mildly relieved that our ordeal has been postponed, though we believe that we have no reason for such relief, we are at most open to weak rational criticism. When my imagined man prefers agony next Tuesday to mild pain on any other day, his preference is open to very strong rational criticism, and that criticism is not undermined if we add the assumption that this man believes that agony is good, or that future Tuesdays do not matter. Those beliefs are also open to very strong rational criticism, which in turn is not undermined if we discover that this man believes that his beliefs are rational. I suggest that we should use 'irrational' to mean 'open to the strongest kinds of rational criticism'. We cannot avoid the charge of irrationality by believing that we are not irrational.

There is much more to be said about the relations between rationality and consistency. I have been discussing inconsistency between certain desires and certain normative beliefs. Similar remarks would apply to inconsistency between certain acts and certain beliefs, as when we believe that we ought rationally to do something, but fail to do it.

The most straightforward inconsistency is between some beliefs and other beliefs. That inconsistency, when extreme, is one kind of epistemic irrationality, and is irrelevant here. What is relevant, however, is inconsistency between some desires and other desires.

Desire-based theories can appeal to one kind of inconsistency between our desires: that in which, though wanting to achieve some aim, we do not want the necessary means. If we add two further assumptions, such inconsistency is one kind of irrationality. These are the assumptions that our aim is rational, and that we have no reason not to want the necessary means. If our aim is not rational, or we have reason not to want the means, failure to want the means to some aim may involve no irrationality. Though desire-based theories cannot make these further claims, they can claim that, in wanting or failing to want the means to our aims, our desires can be instrumentally rational or irrational.

The more important question though, is about the rationality of our intrinsic desires. Many writers claim that the rationality of such desires is at least partly a matter of their consistency. Of the views that are widely advanced, this is the main group of views that still need to be considered. On these views, if our desires are inconsistent, that makes them in one way irrational, or at least open to rational criticism, even if their being consistent would not be enough to make them rational.

Two beliefs are inconsistent if they could not both be true. That definition cannot apply directly to desires, since desires cannot be true. But two desires are inconsistent, several writers claim, if they could not both be fulfilled.

Such inconsistency does not involve irrationality. Suppose that, in some disaster, I could save either of my children's lives, but not both. Even when I realize this fact, it would not be irrational for me to go on wanting to save both my children's lives. When we know that two of our desires cannot both be fulfilled, that would make it irrational for us to *intend* to fulfil both; but it would still be rational to want or wish to fulfil both, and to regret that impossibility.

When our desires are, in this sense, inconsistent, that might make our having them unfortunate. But, as I have claimed, that does not make such desires irrational. It would at most make it irrational for us, if we could cause ourselves to lose these desires, not to do so.

For inconsistency to be a fault, it must be defined in a different way. Though our desires cannot themselves be true or false, they may depend on evaluative beliefs; and such desires can be said to be inconsistent when the beliefs on which they depend could not all be true, or justified.

That would be true, it may seem, if we both wanted something to happen, and wanted it not to happen. In having these two desires, we might seem to be assuming that it would be both better and worse if this thing happened. But, in most cases of this kind, we are assuming that some event would be in one way good and in another bad. Thus, I might both want to finish my life's work, so as to avoid the risk of dying with my work unfinished, and want *not* to finish my life's work, so that, while I am still alive, I would still have things to do. Such desires involve no inconsistency.

For two desires to be irrationally inconsistent, in this belief-dependent sense, they must depend on beliefs that the very same feature is both good and bad, and in the very same way. Thus it would be irrational both to want to avoid some ordeal because it would be painful, and to want to endure this ordeal because it would be painful. It is not clear that it would be possible to have such desires; but, if it were, the objection to inconsistency would here be justified.

When it takes this form, however, this objection cannot apply to those who accept desire-based theories. The objection assumes that, in having such desires, we would have inconsistent beliefs about what is relevantly good, or worth achieving. If we really accepted a desire-based theory, we would believe that nothing could be, in itself, worth achieving.

Turn next from particular desires to our overall preferences, or what we want all things considered. It might be claimed to be irrational to prefer X to Y, and Y to X; but that would also be impossible. We might prefer X to Y, Y to Z, and Z to X. For these three preferences to be irrational, however, they must again depend upon beliefs of a kind that desire-based theories reject. We must believe that X is in itself better than Y, which is better than Z, which is better than X. If these were brute preferences, which did not depend on such beliefs, it is not clear that they could be claimed to be irrational.

Such a claim is often defended with the remark that, if we had such intransitive preferences, we could be exploited. Thus we might be induced to pay first for having Z rather than X, then for having Y rather than Z, and then for having X rather than Y. Our money would be wasted, since we would be back where we started. But this objection again appeals, not to the inconsistency of these preferences, but to their bad effects. And such intransitive preferences might have good effects. Suppose that, whenever our situation changed for one that we preferred, that change would give us some pleasure. If we had three intransitive preferences about three possible situations, that would be, in a minor way, good for us. We could go round and round this circle, getting pleasure from every move. This merry-go-round would be, hedonically, a perpetual motion machine.

There is one kind of inconsistency to which desire-based theories can plausibly appeal. If we want X, and we know that Y is the only means to X, consistency requires us, it is claimed, to want Y. Failing to want the means to our ends is claimed to be instrumentally irrational. This claim applies to our desires the central claim of desire-based theories about the rationality of acts. According to these theories, it is rational to do, and irrational not to do, what we know to be needed to achieve our aims.

These claims do describe an important kind of rationality. But, as several writers have argued, it cannot be the only kind. Like instrumental reasons, instrumental rationality only matters when, and because, our aims are intrinsically rational, or worth achieving.

5

Why has such intrinsic rationality been so widely rejected, or ignored? Why has it been so widely thought that, while there can be reasons for acting, there cannot be intrinsic, object-given reasons for desiring: reasons to want some thing for its own sake, given by facts about this thing?

There are some bad arguments for this view. Thus Hume claimed that, since reasoning is entirely concerned with truth, and desires cannot be true or false, desires cannot be supported by or contrary to reason. If this argument were good, it would show that, since acts cannot be true or false, acts cannot be supported by or contrary to reason. Most desire-based theorists would reject that conclusion. And Hume's argument is not good. In taking reason to be concerned only with *theoretical* or truth-seeking reasoning, Hume assumed that there is only one kind of reason: reasons for believing. He said nothing to support the view that we cannot have reasons either for caring or for acting.

Since most other writers believe that we can have reasons for acting, why do they deny that we can have reasons for caring? These writers may be thinking of those desires, such as hedonic desires, that we cannot have intrinsic reasons to have, and which therefore cannot be intrinsically rational or irrational. They may wrongly extrapolate from this large class.

Another partial explanation may be this. People may have been influenced by a presumed analogy with our reasons for having beliefs, and with theoretical or epistemic rationality. The rationality of most beliefs depends, they assume, either on their origin, or on their consistency with each other. They may then transfer these claims to our desires.

This analogy is, I believe, mistaken. It is true that, as these people claim, few beliefs are *intrinsically* rational or irrational, in a way that depends only on their content: or what is believed. That can be claimed of some kinds of mathematical or logical belief. And it can be claimed of some empirical beliefs, such as Descartes' *Cogito*, whose content ensures its truth. But few empirical beliefs are self-evident, or self-confirming. Some empirical beliefs – such as those of some psychotics – may seem to be, simply in virtue of their content, irrational. But the irrationality of even these beliefs is still mostly a matter of their origin, and of their conflict with other beliefs. The rationality of empirical beliefs cannot depend solely on their content, because the aim of such beliefs is to match the world. It will depend on our other beliefs, and on the evidence available to us, whether we can rationally believe that this match obtains. In the case of desires, the *direction of fit* is the other way, since we want the world to match our desires. When we want something for its own sake, the rationality of this desire can be intrinsic, or depend only on what it is that we want. And what is relevant here is only our desire's *intentional* object, or what we want as we believe that it would be.

Similar points apply to the appeal to consistency. Since beliefs aim to match the world, and inconsistent beliefs cannot all be true, the rationality of our beliefs is in part a matter of their consistency. But, as I have said, there are only very restricted ways in which our intrinsic desires could be claimed to be irrational because they are mutually inconsistent. In rejecting this analogy between our beliefs and desires, I am not denying that, as Scanlon and others argue, most of our intrinsic desires depend on evaluative beliefs. The relevant evaluative beliefs do not conflict. If we believe that some aim would be worth achieving, that does not imply that other aims are not worth achieving.

I turn now to what may be the most influential ground for ignoring, or rejecting, our intrinsic reasons to have desires. On desire-based theories, the source of all reasons is something that is not itself normative: it is the fact that some act would fulfil one of our desires, or the fact that, if we knew more, we would be motivated to act in some way. On value-based theories, the source of reasons is, in contrast, normative. These theories appeal, not to claims about our actual or counterfactual desires, but to claims about what is relevantly good or bad, or worth achieving or avoiding. Unlike facts about some act's relation to our desires, such alleged normative truths may seem to be metaphysically mysterious, and inconsistent with a scientific world view.

The relevant distinction here is not, however, between desire-based and value-based theories. It is between reductive and non-reductive theories. For desire-based theories to be about normative reasons, they must, I believe, take a non-reductive form. Even if all reasons for acting were provided by facts about our actual or counterfactual desires, the fact that we had these reasons could not be the same as, or consist in, these empirical facts about our desires. Desire-based theories should claim that, because some way of acting would fulfil one of our actual or hypothetical informed desires, a *different* fact obtains: we have a reason to act in this way. In making that claim, such theories should be committed to one kind of irreducibly normative truth. That undermines their reason to deny that there can be such truths about what is good, or worth achieving.

This point is reinforced if, as Scanlon suggests, something's being good consists in its having certain reason-giving natural properties. If that is so, in believing that certain aims are good, or worth achieving, we are not committed to normative properties other than the property of being reason-giving, or committed to normative truths other than truths about reasons.

We can next remember that, besides practical reasons, we have reasons for having beliefs. When we have such an epistemic reason, that is another irreducibly normative truth.

Since there are such truths about these other kinds of reason, we have no reason to deny that there can be such truths about reasons for desiring. If there can be certain things that we have most reason to believe, and certain things that we have most reason to do, there can also be certain things that we have most reason to want.

According to desire-based theories, in their only normative form:

> Some acts really are rational. There are facts about these acts, and their relations to our motivation, which give us reasons to act in these ways.

According to value-based theories:

> Some aims really are worth achieving. There are facts about these aims which give us reasons to want to achieve them.

This claim is, I believe, no less plausible. If jumping from a burning building is my only way to save my life, desire-based theorists agree that I have a reason to jump. If that fact can give me such a reason, why can't facts about my life give me reason to want to live? And, if one of two ordeals would be more painful, why can't that give me a reason to prefer the other?

It is amazing that such truths still need defending.

Notes

1   This last claim assumes that we can have reasons of which we are unaware. Some would say that, in this example, *there is* a reason for you to take this treatment, but you don't *have* this reason. But that is merely a different description, not a different view.

2   I make some brief remarks in my 'Reasons and Motivation', *Proceedings of the Aristotelian Society, Supplementary Volume*, 1997. I shall say more in the book I am now writing, *Rediscovering Reasons* (Oxford: Oxford University Press).

3   In denying that reasons are provided by desires, I am following such writers as Warren Quinn, *Morality and Action* (Cambridge: Cambridge University Press, 1993), Chapters

11 and 12, and Thomas Scanlon, *What We Owe to Each Other* (Cambridge, Mass.: Harvard University Press, 1998), Chapter 1.

4   *What We Owe to Each Other, op. cit.*, pp. 95–100.

5   Discussed in my *Reasons and Persons* (Oxford: Oxford University Press, 1984), Section 46.

6   Richard Brandt, *A Theory of the Good and The Right* (Oxford: Oxford University Press, 1979) pp. 10–16.

7   Christine Korsgaard, *The Sources of Normativity* (Cambridge: Cambridge University Press, 1996), p. 44.

What to Do about Dead People

Fred Feldman

Introductory comments

Dead people are legal troublemakers. Should we count their votes? Does it make sense to let them keep their driver's licenses? Should we remove them from their jobs and public offices without any hearing; without even giving them a chance to show they are still capable of performing? These are important questions, but they are not my questions here.

Dead people are *metaphysical* troublemakers, too. Some philosophers find them so troublesome that they deny that there are any dead people. They think people literally 'go out of existence' when they die. Others think people continue to exist after death. But even those who think that people continue to exist after they die disagree about other important questions. Some of them think that people continue to be people after they die. On this view, there really are some dead people. Yet others think that when people die they continue to exist but stop being people. We might call them 'dead people' but the phrase is misleading. Since in fact they are not people any more, it would be better to call them 'dead things that formerly were people'. Other philosophers hold other views – some even stranger than the ones I have mentioned.

My aim here is to sketch some of the main views concerning the metaphysics of dead people. In several cases, I will point out some features of the view that seem to me to make it less attractive. Toward the end, I will describe what I take to be the most plausible and natural account of the metaphysics of dead people. Before I turn to a discussion of these views, I need to make note of some of my assumptions.

Some background assumptions

My first assumption is difficult to state clearly, and may seem too trivial to be worth mentioning. It is the assumption that there really are some people. I will proceed here on the assumption that people are genuine objects, and not 'logical fictions', or 'conceptual constructions', or otherwise ontologically degenerate.

We are not like holes, or shadows, or borders; nor are we like clubs and commit-
tees. Each of us has a kind of ontological independence. I will not be discussing
any views according to which, strictly speaking, there are no people.

Another assumption is that there are plenty of ordinary material objects. When
I say they are 'ordinary', I mean to suggest that typical material objects have
features such as these: they last through time; they undergo change from time to
time; they have other material objects as parts; they have weight, and shape, and
color and all sorts of chemical and physical properties. Examples include such
natural living objects as the big tree outside my office window, such natural non-
living objects as the Earth and the moon, such artifacts as this desk and that chair.

I also assume that there are plenty of ordinary properties. I have alluded to
quite a few already: the property of weighing so-and-so much; the property of
having thus-and-so chemical make-up; the property of being green; the property
of being a tree. I will talk in a realistic way about these properties, but if you
prefer to translate my realistic property talk into something more austere, you
are welcome to do so. It makes no difference to anything I say here.

I will talk as if there are times. It makes it easier to talk about change, which
will be one of my main topics. I think that material objects can change their
properties as they move through time. The big oak tree was covered with green
leaves during the summer; the leaves turned yellow and red in the fall; then in
early winter they fell off. So, as I see it, the tree had different properties at different times. Even the leaves had different properties at different times.

I will also talk as if there are events. In fact I do not accept events as a fundamental ontological kind. But it would be tedious and confusing to replace familiar event-talk with the sort of 'states-of-affairs talk' that I think is closer to the
truth.

Now let me focus on something a bit more controversial. I do not think there
are any souls. Thus, I do not think that people are souls, or that they are body/
soul combinations of any sort. I think people must be material – possibly they are
the objects we ordinarily call 'human bodies'.

Many distinguished philosophers disagree with me here. They believe in souls
(or minds, or transcendental egos). They think that we cannot seriously discuss
the metaphysics of dead people without talking about what happens to a person's
soul when he dies. With due apologies to such philosophers, I will state a proce-
dural assumption: I intend to ignore the views of all those who take people to be
souls, or who take people to be soul/body composites. I mean to be discussing
the issue from the perspective of those who take people (during their prime) to
be complex material objects with interesting brains that somehow give rise to
mentality.

Object-event-property diagrams

As I proceed, I will be making use of a bunch of diagrams. Let me say a word about how the diagrams are to be understood. In the diagrams, a rectangle indicates a material object. The extent of the rectangle in the horizontal axis indicates the duration of the material object. Thus, a very long-lasting material object, such as the moon, might be represented by a rectangle that's tremendously wide, like this:

Moon:

Diagram 1

On the other hand, a material object that lasts for a very short time would be represented by a rectangle that does not take up much space left to right. So, for example, consider this rectangle:

Particle:

Diagram 2

The rectangle in Diagram 2 might represent a certain sub-atomic particle that lasts for just a fraction of a second. (Needless to say, those diagrams were not drawn to scale.)

I guess I could have allowed the size of the rectangles in the vertical axis to indicate something – perhaps the mass of the object. But in fact the height of the rectangles has no significance.

Objects last through time. *How long they last* is represented in the diagrams by the extent of the rectangle in the horizontal axis. But what about *when they last?* For ease of discussion, let us assume a fixed metric of time, with instants lined up in the normal way with earlier times to the left and later ones to the right. Thus, the diagrams can indicate not only *how long* the objects last in time, but *when* they do their lasting.

Various things happen to the objects at various times. For simplicity in exposition, I will write as if these 'things that happen' are events. I will indicate these events by writing names (or abbreviations of names) just under the rectangles. Although I won't make much use of this possibility in this paper, I could indicate the date of an event by inserting the name of the event just above the name of the date. The following diagram concerns the big oak tree outside my office window. The rectangle represents the oak tree. The diagram indicates that the tree lasts a long time – from about 1940 till about 2020. I use 'S' to indicate the event that consists in the mating of the squirrels in the spring of 2000 like this:

Tree:

S
1950 1960 1970 1980 1990 2000 2010 2020

Diagram 3

In the diagrams, I will need a way to indicate that an object has a certain property at a certain time. I will 'flag' the object with a term indicating the property, an arrow, and a line, like this:

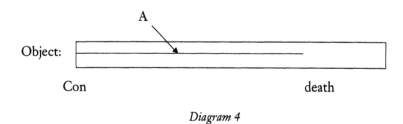

Object:

Con   death

Diagram 4

If 'A' indicates the property of being alive, then the flagging in Diagram 4 indicates that the object represented by the rectangle has the property of being alive throughout the period of time indicated by the line at the tip of the arrow. It started being alive at conception (indicated by 'con') and it stopped being alive at death (indicated by 'death'). It was alive during that period of time.

Some views about people

With all this as background, we are prepared to consider some views about the metaphysics of dead people.

(1) *Type O Animalism.* Animalism is the view that people are animals. The metaphysical principles that are true of animals in general are alleged to be true of people, too. If animals are complex material objects that persist through time, then so are people.

There are several forms of animalism. One form is discussed in detail by Eric Olson.[1] I call this 'Type O Animalism'. Olson's view is that a person comes into existence when the animal he is comes into existence. For reasons he makes clear, Olson maintains that a human animal comes into existence around two weeks after fertilization.[2] That's when the person begins to exist. Olson thinks that a person continues to exist through all sorts of psychological changes so long as he continues to be the same animal. Olson takes this typically to involve having the same body. But Olson thinks that when the person dies he goes out of existence.

Olson thinks that when the person dies and goes out of existence, *no object contin-ues in his place*. The remains of the former person do not constitute any physical object. Thus, strictly speaking, there is no such object as the corpse – not even in the case of a perfectly preserved mummy.

This last claim is strange. It may appear that I have gotten Olson wrong. But here is a passage from his book:

> The changes that go on in an animal when it dies are really quite dramatic. All of that frenetic, highly organized, and extremely complex biochemical activity that was going on throughout the organism comes to a rather sudden end, and the chemical machinery begins immediately to decay. If it looks like there isn't all that much difference between a living animal and fresh corpse, that is because the most striking changes take place at the microscopic level and below. Think of it this way: If there is such a thing as your body, it must cease to exist at *some* point (or during some vague period) between now and a million years from now, when there will be nothing left of you but dust. The most salient and most dramatic change that takes place during that history would seem to be your death. Everything that happens between death and dust (assuming that your remains rest peacefully) is only slow, gradual decay. *So whatever objects there may be that your atoms now com-pose, it is plausible to suppose that they cease to exist no later than your death. There is no obvious reason to suppose that any 150-pound object persists through that change.*[3]

This view has a very simple diagram. It looks like this:

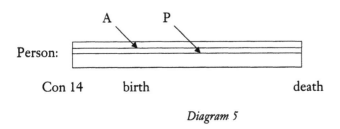

Diagram 5

In this diagram, 'con' indicates the moment of conception, 'A' indicates the prop-erty of being alive, and 'P' indicates the property of being a person. The person does not begin to exist at the moment of conception. It is only about 14 days later when the cells form themselves into something better organized that the person begins to exist. That event is indicated by '14'. The person is alive from its first moment of existence. Note that on the right hand side of the diagram the person ceases to exist at the moment of death. There are no rectangles to the right of the 'person' rectangle. That illustrates Olson's idea that the person ceases to exist at the moment of death, and is not replaced by any other object.

Olson's form of animalism implies that there are no dead people.[4] Indeed, it implies that there are no dead material objects that formerly were people. If Olson's form of animalism is true, then there is nothing to which we can point and correctly say, 'That object used to be a living person'. This implication of Olson's theory seems to me to be pretty unattractive. Surely there is something worth saving about the notion that there are human corpses, and that each of them is an object that formerly was a living person.

(2) *Substantial Change.* In his book *Thinking Clearly about Death*, Jay Rosenberg defends another view on the metaphysics of death. He illustrates his view by discussing a person he calls 'Aunt Ethel'. According to Rosenberg's story, Aunt Ethel died last week. The funeral is going to be held tomorrow. We are inclined to say, 'Aunt Ethel died last week and is being buried tomorrow'. However, Rosenberg insists that this is a very misleading way of talking ('logically a mess') about what is going on. He says this:

> There is no one thing which both died last week and will be buried tomorrow. What died last week was Aunt Ethel. What will be buried tomorrow, however, is not Aunt Ethel but rather Aunt Ethel's remains. What will be buried tomorrow is a corpse, Aunt Ethel's corpse. But a corpse is not a person. Aunt Ethel's corpse is not Aunt Ethel.[5]

While she lives, there is a certain material object – Aunt Ethel. Then when she dies, this object goes out of existence. This feature of Rosenberg's view makes it seem similar to Olson's view. But Rosenberg does not endorse Olson's view about the nonexistence of the corpse. Rosenberg maintains that at the moment of death a new object – the corpse of Ethel – comes into existence. The objects are diverse – two different things. The objects are related in a special way. The former object 'turns into' or is replaced by the latter object. This view comes out pretty clearly in this passage that occurs later in Rosenberg's book:

> The remains of an animal are, to be sure, intimately related to the animal whose remains they are – but this intimate relation is, once again, not identity. It is, in point of fact, a relation which is generated or brought into being precisely by a change in kind. The corpse or remains of an animal are what that animal has changed into or become.[6]

When Rosenberg speaks of a 'change in kind', I think he is alluding to a type of change thought to be discussed by Aristotle.[7] This sort of change may also be called 'substantial change'. If this is right, then there is more to be said about the connection between Aunt Ethel and her corpse. We can say that these allegedly distinct objects are linked by the fact that all the 'stuff' that made up Aunt Ethel at her last moment then makes up her corpse at its first moment.

The diagram for this case then looks something like this:

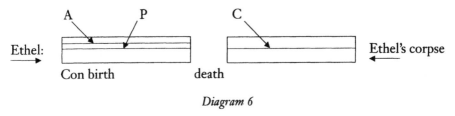

Diagram 6

The rectangle on the left represents Aunt Ethel. She is alive ('A') and a person ('P') throughout her existence. The rectangle on the right represents Aunt Ethel's corpse ('C'). It is not alive and not a person. The two rectangles do not combine to form a larger rectangle. This is as it should be on Rosenberg's view. Aunt Ethel is *not* to be identified with her corpse. The corpse is a new object. It comes into existence when Aunt Ethel disappears. There is no single object that has both Aunt Ethel and her corpse as parts.[8]

Rosenberg's view has some attractive features. At least it acknowledges that there are some corpses! Furthermore, some who find it absurd to say that a corpse is a person will be pleased to see that Rosenberg's view implies that corpses are not people.

However, on balance I have to reject this conception of the metaphysics of dead people. The main problem, as I see it, is that this view implies that the corpse is an object that *never lived*, and Aunt Ethel is an object that is *never dead*. There is no object represented by the diagram as living at an earlier time and then being dead at a later time. This seems to me to fly in the face of our ordinary ways of thinking about people and their corpses. Surely, whether we think that corpses are dead *people* or not, it is quite natural to think that each human corpse is a thing that formerly was alive, and formerly was a person. Rosenberg's view implies that this is strictly false.

(3) *Constitution.* In a collection of recent papers and in a new book, Lynne Rudder Baker defends yet another view about the metaphysics of dead people. Baker thinks that each person is strictly diverse from that person's body. Part of Baker's reason for thinking this seems to be that, as she sees it, the person's history differs from that of the person's body. The person's body starts to exist before the person exists, and the person's body (in a typical case) continues to exist after the person ceases. Another reason is that the person has certain properties essentially, whereas the body has these same properties only contingently. The person and the body are of different 'primary kinds'.

However, Baker stresses that on her view each person is very tightly connected to her body. In each case, the person is a material object composed of exactly the same set of atoms and molecules as the body. During the time when the person exists, the person occupies the same volume of space as the body. The person and body are chemically, materially, and otherwise in many ways indiscernible. Baker describes the link between person and body by saying that the body 'constitutes' the person. One thing constitutes another when, like Aunt Ethel's body and Aunt Ethel, they are of different 'primary kinds', but spatially coincident and sharing all material parts.[9]

I will put an arrow with a 'C' beside it between two rectangles to indicate that one material object constitutes another. Making use of this new symbol as well as symbolism previously introduced, we can diagram the metaphysics behind the case of Aunt Ethel:

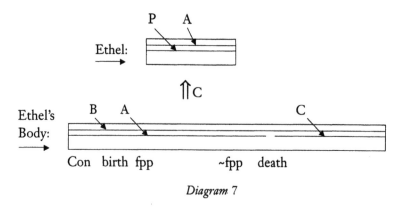

Diagram 7

There are some interesting things to note about persons, their bodies, and death on this view. First, note in the diagram that the person does not begin to exist until quite a while after the body began to exist. Baker thinks that the person begins to exist only when 'the first-person perspective' emerges.[10] Something has the first-person perspective if it is able to conceive of itself as itself – it has a certain sort of reflective self image.[11] When we have a mere fetus or infant on our hands, we have nothing with the first-person perspective. Thus, we have no person. At around age 3, when the first-person perspective emerges, the person begins to exist. That explains why the 'person' rectangle begins later than the 'body' rectangle.[12]

Notice also that the person rectangle terminates well to the left of the spot where the body rectangle terminates. That is supposed to represent the idea that the person ceases to exist when she loses her first-person perspective whereas the body goes on existing until it disintegrates. The loss of first-person perspective is indicated in the diagram by '~fpp'. I am assuming in this case that Aunt Ethel lost her first-person perspective shortly before she died. (Maybe she went into a coma.) That's why Baker would say in this example that Aunt Ethel was already out of existence by the time her body died. The view seems to imply that Aunt Ethel herself never really died. There is only one event labelled 'death' in the diagram. Aunt Ethel did not exist at the time when that event took place.

Baker distinguishes between two ways in which a thing can be a person. Some things are *persons in a nonderivative way* – they are persons in their own right, not because of their connections to other things. They don't 'borrow' their personalities from others. Aunt Ethel is a person in a nonderivative way. But Baker recognizes a second way in which a thing can be a person. When a thing that is not itself a person in a nonderivative way happens to constitute something else that is a person in a nonderivative way, then the constituting thing 'borrows personality' from the thing that is a person in a nonderivative way. When this happens, the constituting thing is a person but only in a derivative way. This just means that it *constitutes* something else that is a person in the nonderivative way.[13] The thing that is a person in a derivative way 'borrows' its personality from the thing that is a person in a nonderivative way.

On Baker's view Aunt Ethel has personality essentially. If she had not been a person, she would not have existed at all. Aunt Ethel's body is also a person, but only derivatively. Furthermore, the body could have existed without being a person at all. If it had not constituted any person, it might still have existed. It has the property of being a person contingently.

Baker's view then implies that Aunt Ethel is a person, and her body is a person, and these are two distinct material objects. In spite of this, Baker would say that the diagram represents a case in which there is just one person. That's because when counting persons, we count not by identity (which would give us 'two') but by constitution-or-identity (which gives us 'one').[14] I will have more to say about this in a moment.

While Baker's view is ingenious and very carefully worked out, I find it unattractive. Frankly, I just don't like the notion that there could be two physical objects occupying the same volume of space at the same time.[15] I am inclined to think that Baker has needlessly multiplied entities. In other words, I am inclined to think that there is really just one thing that is both Aunt Ethel and her body. But this is no objection to Baker's view: it is just an expression of my preference for another view. Let me turn to some comments that may express a genuine objection.

As we have seen, Baker wants to say that there is a difference between the way in which Aunt Ethel has the property of being a person and the way in which her body has that property. Aunt Ethel is a person *nonderivatively*. She is of the primary kind *person*. Her body is a person, but only *derivatively*. It is not of the primary kind *person*.

I find this perplexing. I wonder how it is possible for Aunt Ethel and her body to be so similar, and yet for one of them (Aunt Ethel) to be a *person in a nonderivative way* while the other (her body) is not a *person in a nonderivative way*.[16] I think we may gain some insight here if we take a closer look at what, according to Baker, makes Aunt Ethel a person in a nonderivative way. In all her work on this topic, Baker has consistently claimed that something is a (nonderivative) person iff it has the first-person perspective.[17] And she has described the first-person perspective by saying that one who has this capacity must be able to 'conceive of herself as herself'. She further characterizes this by saying:

> to be able to conceive of oneself as oneself is to be able to conceive of oneself independently of a name, or description or third-person demonstrative. It is to be able to conceptualize the distinction between oneself and everything else there is. It is not just to have thoughts expressible by means of 'I', but also to conceive of oneself as the bearer of those thoughts.[18]

Baker's view is that Aunt Ethel is a person in a nonderivative way precisely because she has the first-person perspective. This comes out clearly in many places. For example, in one place Baker says 'What makes something … a person is a first-person perspective … With the persistence of her first-person perspective, she would still be a person … If she ceased to be a person (i.e. ceased to have a first-person perspective), however, she would cease to exist altogether.'[19] This helps to explain why Aunt Ethel is a person, but it leaves me perplexed about Aunt Ethel's body. I am puzzled here because I find it hard to understand how Aunt Ethel's body could fail to have the first-person perspective in the same way that Aunt Ethel herself does, given that the body is an atom-for-atom duplicate of Aunt Ethel, and Aunt Ethel has the first-person perspective in a nonderivative way. Surely a psychological capacity such as the first-person perspective must have some sort of physical basis, presumably mostly in the brain. How could this physical basis account for the fact that Aunt Ethel has the first person perspective in a nonderivative way, but fail to account for a corresponding fact about her body, given that they are so similar? And if Aunt Ethel's body does have the first-person perspective, then it is a person in a nonderivative way, too. In this case we have too many items of the same primary kind.[20] [21]

Another conception of dead people

In this final section I will sketch what I take to be a more attractive conception of the metaphysics of dead people. I will briefly explain some of my reasons for preferring it.

We have been considering the question whether there really are some dead people. Some of us feel pulled in multiple directions by this question. We want to say 'yes and no'. This is a sign of ambiguity. I think our confusion arises because the word 'person' has several senses. If we understand the question in one sense, the answer should be 'yes'. If we understand it in others, it should be 'no'. Let us distinguish.

I think the word 'person' is sometimes used in a fundamentally biological sense. When so used, it applies correctly to any member of the species *homo sapiens*. Let us make use of the neologism 'bioperson' to express this sense. Thus, each of us is a bioperson, but if there are people on Mars, they are probably not biopersons.

Many philosophers (and perhaps others) use the term 'person' in a fundamentally psychological sense. Baker seems especially interested in this sense, and many other philosophers share her interest.[22] They use the word 'person' in such a way that it applies correctly to a thing only if that thing has a suitably rich mental life. Different philosophers emphasize different psychological features. I prefer to be neutral on the details here. Let us use the term 'psychoperson' to express this sense. Each of us is therefore a psychoperson, but my unfortunate nephew Douglas who is in a coma is not a psychoperson any more. A mere fetus is not yet a psychoperson, but will become one when it develops suitable psychology. It should be clear, then, that even though the vast majority of psychopersons are biopersons, the extension of 'bioperson' is nevertheless slightly different from the extension of 'psychoperson'. Douglas is still a bioperson but no longer a psychoperson. A little fetus is a bioperson, but not yet a psychoperson. A rational, intelligent parrot would be a psychoperson, but not a bioperson.

Something is a *legal person* in some jurisdiction iff it counts as a person under the laws of that jurisdiction. So General Motors (which is neither a bioperson nor a psychoperson) might be a legal person in the state of Michigan. There have been some jurisdictions in which certain psychopersons were not legal persons. Thus, for example, in a sufficiently racist country, members of the oppressed race might not count as persons under the law. Then these psychopersons are not legal persons there. I believe that every psychoperson who lives in Massachusetts is also a legal person here.

Finally, there are *moral persons*. Roughly, a moral person is something that has moral 'standing'; it is 'morally considerable'; it has to be taken account of in our moral decisions. When Mill said that each person is to 'count for one', he may have meant that each bioperson is to taken to be a moral person. Such a person's pleasures and pains are to be incorporated into the utility calculations for the group. I assume that each of us is a moral person. Some philosophers would want to claim that chimps and dolphins and whales are moral persons. They might also be psychopersons. They are clearly not biopersons, and they are not legal persons in Massachusetts (so far, but who can tell about the future).

Now let me introduce some further abbreviations:

BP = the property of being a biological person.
PP = the property of being a psychological person.
LP = the property of being a legal person.
MP = the property of being a moral person.

(These abbreviations blur some important further distinctions. In fact, the 'properties' are relational. Each involves also at least a time; one involves a relation to a jurisdiction. Such subtleties are irrelevant at present.)

Here, at last, is a diagram representing my view concerning the case of Aunt Ethel:

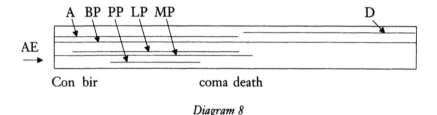

Diagram 8

This looks more like a musical score than a diagram of the metaphysics of death, and so it may be worthwhile to say a few words about what it is intended to mean.

I think that Aunt Ethel is just one (growing, developing, changing) physical object. She does not go out of existence when she dies. She just stops being alive and starts being dead. You can see that the line for *being alive* starts at conception and ceases at death. The line for *being dead* starts at death and carries on until Aunt Ethel goes out of existence when her body finally decomposes.

I think she is a member of the species *homo sapiens* throughout her existence. Thus, I think she is always a bioperson. Thus, the line for biopersonality starts at the extreme left at conception and carries all the way to the right at decomposition.

I have imagined a case in which Aunt Ethel goes into a coma before she dies. That sad event is indicated by 'coma' below the rectangle. You will note that the line for psychopersonality terminates at that point. Aunt Ethel stops being a psychoperson before she stops living and long before she stops being a bioperson. The psychoperson line does not begin at conception or at birth. That's because I am assuming some robust concept of psychopersonality – a concept that does not begin to apply to Aunt Ethel until she is about three years old.

Aunt Ethel starts being a legal person at the time of birth and continues being a legal person until she dies. But she starts being a moral person at conception and continues being a moral person (though perhaps of diminished importance) until some time after she dies. This last judgment is based on the notion that fresh corpses have a sort of moral standing that ancient mummies do not enjoy. We think we have certain moral responsibilities to a fresh corpse – to treat it with a special sort of respect. Of course, this is all very tentative and hazy. I really don't have a clear conception of what is meant by 'moral personality'.

Now let me give my answer to the questions about the metaphysics of dead people. Are there any dead people? Of course. There are plenty of them. Check in the morgue if you don't believe me. The dead human bodies you see there are all things that formerly were living people. We call them 'dead people'. But this leaves open certain further questions. Are these dead people still *people*? Yes and no. They are still biopeople, but they are surely not psychopeople. They might be moral people. They are at best severely diminished legal people.

Do people have any of their personality properties essentially? Certainly none of us is essentially a psychoperson or a legal person. We are just lucky to have those contingent features. I am uneasy about the notion that we are essentially biopersons, since as I see it, the species concepts are somewhat artificial and fairly blurry around the borders. Something that is a borderline bioperson (such as, for example, a prehistoric creature halfway between *homo sapiens* and *homo erectus*) surely might have been a little more like his non-human predecessor, and might have been a little more like his clearly human successor. Thus, there seems to be no principled reason to say that he is *essentially* a bioperson. I am in the dark about whether we are essentially moral persons, largely because I have difficulty understanding what a moral person is supposed to be.

Concluding comments

I'd like to conclude by pointing out some of the advantages of my view – features that make it seem more attractive.

(1) My view is firmly materialistic. I do not posit the existence of any strange or unfamiliar entities. On my view each material object that is a bioperson or a psychoperson is a genuine object – one that we will have to acknowledge in any case if we acknowledge any ordinary physical objects. (It's a bit harder to be clear on the ontological status of certain legal persons. The ones that are not biopersons might not be clear-cut material objects.)

(2) My view does not require us to say that there are cases in which two distinct (neither being a part of the other) physical objects wholly occupy the same volume of space. For on my view (unlike Baker's) the person and the body are related by identity, not mere constitution.

(3) My view (unlike Rosenberg's and Baker's) does not make use of any strange or unfamiliar alleged relations. I do not appeal to the notion that one object may 'turn into' another, or the idea that one object may 'constitute' another.

(4) My view (unlike Olson's, Rosenberg's, and [perhaps] Baker's) respects the intuition that in typical cases when people die, they actually and strictly become dead.

(5) My view (unlike Olson's) respects the intuition that there are material objects that are human corpses. And unlike Rosenberg's view, my view respects the intuition that human corpses are things that formerly were living people. Baker's view implies that there is some truth to the claim that a human corpse formerly was a person. However, on her view, the corpse itself was never a 'hardcore' person. At best, it formerly was a person in a derivative way – something that constituted something else that was a person in a nonderivative way. On my view it is strictly and literally true that the corpse formerly was an actual, hardcore psychological, moral, and legal person.

(6) My view generates correct and straightforward answers to the questions about counting people. Where Aunt Ethel is, there is exactly one person.[23] When a person dies, the number of living persons decreases by one. We do not have to invoke strange and unfamiliar systems for counting people in order to get the right numbers.

(7) My view is consistent with the notion that people are ontologically, psychologically, morally, biologically, and legally 'special'. I can explain our psychological specialness by pointing out that among all the creatures on Earth and beyond, only psychopersons like us have the distinctive features that make a thing be a psychological person. I can explain our biological specialness by pointing out that only biopersons have the distinctive features that make something be a biological person. The same is true of our other forms of personality.

Baker suggests that certain views relevantly like mine must fail to account for the ontological significance of persons.[24] I can't see that there is any objection to my view in this accusation. She suggests that a view like mine is committed to the notion that '... the property of being a person is a temporary and contingent property of things that are essentially nonpersonal.'[25] But this is surely wrong. Since each of us in fact is a bioperson, a psychoperson, a moral person, and a legal person (in Massachusetts), it is clearly a mistake to say that we are 'essentially nonpersonal'. Perhaps Baker meant merely that none of us is essentially personal. Even that claim is open to doubt. We might be essentially biopersons.

But the deeper issue is whether we want our view of persons to imply that each person is essentially a person. I have distinguished among several concepts of personality. I find it hard to believe that Aunt Ethel has each of these essentially. Surely it is just good luck that she was a legal person during her lifetime. Had she been born elsewhere, she might have been chattel. Equally, it is just good luck that she was a psychoperson throughout such a long stretch of her life. Had she fallen into a coma earlier, or had she suffered from some congenital injury or illness, she might never have developed the capacities that made her a psychoperson. As for her moral personality, I am simply unsure. Perhaps she was essentially a moral person throughout her existence. Since the concept of moral personality is so obscure and controversial, I simply don't know what to say.

Thus I admit that my view leaves open many questions about the essentiality of personality. That, as I see it, is yet another advantage of my view.[26]

Notes

1.   Olson discusses his form of animalism in his book, *The Human Animal,* as well as in several papers. Some of these are listed in the bibliography. Another form of animalism is discussed by David Mackie in Mackie (1999). My own view is very similar to Mackie's.

2.   Olson (1997), 91. His reasoning turns on some claims about the level of organization of the cells. Prior to this date we have a somewhat disorganized collection of similar cells. After this date they begin to differentiate and the mass becomes an organism.

3.   Olson (1997), 151–2. (Emphasis added.) In fairness to Olson, I should point out that he is not explicitly discussing the argument of which I find hints in the passage. Olson seems to be engaged in trying to show that there is no such thing as 'my body'. But he does pretty clearly commit himself to the view that no 150 pound material object persists through the death of a 150 pound person. Olson has assured me (in personal correspondence) that the view I here attribute to him is indeed his view.

4.   Of course, Olson can acknowledge that 'there are dead people' can express a truth. If all we mean by this is that there are instances in which it formerly was the case that certain people existed, but they died, then the statement is true enough. However, it would be false if it were taken to mean *that there now exist some things that are dead people*. It would also be false on this view if it were taken to mean *that there now exist some things that are dead and formerly were people*.

5.   Rosenberg, (1983), 27.

6.   Rosenberg (1983), 121.

7.   Aristotle seems to discuss this sort of change in several places, including Bk I, Ch. 4 of 'On Generation and Corruption'. Although I describe this view as Aristotelian, and I think it is to be found in the texts, I recognize that the interpretation of Aristotle is very controversial. I am interested in the view itself; not the question whether it is entirely correct to attribute it to Aristotle.

8.   I should mention a slightly misleading feature of the diagram. The two rectangles are separated by a small gap. That makes it appear that there is a short period of time after Ethel goes out of existence and before the corpse comes into existence. That's not part of Rosenberg's view as I understand it. I'm sure he would say that the corpse comes into existence immediately upon the departure of the person. I found it difficult to draw a diagram that would represent this properly without also suggesting that there is a single object that overlaps Ethel for a while and then the corpse for a while. That also would have been misleading.

9.   In fact there is a bit more to the definition. See Baker (1999c), 149. See also Baker (1999b), 6.

10 Baker (1999b), 2.
11 For a full account of the first-person perspective, see Baker (1998).
12 Someone with an interest in abortion might find this feature of Baker's view attractive. For on this view, there is no fetal person present during gestation. If the fetus is aborted, no person is thereby killed. What dies is a fetus, not a person. It might be argued that abortion does not terminate even a 'potential person' on this view, since the thing that dies is *not* something that would otherwise have become a person in its own right. It is at worst a thing that would later *constitute* something else that will be a person in its own right. But abortion fans should not be overly enthusiastic. Baker's view implies that there is no dramatically important metaphysical difference between abortion and infanticide – provided that the baby is killed before the first-person perspective emerges. If my speculations on abortion are correct, then the same rationale could be used to justify the killing of any poor unfortunate who never develops a first-person perspective. This, presumably, would include quite a few mentally handicapped 'persons'.
13 For a detailed exposition of Baker's views on this issue, see Baker (1999b), 17–18. I discuss this issue in greater detail below.
14 Baker (1999b), 19; (1999c), 157.
15 I don't mind this so much when one is a part of the other. But Baker apparently has no interest in saying that the person is a part of the body.
16 Eric Olson raised this objection in his (1999), and Baker replied in her (1999b), 17–18. Olson presented a long and very impressive version of a closely related argument in his (1996), which anyone interested in this issue will find very helpful.
17 See, for example, Baker (1999a), 154–5; (1999b), 2.
18 Baker (1998), 330. There is much more to be said about the first-person perspective, but for present purposes this should suffice.
19 Baker (1999b), 2.
20 If Aunt Ethel and her body are of the same primary kind, then they cannot stand in the constitution relation. If I am not mistaken, the result would be that Baker would have no basis for saying that Aunt Ethel is distinct from her body.
21 Baker has discussed this objection (in personal communication). I think I understand some of the things she would say in reply. I remain unconvinced. Unfortunately, it would take many pages to explain Baker's views on this issue, and many more for me to explain why I find them unpersuasive. This is not the place to enter into such a long and complex debate.
22 Locke is a prominent example. He says a person is a 'thinking intelligent being, that has reason and reflection, and can consider itself as itself, the same thinking thing in different times and places; which it does only by that consciousness, which is inseparable from thinking, and it seems to me essential to it.' *Essay concerning Human Understanding* II.xxvii.9.
23 To be slightly more exact, I should say that where Aunt Ethel is, there is exactly one thing that is at once a psychoperson, bioperson, moral person, and legal person. That one thing is the material object that has the personality-making properties.
24 Baker (1999b), 24–6.
25 Baker (1999b), 25.

[26] Many thanks to friends and colleagues for comments and criticism. Owen McLeod, Ted Sider, Lynne Baker, Clay Splawn, Kris McDaniel, Jean-Paul Vessel, Elizabeth Feldman, and Jack Hanson all gave especially generous help. I am also grateful to Eric Olson and David Mackie. Though I never met either of them I have benefitted from reading their work.

References

Baker, Lynne Rudder (1997a) 'Persons in Metaphysical Perspective', *The Philosophy of Roderick M. Chisholm* volume XXV in *The Library of Living Philosophers* ed. by Lewis Edwin Hahn (Chicago and La Salle, Illinois: Open Court Publishing Co., 1997): 433–453.

Baker, Lynne Rudder (1997b) 'Why Constitution is not Identity', *The Journal of Philosophy* XCIV, 12 (December, 1997): 599–621.

Baker, Lynne Rudder (1998) 'The First-Person Perspective: A Test for Naturalism', *American Philosophical Quarterly* 35, 4 (October, 1998): 327–348.

Baker, Lynne Rudder (1999a) 'What Am I?,' *Philosophy and Phenomenological Research* LIX, 1 (March, 1999): 151–159.

Baker, Lynne Rudder (1999b) 'Materialism with a Human Face', unpublished manuscript.

Baker, Lynne Rudder (1999c) 'Unity without Identity: A New Look at Material Constitution', *Midwest Studies in Philosophy* XXIII (1999) edited by P. French et al., 144–165.

Baker, Lynne Rudder (2000) *Persons and Bodies: A Constitution View* (Cambridge: Cambridge University Press, 2000).

Carter, W. R. (1999) 'Will I Be a Dead Person?', *Philosophy and Phenomenological Research* LIX, 1 (March, 1999): 167–171.

Feldman, Fred (1992) *Confrontations with the Reaper: A Philosophical Study of the Nature and Value of Death* (New York: Oxford University Press, 1992).

Feldman, Fred (1973) 'Sortal Predicates', *Noûs* (September, 1973): 268–282.

Feldman, Fred (1991) 'Some Puzzles about the Evil of Death', *The Philosophical Review* 100, 2 (April, 1991), reprinted in Fischer (1993): 307–326.

Feldman, Fred (2000) 'The Termination Thesis', *Midwest Studies in Philosophy XXIV,* 2000.

Fischer, John Martin (ed.) (1993) *The Metaphysics of Death* (Stanford: Stanford University Press, 1993).

Mackie, David (1999) 'Personal Identity and Dead People', *Philosophical Studies* 95, 3 (September, 1999): 219–242.

Olson, Eric (1996) 'Composition and Coincidence', *Pacific Philosophical Quarterly* 77 (1996): 374–403.

Olson, Eric (1997) *The Human Animal* (New York and Oxford: Oxford University Press, 1997).

Olson, Eric (1999) 'Reply to Lynne Rudder Baker', *Philosophy and Phenomenological Research* LIX, 1 (March 1999): 161–166.

Rorty, Amelie Oksenberg (ed.) (1976) *The Identities of Persons* (Berkeley and Los Angeles: The University of California Press, 1976).

Rosenberg, Jay (1983) *Thinking Clearly about Death* (Englewood Cliffs: Prentice-Hall, 1983).

Sider, Ted (1999a) 'Global Supervenience and Identity across Times and Worlds', *Philosophy and Phenomenological Research* LIX, 4 (December, 1999): 913–937.

Sider, Ted (1999b) *Four Dimensionalism* (unpublished manuscript).

Wiggins, David (1980) *Sameness and Substance* (Oxford: Basil Blackwell, 1980).

Genetic Therapy and Identity

Roger Crisp

The first time I came across Ingmar Persson was during some seminars on personal identity held by Derek Parfit in Oxford in the mid-1980s. Conversations with Parfit revealed immediately several of Ingmar's qualities: philosophical grip, perspicuity, insight, and a willingness to follow the *logos* wherever it leads. I have continued to learn from him, and look forward each year to a telephone call in May or June which tells me that he is once again in Oxford. Talking with Ingmar is one of the highest pleasures, and I am pleased to have this opportunity to thank him.

My paper concerns a debate to which Ingmar himself has made several important contributions: the question whether genetic therapy on a conceptus changes its identity, and thus may not be supported by person-affecting reasons. As often, I find that I agree to a large extent with Ingmar, but I hope that he might find my differences with him worth talking about when we next meet!

It would not be implausible to claim that a primary purpose of a healthcare system, such as the UK National Health Service, is to improve the health of individual patients. This view is a version of what Parfit has called 'The Person-Affecting View, or V':

V: It is good if people are affected for the better.[1]

Parfit himself finds such views plausible, saying, for example, that it is reasonable to think that 'our choice cannot be wrong if we know that it will be worse for no one.'[2]

If we assume that this is the primary purpose of a health care system, this view gives rise to a potential problem with genetic therapy, especially genetic therapy carried out at very early stages of human development on the conceptus – that is, the organism that initially constitutes the single-celled zygote and then develops into the embryo. In the kind of genetic therapy in question, which may well become common as a result of the Human Genome Project and other research, a conceptus's genetic constitution could be decoded, and genes which would otherwise lead to, for example, spina bifida might be altered, removed, or replaced. It may also of course be possible to enhance capacities as well as remedy defects.

The problem was, to my knowledge, first brought to the attention of philosophers by Noam Zohar, who states it as follows:

> [G]enetic makeup seems to be an important element in the personal identity of human beings. If an embryo's genetic makeup is altered, does this not involve an alteration of identity? If it does, the action cannot be properly conceived as improving an individual's life but rather as *substituting* one individual for another. In professed 'genetic therapy', we must be prepared to ask whether a procedure will be beneficial to the individual before us, or will it in fact involve rubbing out this individual and introducing a new individual in its stead?[3]

In this short paper, I shall suggest that the implications of V for genetic therapy depend on how one understands the notion of a person within V.

Our first question must be: the identity of what? Consider a straightforward example of medical treatment: a doctor gives a patient an aspirin, which relieves a headache. The patient here is of course a person, and thus no problem arises from view V for such treatment. But in the case of genetic therapy on a conceptus (let me call this CT), the subject of the treatment appears to be not a person, but a conceptus. A person is something that *develops* from a conceptus.[4] So, it might be argued, view V has the bizarre implication that no treatment on human beings is justified until they become persons.

One strategy here, often taken in the literature on abortion, would be to argue that the conceptus is in fact a person. But in the present context this is unnecessary, since view V is not to be interpreted as the claim that we should concern ourselves only with existing persons. Rather, the question is one of identifiability: if there is no particular person (past, present, or future) who will be benefited or harmed by my action now, then, on view V, there is nothing to be said for or against it.[5] Consider one of Parfit's examples: *The Medical Programmes*.[6] Imagine that there are two conditions, J and K. If a pregnant woman has J, her child will be born with disability D. A simple treatment will prevent this. If a woman has condition K, any child she conceives will have D, but K always disappears within two months. We have two options: we can initiate either a pregnancy testing programme, so that 1000 children who would have suffered from D are born without it, or a preconception testing programme, so that women with K can delay their pregnancy, with the result that 1000 women who would have had a child with D will in fact have children without D. Now imagine that we carry out preconception testing. On V, the 1000 children with D have been affected for the worse by our decision. Whereas, if we choose the pregnancy testing programme, the 1000 children born with D have not been affected for the worse by our decision (let us assume that, despite their disability, these children have lives which are clearly worth living). For these children are different from those who would have come into existence had the preconception programme been adopted.

Our question, then, is whether CT affects the identity of the person who will develop from the treated conceptus. Note that we are not seeking the identity conditions merely of the conceptus itself, since, logically, it could be that we might change the identity of the conceptus and the same person develop from that conceptus who would anyway have developed, or that the identity of the conceptus remain unchanged and yet a different person develop.

How, then, is the identity of a person related to the conceptus? Does the essence of a person, that is to say, depend in any way on the conceptus from which that person develops? There is a dispute in philosophy about whether essence is best understood on the model of definition, or in modal terms.[7] It is not necessary for me to enter this dispute, since on both accounts the essential properties of x are those properties that x requires if x is to be x. Any other properties x has will be accidental.

Now recall Zohar's question: 'If an embryo's genetic makeup is altered, does this not involve an alteration of identity?'. We might then be tempted by:

Genotype Superessentialism: Any change in the genotype of a conceptus results in a change of identity of the person who develops.[8]

Genotype Superessentialism is too strong. Consider a case in which the genotype of a conceptus is altered slightly, to remove a minor defect in a single toe. It is not plausible to claim that this causes a change in the identity of the person who develops from that conceptus. She can say, perfectly straightforwardly, 'I would have had a defective toe had that genetic therapy not been carried out.'[9]

But, it might be claimed, this is a case of a very minor change in genotype. Major changes will affect identity. Thus we might consider:

Genotype Essentialism: Major changes in the genotype of a conceptus will change the identity of the person who develops.[10]

Consider, for example, the genetically based condition Lesch-Nyhan syndrome, which results in severe mental retardation, spastic cerebral palsy, and involuntary biting of the tongue, lips and fingers. Kahn says: 'How much of our identity is determined by a particular combination of our genes? ... a child with Lesch-Nyhan syndrome is arguably not the same child should the enzyme deficiency causing the syndrome be corrected'.[11]

Here we must pause to ask what it is to be a person. The notion of person is used (pretty loosely) in at least three ways. The first sense is employed in claims such as: 'She has become an entirely different person since her depression was cured'; 'She is not the person she used to be since her partner left her.' Here, the term refers to 'individual human being with a certain set of personality traits', so

I shall call this the *personality* sense of 'person'. I take it that this is not the sense of 'person' intended by those who advocate person-affecting principles, and henceforth I shall ignore it.

In the second sense of 'person', the term is roughly equivalent to 'individual human being'. Thus, to use an example of Paul Snowdon's, we might say: 'Every day, at least one person dies in this hospital'.[12] Let me call this the *human* sense of 'person', and refer to such persons as H-persons.

In the third sense, which dates back at least to Locke, the term refers to a being with certain special mental characteristics, such as sentience, consciousness, or self-consciousness. Let me call this the *mental* sense of 'person', and call such persons M-persons. Note that H-persons may never have any conscious experience whatsoever. Consider a case in which a baby is born severely brain-damaged and kept on life support for twenty years.

Which of these senses should we use in seeking to understand the implications of the person-affecting view for identity and genetic therapy? Notice first that, in either sense, personhood allows for great variability in properties.[13] A (self-conscious) H-person might ask herself: 'I am female, able-bodied, red-haired, of moderate intelligence and considerate of others. Could I have been male, paralyzed, blonde, very intelligent, and unkind?', and answer, 'Yes'. Likewise, an M-person might ask herself: 'I have the experience of being female, of being able-bodied, etc. Could I have had the experience of being male, paralyzed, etc.?', and answer again in the affirmative.[14] This suggests that on either sense of 'person', great changes at the level of genotype in many kinds of property will not affect identity. But we need now to consider what fixes the identity of persons, on each view of personhood.

First, consider H-persons. Since Kripke, it has become common to claim that in many cases the essence of X lies, at least partly, in the origin of X.[15] Consider one of Kripke's examples: a table. He asks: 'could *this table* have been made from a completely *different* block of wood?'.[16] And, of persons, he asks: 'could a person originating from different parents, from a totally different sperm and egg, be *this very woman*?'.[17]

Kripke speaks of our origin as conception. Recently, John Harris has suggested going back even further, proposing:

> *The Gametic Principle*: An individual's life begins when one of the gametes from which that individual will develop is first formed.[18]

Imagine, for example, that someone had irradiated the egg which, once fertilized, developed into the person who is now writing this article, in such a way that this person suffered serious pain. It seems hard to deny that this person would be me; and, according to Harris, because the story of my life would require an account of my serious pain, and its cause, we should claim that I begin with my first gamete.

The Gametic Principle has the following implication. If I am identical with the egg from which I developed, then the same person would have developed had that egg been fertilized by a different sperm – even a sperm from a different father. This is hard to believe.[19] Of course, Harris will claim that the individual who would have developed would in fact have been different. But this suggests strongly that it is not the existence of a gamete, but the fertilization of an egg, that fixes identity.

One objection sometimes made to Kripke's suggestion that our origin lies at conception is that it implies that identical twins are in fact literally identical with one another.[20] For if each twin is identical with the pre-divided conceptus, then each is the same person as the other. To avoid this implication, one might claim that, in a case of twinning, each twin's existence begins at the time of division itself. As Bernard Williams puts it, modifying his own Kripke-influenced 'Zygotic Principle': 'a story is about A if it is about an individual who uniquely developed from the earliest item from which A in fact uniquely developed, where "uniquely developed" refers to development in the course of which there is no splitting.'[21]

I accept this view. A human life, then, begins at conception, or at the time of division in the case of twinning. Now, Kripke's view does not imply that essence depends only on origin. For it may be that my origin in a particular sperm and egg is just one of my essential properties. Return again to the counterfactual questions persons may ask about themselves. An H-person, I am suggesting, cannot sensibly ask: 'Could I have come from a different sperm and egg?'.[22] There is one other question in this category, which follows from the definition of H-persons as 'individual human beings'. A person cannot sensibly ask either: 'Could I have been non-human?'.[23] Imagine a case in which extreme CT is carried out on a conceptus, and the functional genetic material of that conceptus is replaced with the functional material from a chicken conceptus. If a chicken develops, it would not be plausible to claim that this chicken is the person who would otherwise have developed, but now with gallinaceous rather than human properties. H-persons must be human. Once again, there is a good deal of disagreement about which properties determine species membership in general.[24] Biologists tend to employ the notion of interbreeding: a pig is a creature that can breed with other pigs to produce more pigs. But this raises the question of what a pig is in the first place, and here some reference to characteristics is likely to be required. For the purposes of my argument, this is another debate I do not need to enter. So, in the case of H-persons, we are left with what I shall call:

Origin and Species Essentialism (OSE): The essence of a (human) person lies in her origin in a particular sperm and egg, and in her humanity.[25]

What are the implications for V as applied to CT on the basis of OSE? So far we have identified a problem only with CT that changes the species of the treated conceptus.[26] It will harm a particular person by preventing their coming into existence. Such intervention is hardly on the cards at present or in the future! In future, it would seem that the only kind of CT which might run into difficulties here would be positive genetic engineering that vastly enhanced the capacities of the resulting organism to the point where one might doubt whether it was in fact human.

Let me now briefly examine two objections. First, consider the following example:[27]

Gene-swopping: A male child, with Scandinavian ancestry, is conceived at t in Oslo, Norway. A female child, with African ancestry, is conceived at t' in Ouagadougou, Burkina Faso. Through a transfer of functional genetic material, the characteristics of the two developing people are swopped. Ultimately, a black girl is born in Oslo, and a white boy in Ouagadougou, each looking identical to the children who would have been born without the gene transfers.

Is it not plausible that the birth parents of each child would consider the child born to the other couple as their own? This suggests that we have here a case of person-swopping, and that OSE is insufficient to capture what determines identity.

My view is that the identity of the two children is not changed by this procedure. That is, the H-person who develops in Oslo is the same H-person who would have developed without the gene-swopping. The temptation to think otherwise arises, I suggest, partly because insufficient attention is paid to the process of change itself: we tend to think of the case as if it were one in which the two children had been swopped at birth. But one might be tempted to think that gene-swopping must change identity even when fully aware of the gene-swopping process. Often, I suspect, this thought rests on a failure to recognize how resilient certain things can be to change. I now am very different from how I was at the age of five, and even more different from how I was as a conceptus. But the same individual – me – persisted throughout these changes.[28]

Another objection here is not so much to OSE itself as to the claim that, in combination with V, it rules out only CT that changes species. I have already discussed cases in which CT results in great changes to the properties possessed by the resulting person, and claimed that these changes do not affect the identity of the person. But OSE suggests that my identity as a person depends on my origin in the fusion of a particular sperm and egg, and it may be claimed that certain genetic interventions throw doubt on whether this is still true of the resulting person. Here, I think, we *are* concerned with the identity conditions of a conceptus; as Zohar puts it, 'the question is ... if we are substituting one origin for another'.[29] Elliot, for example, claims: 'Certainly nucleus substitution in the case where C [the conceptus] is single-celled, would constitute C's cessation. The same would be true if eighty or ninety *per cent* of C's functional genetic material were replaced'.[30]

A zygote, however, is itself identified through its having its origin in a particular sperm and egg. Thus, even in the case of nucleus substitution or great changes in functional genetic material, the zygote remains the same zygote throughout the change. As Snowdon puts it: 'We regard the persistence in a certain materially continuous form of a fundamental explanatory unity as the persistence of a thing'.[31] So we can conclude that only species-altering CT has person-affecting implications, on the human sense of 'person'.[32]

But what of the mental sense of 'person'? Persson argues that we have here three options: (1) the *origination theory*, according to which 'the (numerical) identity of a ... person is entirely determined by the identity of the (foetal) body in which he originates'; (2) the *type-cast theory*, according to which 'the identity of a person is only *partially* determined by the identity of the (foetal) body in which he originates: it is also determined by some of his distinctive properties ... some distinctive psychological properties of A are so fundamental that he could not possibly exist without them'; (3) the view 'that the numerical identity of a person is *entirely* determined by the psychological type'.[33]

Persson rejects (3) because it is conceivable that there be more than one instance of the same psychological type, and (2) because of the great variability in properties which can be ascribed to the same person in different possible life-stories. And so he advocates (1).

The problem for the origination theory, and hence also for the type-cast view, is that I – as an M-person – can answer 'Yes' to the question, 'Could I have originated in a different body?'. Body-swopping cases, indeed, are one of the main tools used by proponents of the mental view of persons to advocate that view. Persson's objection to the third view, however, seems persuasive.

On one view – reductionism – a person's identity over time consists in the holding of certain more particular facts, and these facts can be described in an impersonal way.[34] To say, 'There is a person' is merely to say something like, 'There is a set of psychologically connected experiences'. On reductionism, questions of personal identity are not all-or-nothing. But we must be able to distinguish one person from another. What makes me a different person from you is that the existence of each of us will be explained in terms of different sets of psychologically related experiences. Now consider Lesch-Nyhan syndrome again. It seems plausible to suggest that the set of experiences of a Lesch-Nyhan sufferer are so different from those of an otherwise healthy individual that they could not plausibly be said to be the same person. This suggests that, on a reductionist understanding, the kind of CT that is likely to be practised could run into person-affecting considerations.

According to non-reductionism, a person is something over and above their experiences. For example, 'I' might be said to be the 'owner' of my experiences. It is this sort of view that underlies the idea that M-persons may have extremely varying experiences in different possible worlds and remain the same person. Nevertheless, on most versions of non-reductionism, psychological connectedness is important to personal identity.[35] What fixes the identity of an M-person, understood non-reductionistically? Here again the notion of origin may be helpful. A mental person might plausibly be said to begin to exist when she has her first conscious experience (or perhaps: her first conscious experience sufficiently connected with subsequent experiences for it to make sense to describe these as experiences of the same person). This suggests that the identity of a mental person depends importantly on *when* that first experience occurs. A mental person could not answer, 'Yes,' to the question, 'Could I have begun to exist at a different time?'.

CT may have serious implications for the identity of mental persons, since it is not unlikely to affect the time of first conscious experience. It is not the purpose of this paper to discuss the plausibility or otherwise of V, but it may be worth noting that many factors may affect the identity of an M-person, non-reductionistically understood: the nutrition of the mother, for example, or postnatal immunization.[36]

So, on either a reductionist or a non-reductionist view of M-persons, CT gives rise to potentially serious person-affecting difficulties. This is not the case with H-persons. Whether we must choose between these different understandings of our nature, and if so which to choose, when interpreting V, are questions I must leave on one side. But certainly those who advocate person-affecting principles ought to answer them.[37]

Notes

[1] D. Parfit, *Reasons and Persons* (Oxford: Clarendon Press, 1984), p. 370. Parfit states the view in terms of badness rather than goodness. I should perhaps register my own doubt about V, if it is taken to give special weight to person-affecting considerations.

[2] D. Parfit, 'Energy Policy and the Further Future', in D. MacLean and P.G. Brown (eds), *Energy and the Future* (Totowa, NJ: Rowman and Littlefield, 1983): 31–37, 166–79, p. 169.

[3] N. Zohar, 'Prospects for "Genetic Therapy" – Can a Person Benefit from Being Altered?', *Bioethics* 5 (1991): 275–88, p. 279. For further discussion, see J. Kahn, 'Genetic Harm: Bitten by the Body that Keeps You?', *Bioethics* 5 (1991): 289–308; N. Zohar, 'Commentary on Kahn's "Genetic Harm: Bitten by the Body that Keeps You?"', *Bioethics*

5 (1991): 309–11; J. Kahn, 'Commentary on Zohar's "Prospects for 'Genetic Therapy' – Can a Person Benefit from Being Altered?"', *Bioethics* 5 (1991): 312–17; R. Elliot, 'Identity and the Ethics of Gene Therapy', *Bioethics* 7 (1993): 27–40; I. Persson, 'Genetic Therapy, Identity and Person-regarding Reasons', *Bioethics* 9 (1995): 16–31; N. Holtug and P. Sandøe, 'Who Benefits? – Why Personal Identity does not Matter in Moral Evaluation of Germ-line Gene Therapy', *Journal of Applied Philosophy* 13 (1996): 157–66; R. Elliot, 'Genetic Therapy, Person-regarding Reasons, and the Determination of Identity', *Bioethics* 11 (1997): 151–60; I. Persson, 'Genetic Therapy, Person-regarding Reasons, and the Determination of Identity – A Reply to Robert Elliot', *Bioethics* 11 (1997): 161–9.

4   Of course, there may be other ways in which persons can come to exist.

5   That is, view V, understood as merely stating a condition of sufficiency for goodness, has no implications in such cases. View V may of course be held alongside other non-person-affecting principles that would have such implications.

6   Parfit, *Reasons and Persons*, p. 367.

7   See K. Fine, 'Essence and Modality', *Philosophical Perspectives* 8 (1994): 1–16.

8   Cf. Elliot's 'Strong Genotype as Essence View', in 'Identity', pp. 31–2.

9   Cf. Zohar, 'Prospects', pp. 285–7; Elliot, 'Identity', p. 33; Persson, 'Genetic Therapy, Person-regarding Reasons', p. 164. Of course, Genotype Superessentialists need not claim that this person is committed to the view that this therapy was carried out on *her*.

10   Cf. Zohar, 'Prospects', p. 279; Elliot, 'Identity', p. 30.

11   Kahn, 'Genetic Harm', p. 291; cf. Zohar, 'Prospects', p. 287.

12   Paul Snowdon, 'Persons, Animals, and Ourselves', in C. Gill (ed.), *The Person and the Human Mind* (Oxford: Clarendon Press, 1990): 83–107, p. 102.

13   Cf. Persson, 'Genetic Therapy, Identity', p. 23.

14   The reference to experience is to keep the distinction between H- and M-persons clear. M-persons are, to put it roughly, streams of consciousness or experience, and it is not clear that such items can have a sex, etc.

15   S. Kripke, *Naming and Necessity* (Oxford: Blackwell, 1980), pp. 112–15.

16   Ibid., p. 113.

17   Ibid.

18   J. Harris, *Clones, Genes, and Immortality* (Oxford: Oxford University Press, 1998), pp. 77, 80. Note that it is not inconsistent to claim that my life begins before I develop. Development may be something that I do or that happens to me.

19   Cf. I. Persson, 'Does it Matter When We Begin to Exist?', in V. Launis, J. Pietarinen, and J. Räikkä (eds), *Genes and Morality* (Amsterdam: Rodopi, 1999): 21–7, p. 21.

20   See Persson, 'Genetic Therapy, Identity', p. 20.

21   B. Williams, 'Resenting One's Own Existence', in his *Making Sense of Humanity* (Cambridge: Cambridge University Press, 1995), p. 230. Italics in original deleted. I am taking the Zygotic Principle to concern identity, and not mere composition.

22   *Pace* David Wiggins, *Sameness and Substance* (Oxford: Blackwell, 1980), p. 116n. Wiggins suggests that one may speculate about how the man whom Brutus murdered in 44 BC would have fared had Marius been his father.

23 See Persson, 'Genetic Therapy, Identity', p. 25.

24 See S. Wulfram, *Philosophical Logic: An Introduction* (London: Routledge, 1989), pp. 229–42.

25 See G. Forbes, *The Metaphysics of Modality* (Oxford: Clarendon Press, 1985), pp. 147–8.

26 The species of a conceptus is presumably to be determined at least partly on the basis of the species of the animal it is to develop into. *Pace* Persson, 'Genetic Therapy, Identity', p. 21, there seems no need to insist that the conceptus itself meet, for example, morphological criteria.

27 Suggested to me by David Edmonds.

28 See C. McGinn, 'On the Necessity of Origin', *Journal of Philosophy* 73 (1976): 127–35, p. 132.

29 Zohar, 'Prospects', p. 282; cf. pp. 285–7. Elliot suggests that if the parts of a bicycle are quickly replaced one after another a new bicycle results. That seems implausible.

30 Elliot, 'Identity', p. 31.

31 Snowdon, p. 97.

32 Zohar says ('Prospects', p. 283): 'If there is any sense at all in considering the embryo's existence to be the beginning (or: origin) of a particular human life, then it surely comes from the fact that once the genotype has been specified, personal identity has been significantly determined.' I prefer his claim on p. 282: 'What justifies viewing the sperm and egg as my origin is precisely the fact that, once they are specified – and not before that – the particular human organism who is me has been uniquely individuated.' Cf. also Bernard Williams, 'Resenting', p. 225: 'The Zygotic Principle is not motivated by any particular belief about the extent to which genetic information is important in causing the characteristics of a human being. (That this is not the point, emerges already from the consideration I just mentioned, that the difference between identity and non-identity does not turn on the question of how much the object that appears in the hypothetical speculation resembles the actual object.)'

33 Persson, 'Genetic Therapy, Identity', p. 22.

34 Parfit, *Reasons and Persons*, p. 210.

35 This may not be true of that version of non-reductionism which postulates the existence of a soul. The identity of a soul may perhaps be quite unrelated to psychological properties.

36 See Kahn, 'Commentary', p. 314; Elliot, 'Identity', pp. 37–8; cf. Persson, 'Genetic Therapy, Identity', p. 24.

37 For comments on and discussion of previous drafts I am grateful to Robert Audi, David Edmonds, Paul Robinson, and participants in the Sion College Conference on Ethical Issues Arising from New Techniques in Human Reproduction held at Corpus Christi College, Oxford, in September 2000.

Hume on Himself [1]

Galen Strawson

Are there such things as selves? It depends on what you mean by 'self', and many people have meant many things. I will restrict my attention to the human case and take it that if anything is to count as a self then it must be a subject of experience and must be non-identical with a human being considered as a whole;[2] whether or not it is also something that has long-term existence, or a personality, or is self-conscious, or capable of discursive thought, and so on.

Do selves exist, on these terms, in the human case? I think they do. I think they exist in every sense in which trees and cats and chairs do; but only for short periods of time.

I call this the *Transience view*. Few if any of those who want there to be such things as selves are drawn to it, because nearly all of them want selves to be things that persist for long periods of time. So most of them think the Transience view of the self amounts to the view that there is no such thing as the self. And this is fine by me. However, the Transience view reminds many of the Bundle view of the self or mind so famously set out and so famously rejected by Hume in his *Treatise of Human Nature*, and this is not so fine by me.

In one way it is unsurprising, because there are many successive selves in the case of a single human being, according to the Transience view, and this rings a loud Humean bell: the selves of the Transience view sound like the sorts of things that get bundled together by Bundle views to make a single self that has some kind of long-term existence. In another way, though, it is very surprising, because the two views are completely different. According to the Transience view a self, considered over time, is a strongly single or *non-compound* thing, a *continuous* thing, and a *fleeting* thing. It is – to introduce a simple scheme of reference –

[+A] diachronically *non-compound*
[+B] diachronically *continuous*
[¬C] a thing that has *short-term* existence.

According to the most natural reading of the Bundle view, by contrast, a self is

[¬A] a diachronically *compound* thing
[¬B] a diachronically *non-continuous* thing
[+C] a thing with *some sort* of *long-term* existence.

So the two views are directly opposed on three fundamental counts.

Contradiction doesn't stop people holding a view, though, and my main motive for trying to sort out what Hume said or thought is to prevent misreadings of Hume interfering with the attempt to make a case for the Transience view. Many do misinterpret Hume's statement of the Bundle view. Worse, many pass over his explicit rejection of the view. Worse, many think the Bundle view incorporates the extraordinary 'no owner' view – the view that there is no subject of experience at all when there is an experience, or 'perception'.[3]

This is easy to deal with, so I will deal with it first. Hume never considers any such position. A perception is not just a content or content-type, an impression-content-type or an idea-content-type, on his view. A perception is a *perceiving*, an experience is an *experiencing*: an actual occurrence, a happening, a clockable event, an occurrent conscious 'tokening' of a particular type of impression or idea. Most simply: an experience is an *experience*; a perception is a *perception*. To hear these tautologies in the right way is to see that the idea that there could be an experience without an experiencer is like the idea that there could be a square without any sides, or a dent without a surface. It is a necessary truth that an experience entails an experiencer, as many have observed.

I will call this the *Experience/Experiencer thesis*. Hume never questions it – he is not so foolish – although he does also use the word 'perception' ('impression', 'idea') in the content-type sense. When he is at the furthest point of his sceptical doubt, in the last section of the first book of the *Treatise*, the one thing he does not doubt (along with the existence of perceptions) is the existence of the subject of perceptions that he is in the heat of his doubt (T268–9). His target in 'Of personal identity' is not belief in the *existence* of subjects of experience. They exist as certainly as experiences do. His target is a certain view of the *nature* of the soul or self or subject, and a correlative view of what can be *known* about its nature.[4] It is the view (routine at the time) of the self or subject as something that has and knowably has 'perfect identity and simplicity' and 'continue[s] invariably the same, through the whole course of our lives' (T251), something that is

    [+A] diachronically non-compound
    [+B] diachronically continuous
    [+C] a thing that has long-term existence
    [+D] diachronically unchanging
    [+E] synchronically non-compound

where [+A] and [+B] and [+C] represent the 'perfect identity' claim,[5] [+D] represents the 'invariableness' claim, and [+E] represents the 'perfect … simplicity' or indivisibility claim.[6]

— These may be Hume's main targets, but I'm still not convinced that he isn't arguing for some form of the 'no owner' view – some form of the view that experiences can exist without an experiencer existing. What about his claim that – I quote – 'perceptions ... may be consider'd as separately existent, and may exist separately' (T233, T252, T634), for example?

What about it? To say that perceptions or experiences may be considered as separately existent, and may exist separately, is in no way to say that they can exist without a subject. It is a necessary truth, a dent/surface truth, that an experience must involve an experiencer or subject. So if experiences do exist separately in the way imagined, all that follows is that there are as many subjects of experience as there are experiences – a version of the Transience view. Hume's fundamental, epistemological, sceptical claim is that we cannot know that this is not how things are, when it comes to the question of the subject of experience or self.

This requires a brief comment. The idea that Hume generally moves from the epistemological claim that

(E)   experiences are all we can *know* of the self or mind

to the semantic claim that

(S)   experiences are all we can legitimately or distinctly *mean* by the words 'self' or 'mind'

to the full-on ontological conclusion that

(O)   selves or minds just *are* (are just) experiences

is (I trust) no longer taken seriously. What Hume does do is to argue from (E) and (S) to the properly sceptical ontological/epistemological conclusion that

(O/E) experiences are all that selves or minds are so far as we have any distinct and positively contentful notion of them.

The argument that this is so has been made enough times recently, and does not need to be done again.[7] Confusion arises from the fact that Hume often expresses his central claim in dramatic ontological terms.[8] Minds or selves or persons, he says, 'are nothing but a bundle or collection of different perceptions' (T252); 'they are the successive perceptions only, that constitute the mind' (T253); a 'succession of perceptions ... constitutes [a person's] mind or thinking principle [or] self or person' (T260, T265; see also T207). But these dramatic ontological statements are shorthand for more sober epistemological claims, and are restated as such when Hume is being more precise: the self or soul *as far as we can conceive it*, is nothing but a system or train of different perceptions' (T657); 'we have no *notion* of [the mind], distinct from the particular perceptions' (T635).[9]

I think it should be obvious that this is Hume's view, but it is worth pausing to prove that Hume takes it that there is more to the mind than a heap of perceptions even though he thinks that we have no notion of its ultimate nature in so far as it is something more than that.

There are at least three decisive points, even when we restrict ourselves to what Hume says specifically about the mind and put aside a number of more general, equally decisive points.[10] First, and most simply, Hume writes that 'to me it seems evident, that the essence of the mind [is] equally unknown to us with that of external bodies' (Txvii). This proves that he cannot think that the essence of the mind is just a heap of perceptions, for he is everywhere committed to the view that 'the perceptions of the mind are perfectly known' (T366), and nothing can be both perfectly known and obscure.

Second, Hume is equally deeply committed to the existence of what he calls 'the imagination'. His philosophy depends on its existence at every moment, and on whatever it is that makes it true that it operates according to the principles of the association of ideas. These things cannot be supposed to be either individual perceptions or collections of perceptions.[11]

A suitably intense empiricist might propose to treat an expression like 'the imagination' or 'the memory' as – roughly – a convenient abbreviatory name for complex patterns among perceptions. That's fine, but Hume never does anything like this. He does not suggest that the imagination might itself be a 'fiction' – if to say that X is a fiction is to allow that it might turn out that there is no such thing as X.[12] That would be a tricky (untenable) position for him to adopt, given that it is the imagination that is the source of all such fictions.

These two points pull together when Hume speaks specifically of our ignorance of the mind. The imagination – the most important single explanatory posit in his philosophy – is, he says, a kind of 'magical faculty in the soul, which … is … inexplicable by the utmost efforts of human understanding' (T24). Reason 'is a wonderful and unintelligible instinct in our souls' (T179). The same goes for the understanding, which Hume identifies with the imagination considered specifically as a faculty that operates according to 'principles which are permanent, irresistable and universal', 'solid, permanent, and consistent' (T225, T226).[13]

The third point is my favourite.[14] Let us call a simple impression of X an *X-impression* and a simple idea of X an *X-idea*. It is a central tenet of Hume's empiricism that an X-idea can arise in a person's mind only if that person has already had an X-impression. But if the mind is nothing but a series of ontologically distinct perceptions then there can be *no possible reason* why this is so. Hume's reason for why it is so is well known: an X-idea, when it occurs, is 'deriv'd from' or 'copy'd from' or 'depends' on an X-impression:[15] when 'an impression first strikes upon the senses', he says, 'there is a copy taken by the mind, which remains after the impression ceases; and this we call an idea.'[16] But if the mind is just a bundle of distinct perceptions with no hidden content (their contents are 'perfectly known'), there is no possible way in which this can happen. *Where* does the idea of X 'remain ... after the impression ceases', given that I go on to experience or think about Y, Z, K, and P, if the mind is just a bundle of distinct perceptions with no hidden content?[17] There is in this case no possible structure or mechanism given which it can possibly be true that the occurrence of an X-impression is the *basis* of the occurrence of any X-idea. It must be a complete fluke that impressions of X always precede ideas of X. The whole phenomenon of memory, furthermore, must be a complete fluke – and an illusion. This point is I think particularly devastating.

— It has no force at all. It not only depends on the view that the outright ontological regularity theory of causation is untenable and reduces all causation to fluke; it also depends on the view that the outright ontological regularity theory is wrongly attributed to Hume; and both these views will be disputed by those who think Hume adopts an outright ontological Bundle theory of mind.

The outright ontological regularity theory is certainly silly (given any sort of realism about the passage of time) and Hume certainly never held it,[18] but one can give these points away, for the third point does not depend on either of them. It must be a complete fluke that impressions of X always precede ideas of X even on the terms of the outright ontological regularity theory of causation.[19] For if the mind is nothing but a series of ontologically distinct perceptions, then the temporal contiguity condition laid down by the regularity theory of causation fails to hold between any X-impression and any later X-idea that is not its immediate successor in the series of perceptions; or, if you like, between the first X-idea (which we may suppose to be the immediate successor of the first X-impression) and any later X-idea. Neither the X-impression nor the first X-idea can be said to be the cause of any later non-contiguous X-idea, if the outright Bundle view is true.

It follows that there must be something more to the mind than just the occurrent series of conscious perceptions, on Hume's view – even if he espouses the outright ontological regularity theory of causation, which he does not. There must be something more to the mind if there is any sense in which ideas derive from, or are copies of, or depend on, impressions that they do not immediately succeed. There must be something – however unknown or unintelligible to us – that *serves to preserve contents through time*, as it were, so that an X-impression (or first X-idea) occurring at a given time can serve as the basis of the occurrence of an X-idea at some later non-contiguous time.

Consider the case, central for Hume, in which an impression of A gives rise to an idea of B because one often saw As followed by Bs in the past – ten years ago, say. How does this happen? How does the B-idea arise in this way after a ten year gap? We don't know, according to Hume. We know that it happens, but we do not understand how. It is a matter of the activity of the imagination, and this activity is 'inexplicable by the utmost efforts of human understanding'. Still, one thing we can know is that it cannot possibly happen if the mind is just a series of ontologically distinct fleeting perceptions.

*

I am preparing to enter the central textual shrine of the rite of 'Hume on personal identity', but there are still a number of things I want to do, beginning with a terminological provision: when quoting from Hume I will use the word 'experience' wherever he uses the word 'perception'. 'Experience' has greater generality in present-day use, its generality corresponds very well to the intended generality of Hume's use of 'perception', and it seems a good idea, when discussing Hume, to try to suspend some of the old interpretative reflexes coded into the word 'perception'.[20]

Let me now list three theses that Hume accepts and that it helps to bear in mind. The first is the Experience/Experiencer thesis, the thesis that an experience entails an experiencer, which I have already discussed, and which Hume rightly never questions. The second is the *Cartesian Certainty* thesis that

> one can know that one exists in the present moment of experience even if there is much one cannot know about what sort of thing one is and even if one cannot know whether one endures beyond the present patch of experience.

This routine sceptical claim is central to Hume's discussion of personal identity and recurs when he is summing up his overall sceptical predicament in the next section. When we go hyperbolic (in Descartes's terms), only our own existence is beyond doubt (T269, ll. 1–2), and when we discount the action of the imagination we can admit to exist 'only those perceptions, which are immediately present to our consciousness' (T265).

The third thesis that Hume accepts is the *Intimate Idea* thesis that

> the idea, or rather impression of ourselves is always intimately present with us, and that our consciousness gives us so lively a conception of our

own person, that 'tis not possible to imagine, that any thing can in this particular go beyond it (T317).

It is widely held that 'when Hume uses the term "self" or "person", he generally means to be referring only to the mind',[21] and this endorsement of the Intimate Idea thesis, which Hume repeats three pages later, is useful because it appears to suffice on its own to show that Hume has no thought of claiming that there is no sort of impression or idea of self at all, rather than claiming that there is (for example) no idea or impression of an uninterrupted, perfectly simple and continuing self.

Is it legitimate to appeal to Hume's endorsement of the Intimate Idea thesis when considering his views on personal identity, given that it occurs in his discussion of the passions in Book II of the *Treatise*? Few doubt that it is, but reference to the Intimate Idea thesis will play no essential role in what follows.

The last thing I want to do before considering Hume's entry into himself is to note some complexities in the Bundle view as he presents it. Hume spends most of his section 'Of personal identity' explaining how we come to believe in the existence of a self that is

[+A] diachronically *non-compound*
[+B] diachronically *continuous*
[+C] something that has *long-term existence*,[22]

whether or not we also come to believe the self to be

[+D] diachronically unchanging[23]
[+E] synchronically non-compound

– either naturally, or because we have some religious or philosophical agenda – and his account of how this belief arises is in certain key respects the same as the account he gives of how we come to believe in continuing physical objects like tables and chairs: it involves what he calls a 'fiction', the natural positing (as a result of the action of the imagination) of a single [+A] diachronically non-compound and [+B] diachronically continuous [+C] persisting thing on exposure to a series of successive experiences that are, considered collectively, [¬A] diachronically multiple, [¬B] diachronically discontinuous, and [¬C] fleeting.

[+A], [+B], and [+C], with or without [+D] and [+E], constitute what one might call the 'simple' version of the fiction view – the *Simple Fiction* view, for short. There is, however, a complication, for Hume does not think that a persisting self, considered as a posit, is a posit of quite the same sort as a table or stone; he thinks it is more like the posit of a persisting plant or vegetable (T255, T259).

At this point a number of ideas are densely concertinaed together, but part of what is going on – very briefly – is this. Consider a stone. In the standard case, according to Hume, we are led to believe in the existence of a single continuing stone by a series of strongly qualitatively resembling experiences [+1]. We also take it that the stone consists of very much the same particles of matter over time [+2]; and that it remains very similar in overall appearance and actual qualitative character [+3].

Plants are different. First, we can be led to believe in the existence of a single continuing plant by a series of experiences that is much more various over time than the series of experiences that leads us to believe in the existence of a stone [-1]. Second, we take a plant to be the same thing over time even though we believe it to be constituted by a succession of different particles [-2], and even if it changes greatly in overall appearance and actual qualitative character over time [-3].

The case of the self is more like the case of the plant than the stone, according to Hume, for, first, the series of experiences that leads us to believe in the existence of a single continuing self is often highly various in qualitative character: 'our thought is ... in a perpetual flux' in which different experiences 'succeed each other with an inconceivable rapidity' (T252) [-1]. Second, we take a self to be the same thing over time even if this involves taking it to be something that changes greatly in overall appearance and actual qualitative character over time, given development of personality, and so on [-3]. Third, we take the experiences that lead us to believe in the existence of a continuing self to be the contents of the consciousness of the very thing we are led to believe in; and these experiences are – in so far as we take them to be (partly) constitutive of the self's being – in this respect comparable to the particles that we suppose to constitute a single plant persisting over time [-2].

Much more can be said about this, but here I will simply extract what one may call the *Vegetable Fiction* view of the self, according to which, as Hume says, 'the identity, which we ascribe to the mind of man, is ... of a like kind with that which we ascribe to vegetables and animal bodies' (T259). The mind or self is a diachronically compound entity, although it is diachronically continuous in every sense in which a plant is, and it is a diachronically changing entity (its substance changes, and not just its states), although it remains the same thing through time in every sense in which a plant does. It is, then,

[¬A]   diachronically compound
[+B]   diachronically continuous
[+C°] a thing that has 'organic' long-term existence
[¬D]   diachronically changing

whether or not it is

[+E]   synchronically non-compound.[24]

The two Fiction views of the self are clearly very different from the outright ontological Bundle view, or *Outright Bundle* view, according to which selves or minds 'are nothing but a bundle or collection of different experiences' (T252). Hume's main task in 'Of personal identity' is certainly not the exposition and defence of the Outright Bundle view; his main task is to give an account of how we come to believe in a continuing single self in the way that we do given that the mind or self 'as far as we can conceive it', as far as we have any distinct or legitimate idea of it, 'is nothing but a system or train of different experiences' (T657). Still, his version of the Outright Bundle view needs to be recorded, and it is most naturally read as stating that the self is a diachronically non-continuous, diachronically compound thing with some kind of long-term existence:

[¬A] diachronically *compound*
[¬B] diachronically *discontinuous*
[+Cᵍ] a thing that has (gappy) *long-term* existence
[¬D] diachronically changing.[25]

PROPERTIES	A *diachronically non-compound*	B *diachronically continuous*	C *(diachronically) long-term*	D *diachronically unchanging*	E *synchronically non-compound*
VIEWS					
Simple Fiction	+	+	+	+	+
Transience	+	+	−	+	+
Outright Bundle	−	−	+	−	±
Vegetable Fiction	−	+	+	−	±

Where is Hume in all this? The Outright Bundle view of the self or mind is Hume's account, couched in outright ontological terms, of the character and content of the information about the nature of the self or mind that is given to us directly in experience, and the relation between the Outright Bundle view and the Fiction views, in Hume's scheme, is as follows. We find we believe in a certain entity, the self or mind, and believe it to have certain properties, as variously set out in the description of the Fiction views above. We believe, for example, that it has some sort of long-term existence. This being so, we next consider the *evidence* for its existence, so conceived. And it turns out that all we have direct experiential evidence for, so far as an entity that by definition lasts longer than the time of single experience is concerned, is an entity that is discontinuous, compound in a strong sense (it is diachronically compound in respect of its substance, being composed of a series of ontologically entirely distinct experiences), and change-ful in an equally strong sense. And yet we tend to *believe* in something quite different: something continuous in its existence, not gappy in any sense, not com-pound in the strong sense just mentioned, and that does not change so far as its basic substantial identity is concerned even though its states change regularly.

That is how things are, according to Hume.

*

> When I enter most intimately into what I call *myself*[26] I always stumble on some particular experience or other ... I never can catch *myself* at any time without an experience, and never can observe anything but the experience (T252).

This is the famous passage. What does it say? It says that when I reflect in this way, two things are true. First, I never catch myself without an experience. Second, when I do catch myself in this way – and this is something that I can certainly do, on Hume's view, for 'the idea, or rather impression of ourselves is always inti-mately present with us' – I never observe anything but the experience. So I never get a *bare view* of the self, a view of the self alone: although I do always catch myself when I enter most intimately into what I call myself, I never catch myself at any time without an experience. And when I catch myself I never observe anything but the experience – the experience-event: I never detect anything that is *distinct* from the overall experience-event in the way that the self or soul is standardly supposed to be.

In other words: I do of course catch myself, when I enter most intimately into what I call myself, but I get no view of a self alone. One might symbolize this by saying that I get no view with just the content

{S}

where 'S' stands for *self*. I get no view of a self alone at all, let alone a view of some continuing unchanging self alone. All views of the self are at the very least views of the self having an experience. That is, they are at least of the form

{S+E}

where 'E' stands for *experience*. But they are not merely of this additive form, according to Hume. For these views of the self having an experience do not present the self as something distinct from the experience in such a way that there is any sense in which I can be said to observe the self, on the one hand, and the experience, on the other hand. Hume expresses this last point very accurately by saying that there is a fundamental sense in which what I observe or catch is just the experiencing

{E},

but this way of putting things has caused confusion over the centuries, because a point Hume takes for granted – reasonably enough, because it is a tautology – gets suppressed by many of his readers. This is the point (the Experience/Experiencer thesis) that the experience is (indeed) an experience: it is an *experience*, an experiencing, an event, a necessarily subject-involving, conscious mental occurrence.

One may express this by saying that {E} can and should be represented as follows:

{S:C}

where 'C' stands for experiential *content* and ':' has some kind of strong intimacy-intimating function. It is {S:C} – where S and C are indissolubly linked in such a way that I cannot have experiences with the content {S} or the content {C} – that I catch or observe when I catch or observe an experience or experiencing {E} and can observe nothing but {E}. {E} is {S:C}.

Is this true? I think it is. In his imperfect terminology, and in spite of his famous looseness of expression, Hume is making an extremely perceptive claim about what it is actually like to encounter oneself as a (mental) subject of experience when one has decided to go looking for oneself considered specifically as a (mental) subject of experience.

There is, no doubt, more than one way to do this, but one way to do it is to have or stage, in expressly introspective mode, an individual, explicitly self-conscious mental episode. You can do it now by thinking 'I'm reading a talk' or 'I'm bored'.

What happens? Once again, there is (as Hume says) no *bare* view or apprehension of the subject, but there is – inevitably – *some* sort of apprehension of the subject. There is (as Hume says) no view or apprehension of the subject as something *saliently distinct* from the content of the experience, but there is none the less – inevitably – *some* sort of apprehension of the subject. There is (as Hume says) nothing that directly presents both (a) as the subject of experience and (b) as an intrinsically persisting thing, but there is nevertheless, and inevitably, *some* sort of apprehension of the subject. The subject is (inevitably) apprehended in the apprehension of the experience, when one is reflective in this way, and is apprehended specifically as the (mental) subject, and not, say, also as something that has arms and legs or a smile, or that is a collection of neurons in a certain state of activation, or a persisting thing. None of this is easy to express in words, but I think it becomes evident if one reflects sufficiently.[27]

To say that the self or (mental) subject does not present itself as an intrinsically persisting thing is not of course to say that people don't *believe* that it is an intrinsically persisting thing. Many do, and they may also believe that they have direct experience of there being such a thing, or at least experience that strongly backs up the belief that there is such a thing. But if we consider what is given in unprejudiced mental reflection we find nothing of the sort, as Hume says. That is why he devotes most of 'Of personal identity' to explaining how it is that we come to believe in a persisting (and simple and unchanging) subject of experience in spite of the fact that no such thing is to be found when we engage in reflection of this kind.

*

The Appendix beckons, and I am going to approach it via William James, a Transience theorist like myself. And just as I replaced Hume's catch-all word 'perception' with my catch-all word 'experience', so I will replace James's Cartesian catch-all words 'thought' and 'thinker' with 'experience' and 'experiencer' or 'subject of experience' respectively.

According to James, the self or subject or

> *I* is an *experience*, at each moment different from that of the last moment, but *appropriative* of the latter, together with all that the latter called its own. All the experiential facts [of mental life] find their place in this description, unencumbered with any hypothesis save that of the existence of passing experiences.[28]

His view is that 'the experiences themselves are the experiencers'.[29] This claim can sound very odd, but it is not the claim some take it to be on first encountering it. It is not the absurd claim that the experiencer is itself nothing but an experiential content. 'Experience' denotes a necessarily subject-involving episode of experiencing, not just an experiential content.

Some may find the oddness of 'the experiences themselves are the experiencers' hardly lessened, but the role James gives to the brain may diminish the sense of oddness. He thinks there are many numerically distinct selves, in the case of a human being, but only one brain. 'The same brain', he says, 'may subserve many conscious selves' that 'have no substantial identity';[30]

successive experiencers, *numerically distinct*, but all aware of the past in the same way, form an adequate vehicle for all the *experience* of personal unity and sameness which we actually have.[31]

Such successive selves are not only all that we have empirically respectable *evidence* for; they are also all we *need* to posit in order to account for all the mental appearances (including the appearances that make the metaphor 'the stream of consciousness' seem apt). In particular, we do not need to postulate a continuing self or subject to account for the evident connections between the experiences of an individual human being and short-lived successive selves are all there are, according to James. They are the subjects of experience intrinsic to the successive experiences that arise constantly in the brain.

— *But doesn't the principle of inference to the best explanation very strongly favour the hypothesis of some sort of continuing self or subject, when applied to the phenomenon of the evident connection of individual human beings' experiences?*

James sees no reason to think so, and this, I take it, is because he has a crucial further resource when it comes to explaining the connection between the experiences of an individual human being – a resource which Hume lacks in his discussion of the self in the *Treatise*; as I will now try to explain.

There are two principal claims before us. First, that there is no direct *evidence* for a continuing self. Second, that there is no *need* to posit such a self to account for the phenomena. James and Hume are on equal terms when it comes to the point about evidence, but Hume seems very much worse off when it comes to the point about need.

This, in effect, is what motivates his rejection of the bundle hypothesis in the Appendix. 'It is evident', as he says in the first *Enquiry*, in his only reference to the problem of personal identity, 'that there is a principle of connexion between the different thoughts or ideas of the mind' (E23), and the problem he faces in the Appendix is that the Bundle hypothesis allows no way of explaining this fact. James is all right. He has the brain to explain the connection. He can be unmoved by the objection that inference to the best explanation supports the idea of some sort of continuing self, when it comes to explaining the connection between the experiences of an individual human being. He doesn't need a continuing self in addition to a continuing brain – any more than one needs a continuing self or subject to explain the regularities and connections between a computer's operations from day to day. It is enough that short-lived selves, numerically distinct, arise successively from brain conditions that have considerable similarity from moment to moment even as they change.[32] Hume, however, does not have the brain, or anything like it – at least in 'Of personal identity' and in the Appendix – to fulfil this crucial explanatory role. This is his problem.

One could put the point dramatically by saying that if one were forced (say on pain of death) to attribute a positive view of the self or mind to Hume, on the basis of his final remarks on the problem in the Appendix, one might do best to attribute to him the view that 'our experiences ... inhere in something simple and individual'. Having restated the argument of Book I, according to which personal identity is just a construct of the mind – according to which

> the thought alone finds personal identity, when reflecting on the train of past perceptions, that compose a mind, the ideas of them are felt to be connected together –

and having judged it to be promising as far as it goes, he realizes that his overall theory depends on there being some kind of real personal identity, some real connection and unity among perceptions that is not just a construct of the mind. He continues, famously, as follows:

> But all my hopes vanish, when I come to explain the principles, that unite our successive perceptions in our thought or consciousness. I cannot discover any theory, which gives me satisfaction on this head.
>
> In short there are two principles, which I cannot render consistent; nor is it in my power to renounce either of them, viz. *that all our distinct experiences are distinct existences*, and *that the mind never perceives any real connexion among distinct existences*. Did our experiences either inhere in something simple and individual, or did the mind perceive some real connexion among them, there wou'd be no difficulty in the case.[33]

Here Hume describes two cases – two outright metaphysical possibilities – given which there could be an explanation of the evident fact 'that there is a principle of connexion between the different thoughts or ideas of the mind' (some form of real, non-'fictional' personal identity exists that is not a construct of the mind). The first is that

(1) 'our experiences ... inhere in something simple and individual'.

This would be a very good basis for an explanation of the fact that they are connected (that some form of real, non-'fictional' personal identity exists); it would already be an explanation, albeit in very general terms, of the fact that they are connected. The second is that

(2) they are distinct existences and 'the mind perceive[s] some real connexion among them',

or, spelt out a bit,

(2) they are distinct existences, but there is some real connexion among them, which the mind perceives.

This would also provide an excellent basis for an explanation of the fact that they are connected in the way they evidently are, for there would be a *real* connection among them, i.e. a connection that was not just a relation of connection that we are led to believe by the operation of the imagination in accordance with the principles of the association of ideas.[34] In the imagined case we would either actually directly perceive what the connection that concerned us was, or we would at least perceive a connection that underlay the connection that concerned us. Hume, however, could *never* accept [2], the overtly epistemological possibility; so it seems that he would have to prefer [1].

This proposal is meant lightly, unless Hume is allowed to appeal to the brain and to count it as something simple and individual,[35] and it assumes that Hume takes the two alternatives to be exhaustive of the possibilities; but this assumption is not unreasonable.

It does, however, need discussion. It is an old point that the two alternatives are not inconsistent or mutually exclusive as they stand, and confusion arises from the fact that one is presented in straightforwardly ontological form, while the other is partly epistemological. But if one takes the two relevant paragraphs of the Appendix (20 and 21) as a whole, and stands back a bit, I think one can see what Hume has in mind, in spite of the ontological/epistemological shifting.

I will now try to set out Hume's problem, but I will not go down all the paths of the 'labyrinth' that he finds himself in. I will revert to his term 'perceptions', rather than using 'experiences' in its place, and I will call the principles of the association of ideas the 'Principles' for short. I will make use of Hume's outright ontological statements of his view, but the point will always be restatable when the outright ontological versions of his claims have been rendered into their more modest ontological/epistemological forms.

I am aware that what follows is somewhat clumsy; but the fundamental point can be put in a sentence: Hume's problem is not a problem about what sort of unity or connection the operation of the mind in accordance with the Principles can account for; it is a problem about what sort of unity or connection can account for the operation of the mind in accordance with the Principles. The crucial point to retain from what has already been said in this section is this: when Hume tells us what would solve his difficulty, he describes two full-on metaphysical possibilities, two outright metaphysical forms of unity and connection, that have *nothing* to do with any unities or connection we may come to believe in as a result of the operation of the mind according to the Principles. This imposes a very clear and strong constraint on any satisfactory account of what his problem is: it shows that his problem *cannot* be a problem with the adequacy of his account of how the Principles generate our belief in a continuing single self, as so many interpretations have supposed. What the two principles that he seems to be calling inconsistent are inconsistent with is the evident fact that there is a real unity (not imagination generated) and connection among our successive perceptions of a kind that could be explained if either there was a 'real' (not imagination generated) connection between them or they inhered in a single substance.

*

Consider the mind of a given individual.[36] The perceptions that wholly constitute this mind, according to the Outright Bundle view, are real existences. They are evidently connected, according to Hume. They are evidently governed by certain *uniting* principles, or a *connecting* principle. Now this is *not* the claim that we *see* them or *believe* them to be connected and united, as a result of the action of the mind in accordance with the Principles. That Humean claim is not at issue here. This claim is the claim that they are *in fact* connected, independently of any unities or connections that the action of the imagination leads us to believe in.

How are they connected? They are connected in (at least) the following respect: they succeed each other in accordance with the Principles. Perceptions are real and this is what actually happens in their case.

I will call this fact about perceptions a *unity-and-connection* fact – a *UC* fact for short. What is its theoretical status? It is an outright metaphysical fact, according to Hume's overall theory of things, whatever its further or ultimate explanation. (In just the same way, the fact that the physical world comports itself in accordance with Newton's laws of motion is an outright metaphysical fact, on Newton's view, whatever its further explanation.) It is a UC fact about minds, which certainly exist, whatever they are. It is a fact about *real* unity and connection, in Hume's terms – an *RUC* fact. It is not a Principles-based UC fact, or *PUC* fact, for short – a UC fact generated by the action of the mind according to the Principles. It is not, in other words, any sort of fiction; it is not any sort of fiction that the mind operates according to the Principles. How could it be? The mind's operation according to the Principles is the *source* of all the fictions that Hume is concerned with.

So the UC phenomena that we consider when we consider the way perceptions succeed each other in a mind are *not* the PUC phenomena that we come to believe in as a result of the operation of the mind according to the Principles – i.e. persisting selves, physical objects, causal necessities, and so on. The former UC phenomena, which are RUC phenomena, are what make the latter possible. It is the fact that our minds (imaginations) operate in accordance with the Principles in the way that they do that accounts for our believing in the UC phenomena we do (physical objects, causal necessities, persisting selves, and so on) in the way that we do.

If this is right, the general mistake is to confuse (1) Hume's concern to explain the existence of the RUC phenomena that *consist* in the mind's operating according to the Principles with (2) his concern to explain the existence of the PUC phenomena (physical objects, causal necessities, persisting selves, etc.) that we come to believe in because they are the *product* of the mind's operating according to the Principles. In the particular case of personal identity, therefore, the mistake is to confuse (1) with the concern to explain the PUC phenomenon (the persisting self) that we come to believe in because it is the product of the mind's operating according to the Principles.

Who is to blame for the misunderstanding? Hume. It is very easy to be misled by the passage

> ... having thus loosen'd all our particular perceptions, when I proceed to explain the principle of connexion, which binds them together, and makes us attribute to them a real simplicity and identity; I am sensible, that my account is very defective ... (T635; Hume's own footnote in this passage refers back to T260)

This passage, which states Hume's worry about how, given the resources of his theory, he can account for the fact that an individual's successive experiences are connected in the ways they evidently are (the ways described by the Principles), is often misread as a concern about the adequacy of his account of how two of the Principles (resemblance and causation) operate to give rise to the idea of the continuing self in the way described on T259–262.[37] Why is it misread in this way? Well, Hume's footnote reference misleads some, and he plainly says that the thing that makes him feel his account is defective is the principle that makes us attribute a real simplicity and identity to our perceptions (i.e. the principle that founds our belief in personal identity, i.e. the Principles). So it is natural to think that Hume sees a defect in his account of how the resemblance and causation Principles do what they are said to do.[38]

But this, taken as it is usually taken, is a mistake. His problem is, as he says, 'to explain the principle'. It is not a problem with the adequacy of the principle itself – a problem with whether it is adequate to explain what it is meant to explain. The passage parses like this:

> ... when I proceed to explain [the principle of connexion, which binds them together, and makes us attribute to them a real simplicity and identity] I am sensible, that my account is very defective ...

The noun-phrase in the bold brackets picks out the thing that is his problem: 'when I proceed to explain (the existence of) X I am sensible that my account is very defective'. His problem is to explain the RUC phenomenon that *consists* in the mind's operating according to the Principles, not the PUC phenomenon –

the continuing single self we believe we have experience of – which is the *product* of their operation.

*

Let me try to put this in another way. When Hume says there would be no difficulty in the case if our experiences inhered in something simple and individual, or if the mind perceived some real connection among them, it seems clear that he intends to be putting forward a pair of mutually exclusive and jointly exhaustive metaphysical possibilities, roughly as follows.

(1) Consider the mind of a given individual. The 'thoughts and ideas' – perceptions – of this mind are evidently *connected*; they are evidently governed by certain *uniting* principles.

(2) How can this be? Well, what are these thoughts and ideas, ontologically speaking? There are two serious possibilities. The first is that they are all distinct existences or distinct substances (T233, 259, 634, 636),[39] each with its own subject, and that they are all there is to the mind. The second is that they all inhere in, or are states or modifications of, one single subject or substance. These two options – call them the 'One' and the 'Many' – are mutually exclusive and jointly exhaustive of the (serious) possibilities.[40]

(3) Given these two ontological options, the One and the Many, when it comes to the thoughts and ideas of the mind, there are also two options when we ask how what is evidently the case – the fact 'that there is a principle of connexion between the different thoughts or ideas of the mind' – can be the case.

(4) Consider the One option first. If the successive experiences of an individual human being are not distinct existences but rather 'inhere in something simple and individual' then clearly we have something that can ground the evident fact of the connection between them, even though we will still have to consign the details of the connection to a 'magical faculty in the soul, which ... is ... inexplicable by the utmost efforts of human understanding'.[41] But – we can never have any evidence for – perceive – anything like this. So the One option is just not available to us even as the *bare form* of a positive account of how something that is certainly actual (the RUC phenomenon of the thoughts and ideas of the mind succeeding each other in conformity to the Principles) is even possible.

(5) Is the Many option any better? No. If the successive experiences of an individual are indeed all distinct existences, and if they are indeed all there is to the mind, then the only possible remaining account of the evident fact of their connection (the fact that they really do succeed each other in conformity to the Principles) is the one that simply states that there is indeed some 'real connexion' among them: there is nothing else to the mind, metaphysically speaking, that can provide even the bare form of a positive account of their evident connection, given the Many option, because the ontologically entirely distinct experiences are by hypothesis all that there is to the mind. But we can never perceive real connections in this sense. So we cannot give even the bare form of an account of how what is certainly actual (our thoughts' and ideas' conformity to the Principles) is possible, given the Many option.

So: given Hume's assumption that one must choose between the One and the Many, when it comes to the ontological status of the perceptions of the mind, it is easy to see why he thinks that there are just two possible types of solution to the general problem of how to give some sort of explanation of the connection. And it is equally easy to see what he also sees: that neither will do, given his overall theory and the account of the mind and personal identity that he has expounded up to now. Neither will do, whether one reads his account of the mind in outright ontological terms (Outright Bundle view, the mind is nothing but a bundle of perceptions) or in sceptical epistemological terms (the mind is nothing but a bundle of perceptions so far as we can know). For his overall theory requires that there must be *something* more to the mind than the Outright Bundle view allows (clash with ontological version), and in so doing it entails that we can in fact know that there is something more to the mind (clash with epistemological version).

*

A slightly different angle. When do Hume's hopes vanish? They vanish when he comes 'to explain the [singular] principle of connexion, which binds ... our particular perceptions ... together', 'the [plural] principles, that unite our successive perceptions in our thought or consciousness'. So the question is, what does he mean by 'explain the principle of connexion which binds' or 'explain the principles that unite'? What problem does he have in mind?

To answer that question, we must consider what he thinks might solve the problem. And he tells us directly. One thing that would do the trick is 'something simple and individual' in which our perceptions inhered; another is some 'real connexion' between perceptions, that is, some connection which is not just a

Principles-produced relation of association in the imagination (remember that causal necessity, conceived as something that holds quite independently of any action of the imagination, is Hume's prime example of a 'real connexion'): if either of these two things were available to theory then, Hume thinks, we would have the resources for *some* sort of explanation, however bare or general, of the existence of the indubitably real UC phenomenon of the mind's operation according to the Principles.[42] But they are not available to theory, from Hume's point of view.

Perhaps this is not sufficiently clear. Perhaps we can best work out what Hume's problem is by working out what it is not. If we call our belief or feeling that the self or mind is something that has diachronic continuity 'the Identity Feeling', we can put things as follows. Hume does *not* have a problem with his account of how the operation of the mind according to the Principles produces the Identity Feeling *once it is taken as given that the mind does operate according to the Principles.* He refers back to this account on T635, restates it, *and calls it promising*, in the very same paragraph in which he says that something makes all his hopes vanish. So whatever that something is, it is not (as so many have supposed) his account of how the operation of the Principles produces the Identity Feeling, given that the mind operates according to the Principles.

> ... having thus loosen'd all our particular perceptions, when I proceed to explain the principle of connexion, which binds them together, and makes us attribute to them a real simplicity and identity; I am sensible, that my account is very defective, and that nothing but the seeming evidence of the precedent reasonings cou'd have induc'd me to receive it. **If perceptions are distinct existences, they form a whole only by being connected together. But no connexions among distinct existences are ever discoverable by human understanding. We only feel a connexion or a determination of the thought, to pass from one object to another. It follows, therefore, that the thought alone finds personal identity, when reflecting on the train of past perceptions, that compose a mind, the ideas of them are felt to be connected together, and naturally introduce each other. However extraordinary this conclusion may seem, it need not surprize us. Most philosophers seem inclin'd to think, that personal identity arises from consciousness; and consciousness is nothing but a reflected thought or perception. The present philosophy, therefore, has so far a promising aspect.** But all my hopes vanish ... (T636).

The sentences between the double asterisks restate the account of how the Principles produce the Identity Feeling and pronounce it promising.

So what is making his hopes vanish? We can distinguish the *Internal* problem of explaining the 'principle of connexion' and the *External* problem. The Internal problem has just been described: it is the problem of giving an account of how the operation of the mind according to the Principles gives rise to the Identity Feeling. We know this is not Hume's problem in the Appendix, in spite of the ambiguous passage that heads the last quotation, because he explicitly says that he considers his solution to it promising. His problem is the *External* problem: the problem of explaining how the mind be so constituted as to operate according to the Principles given only the metaphysical resources of the Outright Bundle view; given, in other words, the 'Many' option that was shown to fail in the last section.

The problem is: it can't be done. The mind can't operate according to the Principles if the 'true idea of the human mind' is really just to 'consider it as a system of different perceptions or different existences' (T261) with no 'real connexion' between them. It follows that the true idea of the human mind according to Hume's general empiricist principles (plus his views about what is given in experience) *cannot* be the true idea of the human mind according to his overall theory. This is a catastrophic result; it destroys his hopes of a tenable overall theory.

One might put the point by saying that the Outright Bundle view does not provide any possible *place of residence* for whatever it is about the mind that makes it such that it operates according to the Principles: for those '*original* qualities of human nature, which I pretend not to explain'.[43] It doesn't just say that we can't know the nature of that whatever-it-is; it has the consequence that there cannot be any such thing. The problem is undiminished if Hume's view is not taken to be the outright ontological view that the mind is just 'a system of different ... existences' but rather the more moderate ontological/epistemological view that the mind so far as we have any distinct or legitimate notion of it is just 'a system of different ... existences'. For then his difficulty can be expressed by saying that it follows from one part of his system (his all-pervasive commitment to the Principles) that the notion of the mind that another part of his system (his general empiricism, his theory of ideas) legitimates as 'the true idea of the human mind' cannot be accurate to the reality of that mind.

In conclusion let me repeat a crucial point. Hume's problem is *not* that he can't offer any sort of further *positively descriptive* explanation of the existence of the RUC phenomenon of the mind's operation in accordance with the Principles, given the resources of the Outright Bundle view. He doesn't need to offer any such further positive explanation of the phenomenon, given his general scheme of things; he can appeal, as he regularly does, to unknown causes or ultimate principles, magical, inexplicable, wonderful, things that we cannot know or understand. But that is not the problem. The problem is that the Bundle view – 'the true idea of the mind' – actually *excludes* the possibility of there being any further explanation at all.

*

Like James and myself, all Hume really needs at this point is the brain, realistically understood, in order to explain the connections between the experiences of a single human being. And in fact he doesn't need to appeal to the brain in any way in which he has not already done so in the *Treatise* – although such an appeal is excluded by the dialectical line he is pursuing in 'Of personal identity'. At one point in his discussion of the principles of association of ideas he remarks that he has not so far appealed to the functioning of the brain to explain the operation of the principles of association of ideas. He might very well have done so, he says; but so far he has (as a good Newtonian) restricted his attention strictly to the observable phenomena of association. But now, he says, he 'must here have recourse to it [the brain], in order to account for the mistakes' that occur in the operation of the principles of association of ideas (T60).

Why do mistakes occur? The reason, he says, is that

> ... the mind is endow'd with a power of exciting any idea it pleases; whenever it dispatches the ... animal ... spirits into that region of the brain, in which the idea is plac'd; these spirits always excite the idea, when they run precisely into the proper trace, and rummage that cell, which belongs to the idea. But as their motion is seldom direct, and naturally turns a little to one side or the other; for this reason the animal spirits, falling into the contiguous traces, present other related ideas in lieu of that which the mind desir'd at first to survey. (T60–1).

That's how mistakes happen.

Here Hume makes explicit use of the hypothesis that the mind is based in the brain, and claims that he must do so. But he can't call on this hypothesis in the more radical dialectical context of 'Of personal identity', and makes no appeal to it when he returns to the problem of personal identity in the Appendix and asks what might be the basic 'principle of connexion, which binds ... our particular experiences ... together' (T635). His next brief reference to the problem simply asserts that 'it is evident that there is a principle of connexion between the different thoughts or ideas of the mind' (E23) – as indeed it is – and leaves it at that.

To finish. Hume does not (self-refutingly) deny the existence of subjects of experience. He shows that we cannot know that they are not short-lived, fleeting things; or – if you insist on giving them some sort of long-term existence – gappy bundles of short-lived things. He doesn't dogmatically conclude that this is definitely all that they are, strictly considered; he concludes, sceptically, that we cannot know that this is not all that they are; a conclusion he then finds to be untenable (in both its dogmatic-ontological and sceptical-epistemological version) on other grounds internal to his theory of the mind.

William James and I are more forward than Hume, metaphysically speaking. We are Transience theorists. We both think that selves exist and are short-lived things, at least in the human case. We are not entirely harmonious; James's reasons for being a Transience theorist are excessively empiricist for my taste. But I have my own reasons. [44]

Notes

[1]   When citing a work I give the first publication date or date of composition, while the page reference is to the edition listed in the bibliography. In quoting Hume I refer to the *Treatise* and the *Enquiries* as 'T' and 'E' respectively, followed by page numbers in the Selby-Bigge editions. When quoting I mark my emphases with italics and the author's with bold face.

[2]   It may well be part of a human being, on this view.

[3]   'Perception' is Hume's general word for a conscious mental occurrence, whether it be an 'impression' (sensation, feeling) or an 'idea' (concept, thought).

[4]   Kant has the same target in the Third Paralogism (Kant 1781/7).

[5]   'Identity' is essentially a matter of *diachronic* identity, in the philosophical idiom of the time.

[6]   Compare Descartes 1641, Kant 1781/7, Second Paralogism.

[7]   See e.g. Craig 1987, where the point is made with particular reference to the mind or self. See also Wright 1983, Strawson 2000a, 2000b.

[8]   '...the positive air, which prevails in that book, and which may be imputed to the ardor of youth, so much displeases me, that I have not patience to review it' *Letters* 1:187.

[9]   It is an elementary mistake to take the sentence 'It cannot ... be from any ... impressions ... that the idea of self is deriv'd; *and consequently there is no such idea*' (T252) to show that Hume thinks that we have no idea of the self. This is to fail to read the sentence within the scope of the remark on the previous page that we have no 'idea of self, *after the manner it is here explain'd*': what is in question is an idea of the self considered as something 'constant and invariable' that has 'perfect identity and simplicity' (T251). More generally, it is easy to prove that what Hume means when he says that we have 'no idea' of something is 'no perfect idea', not 'no idea of any sort'. It is enough to cite his argument that 'We have no perfect idea of anything but of a perception. A substance is entirely different from a perception. We have, therefore, no idea of a substance' (T234).

[10] Here I draw on Craig 1987: 111–120 and Strawson 1989: 128–131.

[11] I put aside his commitment to talk of virtues and vices, and so on, in his moral philosophy.

[12] Hume's use of this term is much misunderstood. For one point see Strawson (1989: 55 n).

[13] To say that these faculties are unintelligible and inexplicable is not to say that they do not exist. On the contrary.

[14] I set it out in Strawson 1989: 130, and develop it further below.

[15] T4, T10. I will stick to simple ideas, but in the case of a complex idea Y, composed of simple ideas Z, V, and W, the claim is that Y can arise in the mind only if Z, V, and W have previously arisen.

[16] T7–8.

[17] This 'where' is metaphorical in as much as it is not restricted to space. (I hope no one will think Hume's view that many perceptions exists 'no where' (T235–6) provides material for a response to this point – but they may re-run it for 'perceptions ... of the sight and feeling' (T236).)

[18] I know of no evidence that it ever occurred to him.

[19] According to which an A-type event – A_1 – is the cause of a particular event of a B-type event – B_1 – only if A_1 is prior to and contiguous with B_1 and all A-type events are prior to and contiguous with B-type events.

[20] Those who wish can always resubstitute 'perception' for 'experience'.

[21] Pike 1967: 161. See also Penelhum 1955, Biro 1993: 47–8. Other references to 'self' or 'person' in Books II and III of the *Treatise* do not have a purely or even primarily mental reference (compare T298, T303, T329).

[22] The kind of long-term existence a thing has if it is diachronically continuous and diachronically non-compound.

[23] In respect of its substance: everyone will allow that selves change in respect of their mental states.

[24] I will omit [E] from now on, as nothing much hangs on it.

[25] I am assuming that [¬B], the non-continuity claim, is part of Hume's version of the Bundle view, but Bundle theorists do not have to accept it. They can suppose that a bundle of experiences that seems temporally gappy (from the inside) is not in fact objectively temporally gappy.

[26] I.e. myself considered as a mental phenomenon; see note 21 above.

[27] See Shoemaker 1986.

[28] 1892: 191, 1890: 1.400–401. He makes the same point in other terms in 1890: 1.338 – 42.

[29] 'The thoughts themselves are the thinkers' (1892: 191).

[30] 1890: 1.401; 1892: 181.

[31] 1892: 181. Compare Damasio 1994: 236–243: 'at each moment the state of self is constructed, from the ground up. It is an evanescent reference state, so continuously and consistently reconstructed that the owner never knows that it is being remade unless something goes wrong with the remaking' (p. 240).

[32] Here there are two main points. (1) Given short-term or 'working' memory, the contents of the immediately preceding experience form part of the overall experiential context in which the new experience arises in every sense in which features of the external environment do. (2) All the features of the brain that constitute a human being's character, beliefs, general epistemic and cognitive outlook, general conative and emotional outlook, and so on, also remain highly stable from moment to moment. It may be added that when we are thinking of the similarity relations between successive selves – those that give rise, in many, to the sense that the stream of consciousness is continuous in the sense of unbroken – we need to bear in mind how much of what goes on in the brain is non-conscious or non-experiential.

[33] T636. Note that Hume takes the notions of inherence in a substance and real connection to be *intelligible enough to be used in an informative description of a situation in which he*

would not face the philosophical difficulty he does face.

34   Causal necessity conceived as something that holds quite independently of any action of the imagination is Hume's main example of a 'real connexion'. Causal connection so far as we know it is just a relation of association in the imagination.

35   He cannot on the terms of debate as then understood, although a brain is a single, individual thing by our ordinary lights.

36   Many commentators still think that Hume faces the (deeply silly) problem that many radical empiricists face of how to group perceptions, conceived as floating around independently of mind bundles, into mind-constituting bundles. Craig is certainly right that this is not Hume's problem (there is no evidence that it ever occurred to him): as far as Hume is concerned 'perceptions arrive already done up into bundles and the apparatus of laws of association and the rest goes to work in each case on a *given* bundle' (Craig 1987: 113).

37   See for example Stroud (1977: 127-128).

38   It is this that leads many to the red herring about the problem of distinguishing one mind-constituting bundle of perceptions from another.

39   Note that when Hume *argues* for this claim (T233, T634) he argues (in classic Cartesian style) only for the claim that they *may* exist separately. His conversions of this claim into the outright ontological idiom should always be read in this light.

40   I offer this as Hume's judgement. It is not as if philosophers can't think up other peculiar possibilities, for example one subject for every ten experiences, and so on.

41   T179, T24. Explanation must come to an end; we should not think that we have reached the ultimate cause, or what Newton calls the 'true cause' or *'vera causa'*.

42   Note that we may take the UC phenomenon to include not only the fact that the mind's operation is correctly described by the Principles, but also the fact that ideas derive from and depend on impressions, and all the phenomena of memory.

43   T13; here Hume is explicitly referring to what underlies the holding of the Principles.

44   This is a shortened version of a work in progress. I am grateful, on points of detail, to Harry Frankfurt, James Harris, David Owen, Ingmar Persson, and Udo Thiel.

References

Biro, J. (1993), 'Hume's new science of the mind', in *The Cambridge Companion to David Hume*, edited by David Fate Norton (Cambridge: Cambridge University Press).

Craig, E. J. (1987), *The Mind of God and the Works of Man* (Oxford: Clarendon Press).

Damasio, A. (1994), *Descartes's Error: Emotion, Reason, and the human Brain* (New York: Avon).

Hume, D. (1739–40/1978), *A Treatise of Human Nature*, edited by L. A. Selby-Bigge and P. H. Nidditch (Oxford: Oxford University Press).

Hume, D. (1748–51/1975), *Enquiries Concerning Human Understanding and Concerning The Principles of Morals*. Edited by L. A. Selby-Bigge (Oxford: Oxford University Press).

Hume, D. (1748/2000), *An Enquiry concerning Human Understanding*, edited by T. Beauchamp (Oxford: Clarendon Press).

James, W. (1890/1950), *The Principles of Psychology*, Volume 1 (New York: Dover).

James, W. (1892/1984), *Psychology: Briefer Course* (Cambridge, MA: Harvard University Press).

Kant, I. (1787/1933), *Critique of Pure Reason*, translated by N. Kemp Smith, (London: Macmillan).

Penelhum, T (1955), 'Hume on Personal Identity', *Philosophical Review* 64, 575-86.

Pike, N. (1967), 'Hume's Bundle Theory of the Self: A Limited Defense', *American Philosophical Quarterly* 4, 159–65.

Shoemaker, S. (1986/1996), 'Introspection and the Self', in *The First-Person Perspective and Other Essays* (Cambridge: Cambridge University Press).

Strawson, G. (1989), *The Secret Connexion* (Oxford: Clarendon Press).

Strawson, G. (1993/2000b), 'David Hume: Objects and Power', in *The New Hume Debate*, edited by R. Read & K. Richman (London: Routledge), 31–51.

Strawson, G. (1999) 'The Self and the SESMET', *Journal of Consciousness Studies* 6, 99–135.

Strawson, G. (2000a), 'Epistemology, Semantics, Ontology, and David Hume', in *Facta Philosophica* 1, 113–131.

Stroud, B. (1977), *Hume* (London: Routledge).

Thiel, U. (1994), 'Hume's Notions of Consciousness and Reflection in Context', *British Journal of the History of Philosophy* 2, 75–115.

Wright, John P. (1983), *The Sceptical Realism of David Hume* (Manchester: Manchester University Press).

Worries about Continuity, Expected Utility Theory, and Practical Reasoning[1]

Larry S. Temkin

Some years ago, Ingmar Persson kindly sent me some unsolicited comments regarding an unpublished argument of mine. In fact, he'd only heard about my argument from another philosopher, but this didn't stop him from offering a set of perceptive comments regarding it, as well as important considerations of his own in support of my conclusion. I was grateful and impressed.

Since Ingmar's initial letter, it has been my good fortune to occasionally meet with him, and to participate in an ongoing exchange of papers and views on a variety of topics of mutual interest. These exchanges have been both personally pleasurable and professionally illuminating. Correspondingly, I am happy and proud to contribute an essay to this volume honoring Ingmar. And it is, perhaps, especially fitting that my essay raises issues related to the topic that Ingmar first wrote me about, and about which we have continued to have fruitful exchanges.

Introduction

Expected utility theory is a powerful and widely influential theory. It underlies game theory, decision theory, and much of modern economics. Unfortunately, expected utility theory relies on a principle of continuity – explicated below – that many people reject in certain cases. Most people seem not to worry about this. I suspect this is because they either haven't thought seriously about the issue, or because they have assumed that continuity only fails in certain 'extreme' or 'hard' cases. Specifically, I suspect that most assume that continuity is perfectly plausible for the vast majority of cases, including, presumably, the kinds of cases we are mainly worried about when invoking game theory, decision theory, or economics. I share this intuition. But I deny it is grounds for complacency.

In this essay, I shall argue that *if* one rejects continuity in so-called 'extreme' cases, as many think one should, then there are deep and irresolvable difficulties for expected utility theory. The implications of this result are substantial, though I cannot develop them here.

Three premises of expected utility theory

One premise underlying expected utility theory is that the relation 'all things considered at least as good as' is transitive. Let us call this premise the *axiom of transitivity*. The axiom of transitivity holds that for any three alternatives A, B, and C, if all things considered, A is at least as good as B, and all things considered, B is at least as good as C, then all things considered, A is at least as good as C.[2]

Many believe the axiom of transitivity *must* be true, as a matter of logic. Others believe it is intuitively obvious. For many, the axiom of transitivity is intimately bound up with our conceptions of consistency and rationality, so that to reject the axiom of transitivity would require radical revision in our understanding of practical reasoning. In addition, we implicitly rely on the axiom of transitivity throughout our lives, for example, whenever we choose between a set of alternatives on the basis of a sequence of pairwise comparisons. Thus, in choosing between a set of options we typically consider the first and the second, and remove the second from further consideration if we think the first is better. We then compare the first with the third, again removing the worse of the two options from further consideration, and so on. But this approach depends on the axiom of transitivity, since we cannot remove one of two options from further consideration, if it might be better than another option which itself is better than the initially favored option. It is the axiom of transitivity that rules out such a possibility.

Thus, most think it is uncontroversial that expected utility theory relies on the axiom of transitivity, and hence that game theory, decision theory, and economics do as well.

A second premise that expected utility theory depends on may be called the *principle of substitution of equivalence* (PSE). Roughly, this principle requires that if x = y, then x and y are interchangeable in formulas where they occur. Note, outside of modal or intensional contexts, PSE holds for all x and y. So, x and y may be simple or complex. PSE is difficult to deny. Indeed, perhaps even more than the axiom of transitivity, PSE may appear to be a basic principle of logic or mathematics.

A third premise underlying expected utility theory is the principle of *continuity*. Roughly, this holds that for any three outcomes A, B, and C, if someone, S, prefers A to B and B to C, then there must be some probability p such that rationality requires S to be at least as happy with the prospect of receiving A, with probability p, or C, with probability 1-p, as with the prospect of receiving B for sure. That is, if VX is the value of X to S, then there must be some p (ranging between 0 and 1) such that $VB \leq pVA + (1-p)VC$.

The principle of continuity has many supporters. But it has detractors as well, and lacks the intuitive transparency and plausibility of the other two premises. Correspondingly, it warrants separate elucidation and discussion.

Examining Continuity – Easy Cases versus Extreme Cases

Continuity is important for expected utility theory. But unlike PSE, continuity's appeal rests not on mathematics or logic, but on a particular normative conception of rationality. It is thus more easily challenged, and in fact, as we shall see in a moment, many reject it. Still, there are cases, and there are cases, and it is useful to distinguish between cases where continuity is questionable, and cases where it is difficult to deny. For the purposes of argument, I shall distinguish between four kinds of cases.

> Case I: Outcomes A, B, and C differ little in value. So, what we stand to lose if we get C, rather than B, is relatively insignificant, though so, too, is what we stand to gain if we get A rather than B.

> Case II: Outcomes B and C differ little in value, but outcomes A and B differ greatly. So, what we stand to lose if we get C, rather than B, is relatively insignificant, though what we stand to gain if we get A, rather than B, is very significant.

> Case III: Outcomes A, B, and C differ greatly in value. So, what we stand to gain if we get A, rather than B, is very significant, but so, too, is what we stand to lose if we get C rather than B.

> Case IV: Outcomes B and C differ greatly in value, but outcomes A and B differ little. So, what we stand to gain if we get A, rather than B, is insignificant, while what we stand to lose if we get C, rather than B, is very significant.

Continuity is plausible for instances of case I. For example, let A = having $1,000,001 per year throughout a long life, B = having $1,000,000 per year throughout a long life, and C = having $999,999 per year throughout a long life. (Henceforth, I drop the tag 'throughout a long life.' Unless noted otherwise, each example discussed involves a long life, for which a once-and-for-all-time decision must be made.) Here, outcomes A, B, and C differ little in value, and it seems clear that there would be *some* p such that I should be at least as happy with the prospect of getting A with probability p or C with probability 1-p as with the prospect of getting B for sure. (In fact, in my own case, this would be so for any $p \geq .5$.)

Continuity is even *more* plausible for instances of case II. For example, if A = having $1,000,001 per year, B = having $2 per year, and C = having $1 per year, there is *surely* some p where I should be at least as happy with the prospect of getting A with probability p or C with probability 1-p as with the prospect of getting B for sure. (In my own case, this would be so for almost any p! But for those attracted to a maximin strategy, consider your reaction to the different outcomes if p = .5, or perhaps .9.[3])

I shall call cases I and II the *easy* cases for continuity. There is widespread agreement that continuity holds as a requirement of rationality at least for the easy cases.

Continuity is more dubious for instances of case III. For example, let A = having \$2,000,000 per year, B = having \$1,000,000 per year, and C = having \$0 per year. Many would accept continuity here too, maintaining that surely there must be *some* p such that, rationally, I should be at least as happy with the prospect of getting A with probability p or C with probability 1-p as with the prospect of getting B for sure. And they would point out that if p is close enough to 1, the expected value of the former prospect might be nearly twice that of the latter.[4] Still, some people, most notably satisficers[5] or risk avoiders, would reject this view. They would argue that a bird in the hand – especially a fine bird – is not only worth two in the bush, it is worth two fine birds that are *almost* in hand. They might urge that a million dollars per year is 'enough,' and that rationality doesn't require that one maximize expected utility. On their view, it is not worth taking even the *tiniest* chance of losing a *certain* \$1,000,000 per year, even for the sake of a *substantial* gain that is almost – but not quite – certain to be realized.

For many, instances of case III are enough to raise doubts about continuity. But the strongest objection to continuity arises with instances of case IV. Peter Vallentyne offers an example of the following sort.[6] Consider three possible outcomes. In B, one has \$1,000,000 per year and, indeed, a full, rich, life. In A, one has \$1,000,001 per year and, an *ever-so-slightly* fuller, and richer, life. In C, one has a life of pain and misery that ends with a torturous, lingering, death. Vallentyne denies that there is any p such that rationality *requires* him to be at least as happy about the prospect of receiving either outcome A with probability p or outcome C with probability 1-p, as about the prospect of having B with certainty. That is, Vallentyne denies that there must be some p such that VB ≤ pVA + (1-p)VC.

Many share Vallentyne's intuition about such examples, and the common assumption is that the intuition trades on our attitudes to risk versus certainty. But, clearly, the issue isn't merely one of certainty versus risk, rather it is one of certainty of a great outcome versus risk of a much worse outcome, especially when there is little to be gained by taking the risk. That is, in general people have no objection to risking a certain outcome in hopes of significant gain if the downside risk is relatively small (case II); what they balk at is risking a certain outcome for a slightly better one if the downside risk is huge (case IV). What seems crazy, in Vallentyne's example, is the idea that rationality should require a willingness to trade the *certainty* of a *full rich life* for the prospect of a *slightly* better one, when doing so means taking some risk – no matter how small – that we would end up with an entire life of *pain and misery*.

Vallentyne offers his example as an objection to continuity, and hence as a threat to expected utility theory. Yet many would deny that the example poses a serious threat to expected utility theory. They might readily accept that continuity fails in 'extreme' cases of the sort Vallentyne imagines, yet they might insist that continuity holds for the vast majority of cases. Minimally, they might urge that continuity holds for the so-called 'easy' cases – cases I and II – and hence that expected utility works fine for at least those cases.

This reaction to Vallentyne's example is natural, and intuitively appealing. But it must be rejected. Examples like Vallentyne's pose a much greater challenge to expected utility theory than is normally recognized.

From safe bets to high stake bets – the challenge[7]

The problem facing expected utility can be stated simply. *If* we agree, as many do and I think we should, that continuity fails in 'extreme' cases of the sort Vallentyne describes, then one can generate a contradiction between the axiom of transitivity, the principle of substitution of equivalence, and continuity even for the 'easy' cases for which it supposedly holds. Correspondingly, we must accept continuity for *all* cases, reject it even for easy ones, reject the axiom of transitivity, or reject the principle of substitution of equivalence. (Of course a fifth possibility, accepting an inconsistent set of views, always remains as a final unpalatable option.)

To illustrate the contradiction in question, let us start with a simple 'extreme' example where many would reject continuity.

Let B be an outcome where I receive \$1,000,000 per year, A an outcome where I receive \$1,000,001 per year, and Z an outcome where I receive \$0 per year. According to continuity, there *must* be some probability p, such that $VB = pVA + (1-p)VZ$. I deny this, as do many others. So, let us assume this represents the kind of 'extreme' example for which many agree continuity should be rejected. But consider examples where the gap between the *certain* alternative and the worst *risky* alternative is small. For such cases, I think most people would readily accept the requirement of continuity. For example, if B is an outcome where I receive \$1,000,000 per year, A an outcome where I receive \$1,000,001 per year, and C an outcome where I receive \$999,999 per year, most people would readily grant that there must be some p such that I should be rationally indifferent between the prospect of B with certainty and the prospect of receiving either outcome A with probability p or outcome C with probability 1-p. That is, there must be some p such that (1) $VB = pVA + (1-p)VC$. But then, consider outcomes B, C, and D, where B and C are as above, and D is an outcome where I receive \$999,998 per year. Surely, most will accept that there is some probability q, such that (2) $VC = qVB + (1-q)VD$. But then, by the principle of substitution for equivalence, one can replace VC in (1) with $qVB + (1-q)VD$ (from (2)), at which point one can show via basic, though rather complex and messy, algebraic manipulation, that there is a probability r (where r = p/(1 + pq - q)) such that (3) VB = rVA + (1-r)VD. Thus, from (1) and (2) one can conclude that there must be some probability r such that one should be rationally indifferent between the prospect where one receives $1,000,000 per year for sure, or the prospect where one either receives $1,000,001 per year, with probability r, or $999,998 per year, with probability (1-r).

But then, next consider B, D, and E, where E is an outcome where one receives $999,997 per year. Since the gap between D and E is small, most would readily admit that continuity holds for B, D, and E, that is, that there must be some probability s such that (4) VD = sVB + (1-s)VE. But then, if one replaces VD in (3) with sVB + (1-s)VE (from (4) by the principle of substitution for equivalence) one can then show that there must be some probability t such that (5) VB = tVA + (1-t)VE. Iterations of this reasoning lead to the conclusion that there must be some probability x such that (N) VB = xVA + (1-x)VZ, where Z, as above, is the outcome where one receives $0 per year. But, by hypothesis, those who reject continuity in 'extreme' cases deny (N).

Note, from (1), (3), (5), (N) we have that VB = pVA + (1-p)VC = rVA + (1-r)VD = tVA + (1-t)VE = xVA + (1-x)VZ. But if we reject that VB = xVA + (1-x)VZ, then we know that we must choose between (a) continuity even in 'easy' cases where there is very little difference between the middle outcome and the worst outcome, (b) the principle of substitution of equivalence, or (c) the axiom of transitivity. Each of these choices seriously threatens our common understanding of the rational requirements for comparing and ranking outcomes.

Let us be clear how the preceding argument works. I have shown that if we accept continuity for 'easy' cases, where the gap between the certain 'middle' outcome and the uncertain worst outcome is small, and we accept the principle of substitution for equivalence, then we can prove that there is a sequence of prospects, S1, S2, S3, ..., Sn-2, Sn-1, Sn such that for any two adjacent members of the sequence, Si and Sj, Sj is *equivalent* to Si. That is, it is not merely the case that Sj is not worse than Si, rather, it is that Sj is *at least as good as* Si. Yet, although we think Sn is at least as good as Sn-1, that Sn-1 is at least as good as Sn-2, ..., that S3 is at least as good as S2, and S2 is at least as good as S1, we may, like Vallentyne and others, *deny* that Sn is at least as good as S1. If so, we are denying the axiom of transitivity.

I take it that most economists, game theorists, and decision theorists, will deny that continuity should be rejected in 'extreme' cases of the sort Vallentyne imagines. And they will take the preceding argument as a reductio of the intuition in question, rather than as a threat to the axiom of transitivity, the principle of substitution of equivalence, or continuity even in so-called 'easy' cases. But they will have a hard time convincing me that rationality *requires* that I be willing to trade the *certainty* of a *full rich life* for the prospect of a *slightly* better one, when doing so means taking some risk – no matter how small – that I would end up with a life of pain and misery. Moreover, I am confident that I am not likely to be alone in resisting such a conclusion, even if this requires substantial revision in our understanding and assessment of expected utility theory and practical reasoning.

Objections and responses

In response to the preceding argument, some people defend the principle of continuity even in so-called 'extreme' cases of the sort Vallentyne imagines. One common response to my argument runs as follows.

Many of us believe that we currently have full, rich, lives. Yet we will make a left turn across a busy street to save $1 in filling our car with gas. Likewise, we'll leave a hotel and cross busy intersections to save a few dollars on the cost of a meal. These actions, and countless similar ones that we routinely make, seem perfectly rational. Yet, in such cases, we seem perfectly willing to risk a full, rich, life for the sake of a slight gain. Moreover, though small, the probability of risk to life and limb is still *much* greater in such cases than the probability of risk that the principle of continuity would require us to accept in 'extreme' cases, since that probability, recall, might be inconceivably small. Thus, it is argued, if, as most believe, our actions in such cases are not irrational, one cannot criticize the principle of continuity for requiring us to be willing to take much smaller risks in cases where the potential gains are similarly slight.

This response is initially plausible, but it should, I think, be questioned. First, it might be claimed that our actions in such cases are not, in fact, rational, if the cases are truly as described. That is, if the best way of understanding them truly is in terms of our putting full rich lives at risk merely for the sake of insignificant gains. But setting such a response aside, one might note that it is one thing to grant that such actions might be rationally *permissible*, quite another to maintain that they must be rationally *required*. Thus, it is one thing to maintain that it is not irrational to risk great personal harm for the sake of a slight gain if that is what one most wants to do, it is quite another to maintain, as the principle of continuity does, that rationality *requires* a willingness to accept *some* small probability of great harm – no matter how great – for the possibility of a slight gain – no matter how slight. The former may seem plausible for reasons that do not support the latter.

Second, the real-world cases this response appeals to are not analogous to the possible-world 'extreme' case where, I claimed, continuity fails. In my 'extreme' case I am supposed to trade-off the *certainty* of a full rich life for the prospect of a *slightly* better one, when doing so means taking some risk – no matter how small – that I would end up with a life of pain and misery. In the real-world cases there is no certainty of a full rich life if we don't adopt the more risky alternative. If I turn into the gas station on my right, instead of the one on my left, I may be hit by a fool passing on the right. If I stay in the hotel, I may break my neck tumbling down the escalator, or die of a heart attack from eating the richer food. It is one thing to trade off between different pairs of risky alternatives, preferring one risky alternative with a slightly higher payoff to another less risky alternative with a slightly lower payoff. It is another matter altogether to trade the *certainty* of a high payoff, for the probability of a slightly higher one, if there is also a probability, however small, of a *much* worse outcome.

Third, and most important, my example involves a unique, once-in-a-life-time opportunity to *guarantee* a full, rich, lengthy life with $1,000,000 per year. The decision whether to risk turning left across a busy street, or crossing several busy intersections to save a few dollars, is not analogous. We are constantly con-fronted by such decisions, where, at best, adoption of the cautious alternative merely increases the probability of *temporarily* preserving the status quo. Moreover, and this is the key point, because of the pervasive contingencies of human existence, in general, an inability or unwillingness to expose oneself to slight increases in risk will result in a crimped, impoverished, life.

In saying that one is not being irrational in crossing a busy street for the sake of a few dollars, one is acknowledging the rationality of a certain kind of desire, disposition, or lifestyle. Our judgment reflects a global judgment of the actor, and of the kind of life he has chosen to live. We view the act as the kind of act that rational agents typically do, and precisely because they have good reason to be disposed to do such acts. One *could* minimize one's risks by never venturing out, never meeting others, never eating foods that you have not grown yourself, and so on. But such a life would be lacking in much of what makes human life valuable. We judge the life of someone who *engages* the world as more valuable,[8] even if more risky. Correspondingly, we regard someone as rational in developing and acting in accordance with those desires and dispositions that promote the more valuable life. Crossing busy streets is the kind of activity that rational people do. It involves some increase of risk to the status quo, but the alternative to taking such risks is to preserve a status quo that is not nearly so worth preserving.

In sum, in my example, one has a momentous once-in-a-lifetime choice where a risk avoider can guarantee a tremendously valuable life. In the apparent counterexamples, one's choice is of a kind frequently confronted, where to be a risk avoider regarding such actions is almost certain to lead a crimped existence. The examples are not analogous. Our judgment that a rational person might choose the riskier alternative in the latter case, clearly does not support the judg-ment that a rational person must choose the riskier alternative in the former case.

There is a second objection to apparent counterexamples to continuity. Recall that continuity merely requires that for any alternatives where we prefer A to B, and B to C, there must be *some* p, such that we should be indifferent between X, the alternative where we receive B for sure, and Y, the alternative where we receive A with probability p, or C with probability 1-p. In particular, p can be as close to 1 as one likes, so the probability of the undesirable outcome (1-p) can be as close to 0 as one likes. For example, as Derek Parfit likes to colorfully put it, the probability of C could be as small as .000 ... 001, where the total number of zeros equalled the number of atoms in the universe. But, it is argued, we can't *possibly* accurately imagine probabilities this small. Correspondingly, for 'extreme' cases we should trust theory over intuitions. Since our theory – expected utility theory in general, and the principle of continuity in particular – seems acceptable for the 'easy' cases, where our intuitions seem well-grounded, we should also accept it for the 'extreme' cases, where its judgments may seem counterintuitive, but our intuitions cannot be trusted.

The idea here might be illustrated as follows. Imagine that there is an urn containing some number of white and red balls. We will receive A if a white ball is randomly selected from the urn, C if a red ball is. If we know there are five white balls and five red balls, we may be fairly good at intuitively judging the probability that we shall select a red ball. Similarly, if there are nine white balls and one red ball, or perhaps even 99 white balls and one red ball. But if we are told that while there is only one red ball, the number of white balls is a billion, or a zillion, or equal to the number of atoms in the universe, there is no way we can accurately 'intuit' our probability of randomly selecting a red ball. Thus, we cannot trust our intuitions about such cases – which are precisely the kind of 'extreme' cases where continuity allegedly fails.

This objection raises a legitimate worry. Our intuitions are *not* finely calibrated to reflect extremely small, or large, probabilities. Thus, in 'extreme' cases, we will inevitably attach either greater or less intuitive weight than we should to the likelihood of the worst outcome occurring. It is slightly ironic, however, that one might turn to this kind of defense to defuse our strong intuitive reactions to such cases. Since, typically, the greater danger lies in people *underestimating* the probability of a terrible outcome occurring, rather than in their overestimating the probability of such an outcome. Humans are notorious for treating a very small chance of a bad event happening as if there were no chance of it happening. This is a grave mistake. Of course, it is a mistake that most individuals will get away with most of the time. Still, as Derek Parfit writes, for reasons he amply presents, 'when the stakes are high, no chance, however small, should be ignored.'[9]

In the extreme case of the offered counterexample to continuity, an inflated estimate of the probability of the worst outcome may lead me to choose X, where I receive B for sure, rather than Y, where I receive A with probability p or C with probability 1-p. As the example was described, this would almost certainly cost me an extra dollar a year, and an *ever-so-slightly* fuller and richer life than I would have led had I chosen B. This slight difference in the quality of my life, caused, let us now suppose, by our inflated estimate of C's probability, may be a source of rational regret, but it won't be of much significance.

Suppose, on the other hand, that we underestimate C's probability. Impressed by C's *extreme* unlikelihood, we decide as if there were *no* chance of C's occurring and, on this basis, we choose Y rather than X. Unfortunately, we are the victims of bad luck of cosmic proportions, and we end up with a life of pain and misery rather than the full, rich, life with $1,000,000 per year that we would have been guaranteed had we chosen X. Here, it seems, our underestimate of C's probability could be the source of tremendous rational regret.

Of course, defenders of continuity might deny this. They might insist that we can only *rationally* regret our miscalculation of C's probability, and the corresponding difference in *expected* utility between X and Y, *not* the tremendous difference in *actual* outcome that our miscalculation led to because of horrendous bad luck. But this is precisely what opponents of continuity in extreme cases want to deny. They insist that if we can effectively guard against horrendous bad luck at *very* little cost to our well-being, and we fail to do so, then our choice is open to serious rational criticism. We cannot avoid such criticism by claiming that the bad outcome only occurred because of horrendous bad luck.

So, acknowledging that we are intuitively incapable of accurately assessing extremely small, or large, probabilities, does not yet support the conclusion that we must accept continuity for 'extreme' cases as well as 'easy' cases. We may judge that the dangers of underestimating the probability of the worst outcome far exceed the dangers of overestimating its probability. Such a judgment would provide direct grounds for rejecting continuity in extreme cases, one not based on our intuitive calculation of the expected utilities of X and Y.

Note, by the axioms of expected utility theory, our intuitive calculation of the expected utilities of X and Y *must* either support the principle of continuity or be mistaken. But this is not an *argument* against our intuitions about 'extreme' cases, since those cases are being offered as a *challenge* to the axioms of expected utility theory. Appealing to the axioms of expected utility theory doesn't refute such a challenge, it merely begs the question against it.

In thinking about the rationality of one's choice where probabilities are involved, it is, I think, useful to consider cases where that choice would be made repeatedly. Imagine, for example, that I am a benevolent leader of a large population. I am going to urge on my fellow citizens a principle of choice that each will follow. If they choose X, they will each receive B – $1,000,000 per year and a full, rich, life. If they choose Y, they will either receive A – $1,000,001 per year and an ever-so-slightly fuller, richer, life, or C – a life of pain and misery. Suppose first that if they choose Y, the odds of C are only one in a million. If there are a million people who will follow my advice I would urge each to choose X. I know that with a million people choosing the odds are great that *one* of them would end up with C if each chose Y. Thinking of my fellow citizens as I might members of my own family – remember, I am a benevolent leader – I *much* prefer the outcome where each of them is guaranteed B, to the outcome where virtually every one has A, but one ends up with C. It won't seem worth it to me to trade off an incredibly huge loss for one, for the sake of tiny gains for many others, even for almost a million others.

What if instead of one in a million, the odds are one in a billion, or one in a zillion, or one in the number of atoms in the universe? To be sure, these are inconceivably large numbers. But if I imagine the size of the population increasing proportionally, so the number of my fellow citizens who will follow my advice is a billion, or a zillion, or equal to the number of atoms in the universe, then my advice would be the same. I would urge each to choose X, knowing that if each chose Y, the odds would be high that *one* of them would end up with a life of pain and misery.

In considering my position, it may help to recall a familiar objection to (total) utilitarianism, which may be referred to as 'the problem of additive aggregation.' One example of the objection is Derek Parfit's *Repugnant Conclusion*: 'For any possible population of at least ten billion people, all with a very high quality of life, there must be some much larger imaginable population whose existence, if other things are equal, would be better, even though its members have lives that are barely worth living.'[10] Another example is what I call the 'lollipop for life' case. Suppose one could construct a *very* large lollipop. Suppose, for reasons we don't understand, that the only way of creating this lollipop would unavoidably involve an innocent person dying, but only after first being subjected to prolonged agony. But, then, suppose that we can take the lollipop around the universe, and give *many* people one lick each. Should we do so?

Most people firmly believe that the Repugnant Conclusion is, indeed, repugnant. They believe that an outcome, A, of at least ten billion people, all with a very high quality of life, would be better than an outcome, Z, with a large population all of whom have lives that are barely worth living, no matter *how many* people live in Z. Similarly, most firmly believe that no matter *how many* people would get one lick of the lollipop, we ought not to make it, if doing so would require an innocent person to suffer unbearable agony and die. Notoriously, total utilitarians have to reject these claims. However counterintuitive it may seem, they are committed to the additive aggregative view that if only there are *enough* people in Z, Z would be better than A, and if only *enough* people get a lick, we should make the lollipop.

Should we regard such examples as serious objections to total utilitarianism? Total utilitarians, of course, think not. They deny that the so-called 'problem of additive aggregation' is in fact a problem. Insisting that more of the good is better than less of the good, they respond to such examples along the lines of those who reject my intuitive reaction to the 'extreme' cases of continuity. They offer a number of sophisticated explanations for why we have the intuitions we do about such cases, arguing, in essence, that our intuitions were not developed to adequately respond to wild science-fiction type cases involving unimaginably large numbers of relatively small amounts. Correspondingly, they contend that we don't intuitively grasp how *much* total good is dispersed among Z's innumerable masses, or how *much* total pleasure would be enjoyed by countless people each licking a lollipop. So, they claim, our intuitions about such cases are mistaken. No matter *how* small the amount of good may be in a life that is barely worth living, or *how* small the amount of pleasure may be from one lick of a lollipop, if only there are *enough* such lives, or licks, *eventually* the total amount of good or pleasure *will* outweigh, and then be better than, any finite amount of good or pain that might be balanced off against it. Here, our understanding supposedly leads us to recognize truths that our imagination fails to appreciate. Both the Repugnant Conclusion and the 'lollipop for life' example can be rejected as objections to total utilitarianism.

The problem of additive aggregation has been much discussed, and I have little to add to that discussion. My point is mainly to remind the reader that the response people make against trusting our intuitions about continuity in 'extreme' cases is the same kind of response total utilitarians make to the problem of aggregation. Few people are willing to 'bite the bullet' and accept the total utilitarian's response for the Repugnant Conclusion and the 'lollipop for life' examples. I believe they are right not to do so. Similarly, I believe one should reject such a response to my claims about continuity.

Just as I think one cannot trade off between lollipops and lives, so I think one cannot trade off between tiny increases in well-being for many, and an *immense* loss in well-being for one. On my view, well-being is not aggregative in the way it would need to be for me to urge my fellow citizens to choose Y. Just as I think the moral value of a human life exceeds *any* number of lollipop licks, so I think no matter how large the population might be, the outcome in which *everyone* has B – $1,000,000 per year and a full, rich, life – is *better* than the outcome in which everyone has A – $1,000,001 per year and an ever-so-slightly fuller, richer, life – except, regrettably, for one person who has C – a life of pain and misery.

Similarly, imagine that I am to live a large number of lives successively. Each life will be confronted with the choice between X and Y, and I must adopt a principle of choice for each of my future selves. If the number of my future selves was large enough that the odds were that even *one* of them would end up with C if they each chose Y, then I would want each to choose X. I realize that this would cost each of an innumerably large number of future selves a small amount of well-being (equal to the difference between A and B), but I think that that would be a cost well worth innumerable future selves bearing, to prevent one of my future selves having C rather than B. Here, as before, I think the tiny differences between A and B don't aggregate as they would need to to outweigh the difference between B and C.

I think, then, that unless one is willing to bite the bullet regarding the problem of aggregation, one has good reason to recommend X rather than Y to innumerable citizens, or future selves, confronting that choice. But this suggests it may be rational to choose X rather than Y for oneself. Though the risk of ruining one's life might be small, it is not worth taking, for the rough equivalent of a few extra licks of a lollipop.

In sum, there remains reason to doubt the principle of continuity for 'extreme' cases. Correspondingly, there remains reason to question the axiom of transitivity, the principle of substitution of equivalence, or continuity even in so-called 'easy' cases.

Conclusion

I have argued that *if* one rejects the principle of continuity in certain 'extreme' cases, then expected utility theory is deeply problematic. One cannot simply assume that expected utility theory may only fail in rare 'extreme' cases, but will work fine for the vast majority of 'normal' cases. To the contrary, *if* one rejects the principle of continuity in certain 'extreme' cases, then one must reject continuity even in the 'easy' cases for which it seems *most* plausible, reject the axiom of transitivity, or reject the principle of substitution of equivalence.

To give up the principle of continuity even for easy cases would have radical implications for practical reasoning. But so, too, would giving up the axiom of transitivity or the principle of substitution of equivalence. Indeed, I suspect the implications of any of these moves would be so great, that many people will be tempted to reject the position causing all the trouble – namely the view that continuity should be rejected in certain 'extreme' cases. I am tempted to this view myself, but for reasons indicated in section V, find it deeply problematic.

Ultimately, I believe serious revision may be in order in our understandings of expected utility theory, practical reasoning, aggregation, and the good. But to fully defend this claim would require at least a book.[1]

Notes

[1]   My thinking about this essay's topic has evolved over many years, and there are many to whom I am indebted for their comments and support. The essay was first begun while I was a Fellow at Harvard's Program in Ethics and the Professions, and it was completed while I was a Visiting Fellow at All Souls College. I am most grateful to

both the Program, and All Souls, for providing ideal research environments. I am also grateful to numerous audiences for their reactions to this paper's ancestors, including those at Brown University, Harvard University, New York University, the University of Massachusetts at Amherst, St. Andrews University in Scotland, the Program in Economics, Justice and Society at the University of California at Davis, the Society for Ethics and Legal Philosophy in Cambridge, and the World Health Organization. My memory is too faulty to properly acknowledge all those who have given me useful comments on this topic, but they include Baruch Brody, Gerald Cohen, Tyler Cowen, Roger Crisp, Keith DeRose, Fred Feldman, Charles Fried, David Gauthier, James Griffin, Susan Hurley, Shelly Kagan, F.M. Kamm, Liam Murphy, Thomas Nagel, Ingmar Persson, John Roemer, Tim Scanlon, Amartya Sen, Ernest Sosa, Peter Unger, and Peter Vallentyne. John Broome, Stuart Rachels, and J. David Velleman deserve special mention for their influence on this essay. Finally, Derek Parfit initially inspired my work on this topic, and he has consistently been both my biggest source of encouragement and my most penetrating critic.

[2]   More generally, any relation R will be transitive, if and only if, for any a, b, and c, if aRb and bRc, then aRc. 'Taller than' is a standard example of a transitive relation, since if Andrea is taller than Becky, and Becky is taller than Claire, then Andrea is taller than Claire. By contrast, 'being the birth mother of' is clearly not a transitive relation, since Andrea's being the birth mother of Becky, and Becky's being the birth mother of Claire, does not entail – and in fact is incompatible with – Andrea's being the birth mother of Claire.

[3]   This example assumes that the value of $2 is not significantly different from the value of $1. If we imagine a scenario where the difference of one dollar meant the difference between life and death, then this wouldn't be an example of case II.

[4]   For the sake of discussion, I assume, contrary to fact, that there is no significant diminishing marginal utility of income between $1,000,000 per year and $2,000,000 per year.

[5]   Satisficers are people who believe there is a point where 'enough is enough,' after which they eschew a maximizing strategy in decision making. For an interesting discussion of the attractions of satisficing, see Michael Slote's *Beyond Optimizing: A Study of Rational Choice* (Harvard University Press, 1989).

[6]   Vallentyne's example is contained in his illuminating review of John Broome's *Weighing Goods* (Basil Blackwell Inc., 1991); see 'The Connection Between Prudential and Moral Goodness', *The Journal of Social Philosophy* 24 (1993): 105-28.

[7]   The argument of this section is taken from my 'Weighing Goods: Some Questions and Comments', *Philosophy and Public Affairs* 23, no. 4 (1994): 350-380. However, most of the discussion of the argument is new.

[8]   Or at least as not less valuable, which is all one really needs to defend this position.

[9]   *Reasons and Persons* (Oxford University Press, 1984), p. 75.

[10] *Reasons and Persons*, p. 388.

[11] I have been working on such a book for many years now, tentatively entitled *Rethinking the Good, Moral Ideals, and the Nature of Practical Reasoning*. Unfortunately, the ground is treacherous, and so far my work has yielded more problems than solutions.

The Resentment Argument[1]

Michael Smith

The holy grail of moral philosophy must surely be an argument that would show how and why certain facts, when properly appreciated by people, no matter who those people are or what their antecedent inclinations might happen to be, rationally require of those people a certain kind of response. Perhaps the required response would be a desire that those facts be realized, or perhaps indifference to those facts being realized, or perhaps an aversion to those facts being realized. That doesn't matter. What matters is not the nature of the response rationalized, but rather the fact that appreciation of the specified facts would rationalize some response or other.

The argument I have in mind would, of course, straddle the divide between meta-ethics and normative ethics. Like arguments in meta-ethics it would proceed without making any, or at any rate without making any undefended, normative assumptions. But like arguments in normative ethics it would enable us to draw a substantive normative conclusion. In other words, it would be no less than an argument taking us from an 'is' to an 'ought'. While no one much likes to describe themselves as attempting to derive an 'ought' from an 'is' these days, my own view is that at least some of the best work that has been done in moral philosophy in the last thirty years or so is best understood in just these terms. My aim in this essay is to focus attention on one such argument, the role reversal argument, which proceeds by way of asking the question 'How would you like it if someone did that to you?'.

The role reversal argument seems an especially fitting topic for a volume of essays in honor of Ingmar Persson. I first got to know Ingmar as the author of a critique of a well known presentation of this argument, a presentation that was subsequently described quite explicitly as an attempt to derive an 'ought' from an 'is' (Robinson 1982). Persson's target was, of course, Hare's famous attempt to derive utilitarianism from the formal features of moral thinking: that is, from the fact that, if thinking is to count as moral thinking at all, then the thinker must be trying to figure out what she can overridingly and universally prescribe (Hare 1981). Whenever I teach Hare's argument to my students, I teach it alongside Persson's careful and devastating critique (Persson 1983). It seemed to me when I first read Persson's critique, and it still seems to me now, that it provides an excellent illustration of just how much we can learn when we subject an apparently convincing argument – an 'intuitive' argument, as we might say – to rigorous analysis.

The argument is a fitting choice for another reason as well. For while Hare's argument, partially under Persson's influence, is no longer seriously supposed by anyone to have any hope whatsoever of allowing us to derive an 'ought' from an 'is', another presentation of the role reversal argument from much the same period is still alive and well. The alternative presentation of the argument first appeared in Chapter Nine of Thomas Nagel's *The Possibility of Altruism*. Here is what Nagel says.

> The rational altruism which I shall defend can be intuitively represented by the familiar argument, 'How would you like it if someone did that to you?' It is an argument to which we are all in some degree susceptible; but how it works, how it can be persuasive, is a matter of controversy. We may assume that the situation in which it is offered is one in which you would not like it if another person did to you what you are doing to someone else (the formula can be changed depending on the type of case; it can probably be used, if it works at all, to persuade people to help others as well as to avoid hurting them). But what follows from this? If no one is doing it to you, how can your conduct be influenced by the hypothetical admission that if someone were, you would not like it?
>
> It could be that you are afraid that your present behavior will have the result that someone will do the same to you … It could be that the thought of yourself in a position similar to that of your victim is so vivid and unpleasant that you find it distasteful to go on persecuting the wretch. But … why cannot such considerations motivate you to increase your security against retaliation, or take a tranquilizer to quell your pity, rather than to desist from your persecutions?
>
> There is something else to the argument; it does not appeal solely to the passions, but is a genuine argument whose conclusion is also a judgement. The essential fact is that you would not only *dislike* it if someone else treated you in that way; you would resent it. That is, you would think that your plight gave the other person a reason to terminate or modify his contribution to it, and that in failing to do so he was acting contrary to reasons which were plainly available to him. In other words, the argument appeals to a *judgement* that you would make in the hypothetical case, a judgement applying a general principle which is relevant to the present case as well. It is a question not of compassion but of simply connecting, in order to see what one's attitudes commit one to. (Nagel 1970, pp.82–3)

Let's call this the 'resentment argument'.

According to Nagel, the resentment argument provides merely 'intuitive' support for rational altruism. But though in the remainder of *The Possibility of Altruism* he goes on to give a much more complicated and sophisticated argument for that same conclusion, it is the intuitive argument that has had a lasting impact. Nagel himself has since abandoned the sophisticated argument (Nagel 1986), for example, but he quite happily continues to repeat the intuitive argument (Nagel 1987). More recently, Christine Korsgaard relies exclusively on the intuitive argument at a crucial point in *The Sources of Normativity* (Korsgaard 1996). In response to her own question 'Now how do we get from here' (where 'here' is an argumentative situation in which we are a long way short of rational altruism) 'to moral obligation?' (which is an argumentative situation in which we have derived some obligations towards others, and have hence committed ourselves to some form of rational altruism), Korsgaard responds 'This is where Thomas Nagel's argument ... comes into its own' (Korsgaard 1996, p.142). The argument she goes on to give is none other than the resentment argument.

Despite its evident impact it is, I think, less than clear both what the resentment argument is meant to be and whether, when properly understood, it has any real force. Accordingly, my aim in this paper is to spell out the resentment argument in some detail and to provide an evaluation of it. Though I would be delighted if subjecting the resentment argument, Nagel's version of the role reversal argument, to rigorous analysis enabled us to learn as much as we learned from Persson's analysis of Hare's version of that argument, I will be content if the conclusion is the more plonking one that Nagel's intuitive argument for rational altruism, much like Hare's for utilitarianism, collapses under close scrutiny.

Clarification of the resentment argument's main premise and conclusion

Let's begin by clarifying the main premise of the resentment argument.

I am to imagine that I have acted in some way such that I would not like it if someone acted in that way towards me. Nagel suggests that it might be a situation in which I have harmed another person, or a situation in which I have failed to provide the other with some benefit. To make things simple, in what follows I will focus on cases of harming another. Nagel does not say so, but it must also presumably be imagined that the alternative action was available to me in the circumstances. In other words, I am to imagine a situation in which I harm another when I could have failed to harm him instead.

The crucial observation to make about this main premise of the resentment argument is that, being about a harm done in circumstances in which a harm might not have been done, it is a premise that falls fairly and squarely on the 'is' side of the 'is-ought' gap. This premise is about a non-evaluative matter of fact. Acceptance of it does not, all by itself, entail acceptance of the rightness or wrongness of what was done, and nor does it fix a subject's orientation to what was done either. Those who believe themselves to be harming someone in the circumstances described could be in favor of their so acting, or they could be indifferent to so acting, or they could be averse to so acting. Acceptance of the premise does not yet tell us which of these states they are in, still less does it tell us whether their being in one or another of these states would be rationally required or forbidden.

Consider now the conclusion of the resentment argument. Nagel tells us that the argument is meant to be 'persuasive'. In context, it is plain what he means by this. He means that the argument is meant to have a rational influence on the conduct of those who appreciate its force. The conclusion of the resentment argument is thus supposed to be a motivation to act. Moreover, and much more importantly for the argument's claim to be an *argument*, Nagel tells us that when the resentment argument exerts this influence on conduct, it exerts it by way of supporting a 'judgement', or, if you like, by way of supporting an intermediate propositional conclusion. The intermediate conclusion is the claim that, when I harm another in circumstances in which I could have failed to harm them, I act in a way that I have a reason not to act and hence have a reason to stop so acting.

Just as we saw that the main premise of the resentment argument fell on the 'is' side of the 'is'-'ought' gap, we can therefore see that the intermediate conclusion of the argument, which is a claim about what there is a reason to do, a claim whose acceptance is in turn supposed to rationalize the main conclusion of the argument, a corresponding motivation, evidently falls on the 'ought' side. So if the resentment argument contains no further premises – in other words, if everything is meant to follow a priori from the main premise – then it seems that the argument does indeed purport to take us from a non-evaluative premise to an evaluative conclusion. The resentment argument thus really does look like it is meant to be the holy grail of moral philosophy: little wonder that Korsgaard thought she should appeal to it at that crucial juncture in *The Sources of Normativity*!

Even if the resentment argument is everything it purports to be, however, note that this is not to say that those who accept the 'is' main premise of the resentment argument cannot fail to accept the 'ought' conclusion. Since the argument purports to be an *argument*, they may of course fail to accept that conclusion. They may fail to accept it either by failing to accept the intermediate conclusion that they have a reason not to do what they did, or, if they accept that intermediate conclusion, by failing to be correspondingly motivated. The important point is simply that, on the assumption that the resentment argument is everything it purports to be, to the extent that people who accept the 'is' premise fail to accept the 'ought' conclusion they thereby become liable to rational criticism.

Moving beyond the main premise: role reversal

Consider now the first move beyond the main premise of the resentment argument.

Informally, remember, the argument proceeds by making us confront the counterfactual question 'How would you like it if someone did that to you?' Put slightly more formally, what this counterfactual question assumes is that it follows from the fact that I have harmed another person in circumstances in which I might not have harmed them, that there is a possible situation which is exactly like this one in various respects, including the nature of the harm that is done, but which differs in that I am the one who is harmed and another person is the one who does the harming.

Note that this is an 'is'–'is' move, not yet a move from an 'is' to an 'ought'. More precisely, it is a move from an 'is' that characterizes actuality to an 'is' that characterizes a mere possibility. Even so, it might well be questioned whether the move is valid. Suppose, for example, that I am a doctor and that what I have done is harm a woman by, say, damaging her reproductive system during an operation. Can we really suppose that there is a possible situation in which I suffer that harm? That would seem to require, falsely, that there is a possible situation in which my natural reproductive organs are those of a woman. Or suppose that I harm an Australian Aboriginal by making a racist remark about the genetic pool from which he came. Can we really suppose that there is a possible situation in which I suffer that harm? That would once again seem to require something impossible, namely, that there is a possible situation in which I come from the genetic pool of the Australian Aboriginals.

Having noted this problem, however, it seems to me that we can safely put it to one side. Either there is a relevant sense of 'possibility' in which these claims do state genuine possibilities, notwithstanding the fact that in the most familiar sense of 'possibility' they do not, or we can ascend to a more general characterization of the harm done so that it is plausible to suppose that, in the more familiar sense of 'possibility', it is possible for me to suffer a harm so characterized. Of course, once we ascend to this more general characterization of the harm done it might be extraordinarily difficult to specify the *respect* of similarity in non-evaluative language. The easiest way to characterize the similarity might well be in evaluative terms, for example by saying that the harm done to me in the possible case is just as bad as the harm done to the person I harm in actuality. But even if this is right it seems to me that we should resist drawing the conclusion that there is no *non*-evaluative respect of similarity in such cases. Indeed, given that a quite radical particularism is false, it seems to me that there must be some non-evaluative respect of similarity (Jackson, Pettit and Smith 2000). It is the possibility of these sorts of harms that we must countenance, harms which must be identical in non-evaluative respects, even if it is difficult for us to characterize the nature of such harms in English without recourse to evaluative language.

To sum up: we should grant the first move beyond the main premise of the resentment argument. It does indeed seem to follow from the fact that I have harmed another person in circumstances in which I might not have harmed them, that there is a possible situation which is exactly like this one in respect of the harm that is done – or, at least, similar in crucial non-evaluative respects – but which differs in that I am the one who is harmed and another person is the one who does the harming.

Moving beyond the main premise: feelings of resentment

The second move beyond the main premise is the observation that, in the possible situation imagined in which it is me who is harmed, and another person who does the harming, I do not just find the fact that I have been harmed by the other unpleasant, or a cause of feelings of insecurity, or to be something that I dislike. Rather I find that I resent what he does to me.

The second move thus presents itself as another 'is'–'is' move. The fact that someone feels resentment is a non-evaluative fact about them, albeit, as we will see, a fact which presupposes that the person who feels resentment is committed to certain evaluative claims. I will have more to say about this in the next section. Even putting the connection between resentment and evaluation to one side, however, the transition is still problematic. For we must ask why we should suppose that I would have any such feelings at all in the possible situation in which it is me who is harmed. What is the connection supposed to be between imagining myself being harmed and imagining myself feeling resentment? Various suggestions might be made.

To begin, it might be suggested that I have to imagine myself feeling resentment because, as we saw in our discussion of the first move beyond the main premise, we have to imagine a possible situation which is as similar as possible to the actual situation, except that our roles are reversed. Since we can assume that the person I harm in actuality resents my harming him, the suggestion might be, it follows that I have to imagine myself resenting him in the imagined situation in which our roles are reversed. Role reversal means not just taking on the other person's harm, but taking on his resentment as well. But I do not think that this can be right.

As I understand it, the resentment argument is supposed to show that I have a reason not to harm another person even if, for some reason, perhaps because he is so child-like in his appreciation of what happens to him, he feels no resentment at all when I harm him. If this is right, however, then it cannot be that the felt resentment that the person in the actual case feels towards me, even assuming that that person does feel such resentment, is what explains why I have to imagine myself feeling resentment towards him when our roles are reversed. The resentment that the person in the actual case feels towards me, even assuming that he does feel such resentment, though perhaps perfectly legitimate, is therefore not something that I must take on board when our roles are reversed. The fact that he feels resentment for the harm I do to him is incidental and inessential for the resentment argument to gain purchase.

Another suggestion might be that I have to imagine myself resenting being harmed by the other because it is literally impossible for me to imagine being harmed without, thereby, imagining myself feeling resentment. But this cannot be right either. If it is so much as possible for there to be someone who feels no resentment when I harm him – (say) because he is so child-like in his appreciation of what happens to him – then there is at least one possible situation – the situation in which I am as child-like in my appreciation of what happens to me – in which I feel no resentment when he harms me. The claim that it is literally impossible for me to imagine myself being harmed without feeling resentment is therefore implausible.

A final suggestion, and I suspect that this must be what Nagel has in mind, is that I am supposed to imagine myself feeling resentment because, at the role reversal stage of the argument, I am not supposed to imagine just any old possible situation in which it is me who is harmed by another, but rather a situation which is as similar as possible to actuality in which it is me who is harmed by another. Informally, remember, the argument begins by asking us a counterfactual question: 'How would you like it if someone did that to you?' The assumption might be that since I actually feel resentment for similar harms that are done to me in actuality – after all, I am not in actuality child-like in my appreciation of what happens to me – so, in the counterfactual case in which a harm exactly like the one that I do to another is done to me, we must suppose that I would, in that case, feel resentment as well.

If this is right, however, then the resentment argument has been underdescribed. The argument must contain an extra premise. It must contain an extra premise because, without that extra premise, it is simply invalid. There is, after all, a possible world in which I accept the premise that there is a possible situation, maximally similar to the possible world in which the argument is being offered to me, a possible world in which I cause someone to suffer a harm, in which I suffer a harm exactly like that, but in which I quite correctly resist drawing the alleged conclusion that, in that possible situation, I would feel resentment. There is such a possible world because, in some such possible worlds in which the argument is being offered to me, completely child-like as I am in my appreciation of what happens to me. I don't ever feel resentment and hence it simply isn't true that I would feel resentment. The truth of the premise thus doesn't entail the truth of the conclusion all by itself.

What the extra premise needs to capture is the crucial assumption that the resentment argument is only being offered to people who, not being child-like in their appreciation of what happens to them, do in fact feel resentment when they experience harms like the one that I have caused the other person. But what, exactly, would this extra premise be? One possibility is that the extra premise is simply a statement to the effect that none of the possible explanations of why someone might fail to experience resentment obtain. In other words, the extra premise would state that (for example) I am not child-like in my appreciation of what happens to me, and, if there are other conditions whose obtaining would prevent me from feeling resentment, then it would state that none of these conditions obtain either. Another possibility is that the extra premise is simply a more bald statement to the effect that I am a person who feels resentment when I experience a harm like the one that I have caused the other person.

Whichever of these is the ultimate form of the relevant premise, the crucial point to make here is that some such extra premise is required. To be sure, it is another 'is' premise, not an 'ought' premise. The fact that I feel resentment is a non-evaluative fact about me, albeit, as we will shortly see, a fact which presupposes that I am committed to certain evaluative claims. As will then eventually become clear, the fact that some such extra premise is required is thus problematic.

Moving beyond the main premise: evaluation

The third move beyond the main premise of the resentment argument is this. Granting that I feel resentment in the possible situation in which I am harmed by another, it is supposed to follow that I negatively evaluate his harming me, that is, that I judge his doing so to be undesirable.

Note that this is once again a move from an 'is' to an 'is'. The fact that I negatively evaluate someone's conduct is a non-evaluative fact about me, albeit a non-evaluative fact about my commitment to certain evaluations. Even so, we must ask why we should suppose that resentment does entail a negative evaluation. The reason, I take it, is that resentment is supposed to be a prime example of those emotions that, by their very nature, have an evaluative aspect. Other prime examples are supposed to include anger, which is said to be connected with the judgement that one has been wronged, and fear, which is said to be connected with the judgement that something is dangerous.

However, without questioning whether there are such emotions, it is important to remember that the claim that there are such emotions is subject to two quite different interpretations (contrast Solomon 1976 and Gibbard 1990). It can be interpreted as saying something quite strong, namely, that when I experience certain emotions, things don't just appear to me to be a certain way, but that I actually judge things to be that way: I *judge* that someone has wronged me, I *judge* that something is dangerous, I *judge* that someone has acted in an undesirable way towards me, and so on. Or, alternatively, it can be interpreted as saying something much weaker: that when I am angry at someone, it *seems* to me that he has wronged me, whether or not I go on to make the judgement; that when I am afraid of something, it *seems* to me that that thing is dangerous, whether or not I go on to make the judgement; that when I resent the way that someone behaves, it *seems* to me that he has acted in an undesirable way towards me, whether or not I go on to make the judgement; and so on.

The third move beyond the main premise of the resentment argument plainly requires that we interpret the claim that emotions have an evaluative aspect in the stronger of the two ways just described. But the problem with interpreting the claim in this way is that it would seem to be quite plainly mistaken. It would seem to be mistaken because emotions that have an evaluative aspect would seem, in this respect, to bear a certain striking similarity to ordinary perceptual states. Just as when we ordinarily perceive something we systematically have appearances of objects being a certain way, so, when we experience such emotions, we systematically have appearances of value and disvalue. Crucially, though, just as when we perceive things we can know that the appearances are misleading, even while they continue to appear to us in the way that they do – think of the way in which the two lines in the Muller-Lyer illusion persist in seeming to be of different lengths even after we have measured them and convinced ourselves that they are of the same length – so, when we experience the evaluative emotions, it can continue to seem to us that there is value or disvalue even after we have convinced ourselves that such an evaluation would be mistaken. Allan Gibbard gives us a nice example of this sort of evaluative illusion.

> Most of us have experienced being angry and yet thinking that no wrong has been done, so that the anger is unjustified. In such cases, one *feels* as if a wrong had been done, but thinks that no wrong has been done. ... [I]f the anger is indeed irrational, as one thinks, then there is a belief it would be irrational to have. It would be irrational to believe that a wrong has been done. That, however, is precisely what one doesn't believe; that is why one considers one's own anger irrational. (Gibbard 1990, p.40)

If this point is agreed, however, then it follows that the resentment argument goes wrong in moving straight from the fact that I feel resentment, in the possible situation in which it is me who is harmed, to the fact that I make a negative evaluation of the conduct of the person who harms me. From the fact that I feel resentment in that possible situation all that strictly follows is that it seems to me that someone has acted in an undesirable way. But that seeming might be mere appearance, an evaluative illusion. I might not judge that he has acted in an undesirable way.

In order to get from the fact that I would feel resentment to fact that I would judge that he acted undesirably, we therefore need to add a further premise. But what premise? Following from the earlier discussion it seems that the argument needs to make explicit the fact that the person to whom the argument is being addressed is not someone who suffers evaluative illusions in situations like this. That is why, when we ask that person to imagine how he would feel if the harm were done to him, he can not only say that he would feel resentment, but that he would judge that the person who harmed him did something undesirable.

Once again it therefore seems that we have two choices. One possibility is that the extra premise is simply a statement to the effect that the argument is being addressed to someone who does not suffer from any evaluative illusions. But since, as Gibbard points out, that amounts to the claim that the person is not irrational, it follows that the extra premise would have to be that I am not irrational. Another possibility is that the extra premise would simply be the bald statement that I judge that people who cause harms like the one done to me in the imagined case act in a way that is undesirable. This is why, in the closest possible world in which it is me who is harmed, I would judge that the harm done to me is undesirable.

This time, however, it seems that we have a decisive reason to prefer the second formulation of the extra premise to the first. For the first formulation is an 'ought' claim, whereas the second is still an 'is' claim. The fact that I make a certain evaluative judgement is a non-evaluative claim about me, albeit a non-evaluative claim about the evaluative claims to which I am committed.

Moving beyond the main premise: reasons

Let's now consider the remaining steps in the resentment argument.

Granting both that I feel resentment in the possible situation in which I am harmed by another, and that I negatively evaluate his harming me, it is supposed to follow that, in the imagined situation, I thereby commit myself to the claim that he has a reason to stop harming me. This is plainly meant to be another 'is-is' transition: a move from a claim about a belief I would have in the imagined situation about the undesirability of the way in which the other person acts towards me to a claim about a belief I would have in the imagined situation about the reasons that that person has. From this claim, the claim that in the imagined situation I would believe that the person who harms me has a reason to stop, I am then supposed to derive, via universalization, the intermediate conclusion of the resentment argument, the conclusion that I have a reason to stop harming the person I am harming in the actual situation. Here, at last, we have a move that is supposed to take us from an 'is' to an 'ought'. This intermediate conclusion is then, in turn, supposed to give rational support to the main conclusion of the argument: a motivation to stop.

Now it might be thought that at least some of these steps are relatively straight-forward. After all, it is widely acknowledged that the term 'reason' has many senses, and that in at least one of these senses it is simply analytic that people who act in a way that is undesirable, act in a way that they have a reason not to act (see e.g. Foot 1972). If this is right, however, and if, as seems plausible, the judgement that someone acts in a way that is undesirable commits the judge to judging that it is desirable that the person stops so acting, then it follows that there is at least a sense of the term 'reason' in which the judge is committed to judging that that person has a reason to stop. If the universalization stage of the argument is acceptable then it might well be thought that we should concede these final steps in the argument. However it seems to me that it would be a grave mistake to grant all of these steps so quickly.

The first problem concerns the very first of these steps. True enough, there is a sense of the term 'reason' in which it is analytic that people who act in a way that is undesirable act in a way that they have a reason not to act. However that is not a sense of the term 'reason' that can support the main conclusion of the resentment argument which, you will remember, is a motivation to act. In order to see why this is so, consider a completely conventional mode of normative assessment, such as etiquette. Norms of etiquette are, I assume, all too often completely arbitrary from the rational point of view. Indeed, in some cases at least, they are positively pernicious, improving the position of the ruling class and undermining that of the underclass. This is why each of us can recognize, while yet quite reasonably rejecting wholesale, at least some requirements of etiquette. The mere fact that there is *a* sense of the term 'reason' in which it is analytic that what it is desirable for us to do, from the point of view of etiquette, is something that we have a reason to do, thus does nothing to show that a failure to be motivated in the way that we acknowledge ourselves to have reason to act, in *this* sense of the term 'reason', makes us liable to rational criticism. Quite the opposite. The mere existence of a reason to stop harming another, if this is the sense that the term 'reason' has, would thus likewise do nothing to give rational support to the main conclusion of the resentment argument, which is a motivation to stop.

What this shows, I think, is that the resentment argument plainly requires that we have, in the background, a particular conception of evaluative judgement, a conception that permits us to infer not just that an agent has a reason to act in a certain way from the fact that it is desirable that he acts in that way, but also that, in that sense of the term 'reason', when someone believes that they have reasons, they are liable to rational criticism if they are not correspondingly motivated.

Of course, I am happy to admit that there is such a conception of evaluative judgement, as it is a conception according to which such judgements conform to what I have elsewhere called the 'Practicality Requirement' (Smith 1994, 1997). But not everyone is happy to agree that evaluative judgements conform to such a requirement (Brink 1997). It is thus crucial to remember that the resentment argument itself presupposes that some such conception of evaluative judgement is correct.

The other much more serious problem concerns the move from 'is' to 'ought': that is, the move, via universalization, from the claim that I have to imagine myself believing that the other person has a reason to stop harming me, in the imagined situation, to the conclusion that I have a reason to stop harming the person I am harming in the actual situation. The glaring problem with this move is that, in order to be valid, it requires not just that I imagine myself *believing* that the other person has a reason to stop harming me, in the imagined situation, but that this belief is *true*. But nothing so far granted in the premises guarantees that the belief I imagine myself having is true.

Now it might be suggested that, whether or not the belief is true, I must certainly *believe* that that belief is true as I rehearse the premises of the resentment argument to myself. After all, the reason I have to imagine that I would believe that the other person has a reason to stop harming me is because this is supposed to follow from the fact that I would believe that he is acting undesirably, and the reason that I had to imagine that I would have that belief is that I in fact believe that people causing such harms act undesirably: remember how we got to make the third move beyond the main premise (section 4 above).

But while this does indeed explain why I must believe that the beliefs I imagine myself having are true, as I rehearse the premises of the resentment argument to myself, it also highlights what seems to me to be the argument's central flaw. For, as should now be plain, we can in fact by-pass all of the steps that go via role-reversal and resentment. They are all completely irrelevant. What is relevant is rather a single premise, the premise that we saw was required in order to make the third move beyond the main premise. The really crucial reasoning in the resentment argument goes like this. Premise: I judge that people who cause harms like the one that I cause to the person I harm in actuality act in a way that is undesirable. First intermediate conclusion: I should believe that what I did when I harmed that person in actuality was undesirable. Second intermediate conclusion: what I did when I harmed that person in actuality was undesirable. But this argument is plainly fallacious. We simply cannot infer from the fact that I have a belief that that belief is true. Yet that is, in effect, what the resentment argument asks us to do.

Conclusion

Now that we have seen the premises of the resentment argument fully laid out it seems to me that we must conclude that it is a very disappointing argument indeed. What we were after, and what the resentment argument promised, is the conclusion that I have a reason to stop harming the person I am harming in actuality. But all that the premises of the resentment argument really entitle us to is the conclusion that I ought to believe that I have such a reason. Nothing in the premises supports the conclusion that this belief is true because the crucial premise that drives the conclusion is simply a premise to the effect that I believe that people who cause harms like the one that I cause to the person who I harm in actuality act undesirably. And, as with any belief, the mere fact I have this belief does nothing to show that it is true. The premises about role reversal and resentment were all completely irrelevant.

Notes

1 An earlier version of this paper was read under the title 'In Search of the Philosopher's Stone: The Resentment Argument' at *Emotion and Value*, a conference held at Ohio State University, October 1999. I would very much like to thank all of those who participated in this splendid conference. I am especially grateful for comments received from Simon Blackburn, Miles Burnyeat, Justin D'Arms, Allan Gibbard, Philip Pettit, and Neil Tennant.

References

Brink, David (1997), 'Moral Motivation', *Ethics*, 4–32.
Foot, Philippa (1972), 'Morality as a System of Hypothetical Imperatives' reprinted in Philippa Foot, (*Virtues and Vices*. Berkeley: University of California Press) 1978: 157–73.
Gibbard, Allan (1990), *Wise Choices, Apt Feelings* (Oxford: Clarendon Press).
Hare, R.M. (1981), *Moral Thinking* (Oxford: Oxford University Press).
Jackson, Frank, Philip Pettit and Michael Smith 2000, 'Ethical Particularism and Patterns' in Brad Hooker and Maggie Little (eds) *Moral Particularism* (Oxford: Oxford University Press) 79–99.
Korsgaard, Christine (1996), *The Sources of Normativity* (Cambridge: Cambridge University Press).
Nagel, Thomas (1970), *The Possibility of Altruism* (Princeton: Princeton University Press).
Nagel, Thomas (1986), *The View from Nowhere* (Oxford: Oxford University Press).
Nagel, Thomas (1987), *What Does It All Mean?: A Very Short Introduction to Philosophy* (New York: Oxford University Press).

Persson, Ingmar (1983), 'Hare on Universal Prescriptivism and Utilitarianism', *Analysis*, 43–49.

Robinson, H. M. (1982), 'Is Hare a Naturalist?', *Philosophical Review*, 73–86.

Smith, Michael (1994), *The Moral Problem* (Oxford: Basil Blackwell).

Smith, Michael (1997), 'In Defence of *The Moral Problem*: A Reply to Brink, Copp and Sayre-McCord' in *Ethics*, 84–119.

Solomon, Robert C. (1976), *The Passions* (Garden City, N.Y.: Doubleday/Anchor).

Intrinsic Value and Individual Worth

Michael J. Zimmerman

The headline in this morning's *Daily News* proclaims, in block letters 5 cm tall:

DIANA'S DRESS CAUSES BIG SENSATION!

We all understand what it means, but should any of us take it literally?

What the headline means is that there was something about Diana's dress that caused a big sensation. The headline is intended to entice us to read further and discover what this something was. (Was the dress especially lavish? Was it shockingly revealing? Was its design outrageous? What exactly was it that caused such a stir?) Once we have learned these details, we will have a better understanding of what took place.

Suppose the dress was especially lavish, carrying a price tag of £30,000. It is this that caused the sensation. Once we have discovered this, what will our attitude be toward the claim made in the headline? Will we accept it as literally true? Will we, that is, still want to say that *the dress* caused the sensation, once we have learned that *the dress's being lavish* caused the sensation? Perhaps, but, if so, we surely wouldn't want to say that these causes are on a metaphysical par; for that would put us at risk of having to say that the sensation was causally overdetermined, which (we may assume) it was not. If we are not to be eliminativists of a certain sort and deny that the dress was, literally, a cause of the sensation, we must at least be reductionists and say that its being such a cause was nothing above and beyond some state of the dress being a cause of the sensation. Object-causation, if there is such a phenomenon at all, is metaphysically parasitic on state-causation, and so talk of the former is reducible to talk of the latter.[1]

The next morning's headline declares:

DIANA'S DRESS OF GREAT VALUE!

Is this something we should take literally?

That depends on the sort of value at issue. If it is economic value, then it seems quite natural to take it literally (and also to accept it as true; £30,000 is a lot of money for a dress). But suppose that this headline appears, not in the *Daily News*, but in the *Axiological Gazette*, and that the value at issue is intrinsic value. Then, I believe, either we should not take the headline literally, or we should understand the value at issue to be metaphysically parasitic on the intrinsic value of states.

1

To defend this position, I must say what I mean by 'intrinsic value.'

Often, when introducing students to the notion of intrinsic value, I set it in the context of hedonism. I don't try to define the notion, merely to illustrate it.

'Is charity a good thing?' I ask.

'Yes,' comes the reply.

'Why?'

'Because it provides people with food, clothing, and shelter.'

'What's good about that?'

'It satisfies their needs.'

'What's good about that?'

'It gives them pleasure.'

'What's good about that?'

At this point, some of the students try to think of something else that might in turn explain the value of pleasure, but I tell them that it is here that the hedonist puts a stop to this line of inquiry by saying simply, 'It just is.' And then I elaborate by telling them,

'What the hedonist is saying is that charity is (usually) good because of what it produces, which is, ultimately, pleasure, whereas pleasure is good, not because of what it produces, but rather because of what it is. That's the difference between intrinsic value and instrumental value.'

I then provide a second, briefer illustration.

'Is hitting someone on the head with a hammer bad?'

'Yes.'

'Why?'

'Because it causes pain.'

'What's bad about that?' I ask rhetorically, and continue, 'This is where the hedonist would stop. He'd say that pain just is bad. It's bad because of what it is, not because of what it produces.'

Of course, this is all very rough, but the students seem to get the idea. Many philosophers, however, would accuse me of misleading my students. They'd claim that to say that pleasure is good 'because of what it is' and that pain is bad 'because of what it is' is to say nothing helpful, since it provides no insight into the type of value at issue. They'd also say that I am confusing two types of value that Christine Korsgaard has famously argued must be kept distinct: first, there is intrinsic value, which is the value that something has 'in itself' and which is to be contrasted with extrinsic value; then there is final value, which is the value that something has 'for its own sake' and which is to be contrasted with instrumental value.[2] The charge is that, in contrasting intrinsic value with instrumental value, I am confusing intrinsic value with final value.

I shall try to explain why both objections are mistaken, since states, and only states, are the bearers of intrinsic value.

2

Let me begin by conceding that the crucial value at issue is that which Korsgaard calls final value. It is the value that something has for its own sake that is the ground of all attributions of value (or, at least, all attributions of the sort of value I'm concerned with here[3]). Consider the claim that pleasure is good for its own sake. I take this to mean that every state of pleasure, every state consisting of someone's being pleased, is good simply in virtue of being such a state. There is no helpful explanation why the state is good; it just is good 'as such,' that is, good in virtue of its own nature. But though unhelpful, in that this account of the goodness of pleasure does not cite something else in terms of which the goodness of pleasure may be understood, it does, contrary to the first objection, provide some insight into the nature of final value. Such value is *nonderivative*; it is the ground or source of nonfinal values (such as those of charity and of hitting someone on the head with a hammer), values that may thus be declared derivative.[4] All explanation must come to an end somewhere; the explanation of values stops with the citing of final values.[5]

Consider, now, the claims about final value that are sometimes made when it is individual objects, rather than states, that are said to have such value. Korsgaard, for instance, suggests that mink coats, handsome china, and gorgeously enameled frying pans might all be good for their own sakes.[6] Shelly Kagan claims that the pen used by Abraham Lincoln to sign the Emancipation Proclamation is something that might well be good for its own sake.[7] And Wlodek Rabinowicz and Toni Rønnow-Rasmussen are prepared (for the sake of illustration) to declare Princess Diana's dress good for its own sake.[8] If we were to ask these authors why the objects in question are good, we might expect, given what was said in the last paragraph, that they would simply answer, 'They just are good "as such." They're good in virtue of their natures.' But this is *not* what they say. Korsgaard attributes the value of the objects she mentions to their 'instrumentality,' that is, to their helpfulness in allowing us to accomplish certain tasks. Kagan attributes the value of Lincoln's pen to the unique historical role it played. Rabinowicz and Rønnow-Rasmussen attribute the value of Diana's dress to the fact that it belonged to Diana.

Notice two things about these claims made by Korsgaard *et al.* First, it is precisely because of such examples that they insist on the distinction between intrinsic value and final value; for the final values they claim on behalf of the objects they cite supervene on *extrinsic*, relational features of the objects.[9] And this brings me straight to the second point, which is simply that the sort of claim made by Korsgaard *et al.* is very different from the sort of claim made earlier about pleasure. In the case of pleasure, there was no helpful explanation why pleasure is good, and this fact fits well with the observation that the value of pleasure is nonderivative. But if we explain the values of the coat, the china, the pan, the pen, and the dress by appealing to certain particular relational properties of these objects rather than to their own natures, this seems to me a strong indication that these values are *derivative* and that we must press our inquiry further in order to reach the nonderivative values that are their sources.

A strong indication, I say, but naturally this can be contested. My contention is that a helpful explanation as to why something is good is available if and only if the goodness is derivative. I have also suggested that, where no helpful explanation as to why something is good is available, this is because the thing in question just is good 'as such,' that is, good in virtue of its own nature. Given that something's nature is intrinsic to it, my contention and suggestion jointly imply that *nonderivative value is intrinsic to its bearer*. Each of the assumptions on which this conclusion is based could of course be challenged, but further support for my position is provided by the observation that, given the particular relational properties cited by Korsgaard *et al.*, we don't have to look very far at all in order to find the sources of the values they claim on behalf of the individual objects in question. It is the coat's (the china's, the pan's) being helpful that Korsgaard should identify as having final value; it is the pen's playing the historical role (or, at least, the sort of historical role) that it played that Kagan should say is of final value; it is the dress's belonging to Diana (or, at least, having some such connection to someone of that sort) that Rabinowicz and Rønnow-Rasmussen should claim to be of final value. The attribution of value to the objects is thus eliminable in terms of, or at least reducible to, an attribution of final value to some states of the objects. Just as in the case of causation, so too in the case of value: once the move from objects to states of objects is made, we get a fuller account and a better understanding of what is at issue.

3

The claims that object-causation is parasitic on state-causation and that object-value is parasitic on state-value are, as I have already acknowledged, contestable. Nevertheless, I submit that the thesis is, in each case, an attractive and plausible one. But it is also a controversial one. I won't have much more to say regarding the thesis about causation, since that is not the concern of this paper. Rather, let me now address some objections to the thesis about value.

First objection

If something is valuable, this is because of some other property that it has. Given this, the principle upon which I am relying is unacceptable, for it leads to an infinite regress. The principle is this: if x is valuable because it has some property P, then x's having P is valuable. Now, if x's having P is valuable, this will be because of some further property Q that *it* has. The principle then implies that x's-having-P's having Q is valuable, which will in turn imply, for some property R, that x's-having-P's-having-Q's having R is valuable, and so on.

Response

I am not relying on the principle cited. This principle is in fact ambiguous, since 'because' admits of more than one interpretation. Suppose that 'because' expresses supervenience. Then I grant that, if something is valuable, this is because of some other property that it has. But I deny that its having this other property must be something that is itself valuable. Indeed, when it comes to final value, I think it is true that, if x (which, in my view, must be a state) is valuable because it has P, then x's having P is itself *not* valuable.

Suppose that I agree that Diana's dress is of great value because it belonged to Diana. I am *not* thereby saying that it has a certain final value that supervenes on the property of having belonged to Diana. That is what my *opponents* are saying. I am saying that it has a certain *non*final value that is related in some *other* way to this property. (This nonfinal value will, like all value, supervene on some property, but it won't be the property of having belonged to Diana.[10] More on this in just a moment.) As I am using it, 'because' in this case expresses not supervenience but derivation; and of course, when value is derivative in the present sense, it is derivative from something else that has value. My claim is that Diana's dress derives its value, not from the property of having belonged to Diana,[11] but from the state that consists in its having this property, and it is this state that has final value. (Actually, this is too simple. If there is final value to be found in this case at all, I'm sure it won't be, at bottom, in Diana's dress having belonged to Diana but rather, as indicated earlier, in something more general, such as Diana's dress having a certain sort of connection to someone of a certain sort.) The nonfinal value that Diana's dress has will thus supervene, not on the property of having belonged to Diana, but rather on the property of being a constituent of the state in question.

Second objection

If there is derivation of value, it will go in just the opposite direction from that which I have indicated. Suppose that it is a good thing that Diana's dress exists. This will be precisely because Diana's dress is valuable. To embrace reduction from the value of the object to the value of the state is 'to put the cart before the horse ... [I]t is the state that derives its value from the object it involves and not the other way round.'[12]

Response

The state identified in this objection is not the state identified by me. Whether we call the 'thing' in question, namely, that Diana's dress exists, a state or something else (a fact, for example), and whether we say that it is the sort of thing that can be good, it is not the sort of thing that I have called a state and which I have claimed to be the bearer of final value. The state that consists in Diana's dress having belonged to Diana is quite distinct from the fact that Diana's dress exists. Even if the latter has only derivative value, it doesn't follow that the former does. Indeed, insofar as it is plausible to say that the fact that Diana's dress exists has a value that it derives from Diana's dress, it seems just as plausible to say that it derives this value from the dress's having belonged to Diana.

Third objection

To say that something is valuable is to say that it is the fitting object of a pro-attitude. Pro-attitudes vary with respect to the sorts of things to which they are directed. Certainly, states (and entities of that ilk, such as facts, propositions, and so on) can be the appropriate objects of pro-attitudes (such as preference and desire), but so can individual objects be the appropriate objects of pro-attitudes (such as love, admiration, and respect). Insofar as this is the case, it is individual objects that are the bearers of value.[13]

Response

I accept the general thesis that to be valuable is to be the fitting object of a pro-attitude.[14] (This can of course be challenged, but I think it contains an important insight into the nature of value.) And I also accept that individual objects can be the things toward which certain pro-attitudes are directed. Nonetheless I deny that individual objects can be the bearers of final value.

Notice that in many cases the attitudes that are directed toward individual objects may also be directed toward other things as well. I may love, admire, and respect someone, but I may also love, admire, and respect what he does. The fact that I have these pro-attitudes toward him doesn't itself show that he has final value, for these attitudes may derive from the attitudes I have toward what he does. I may admire what John does for its own sake (for example, I may admire his display of courage), and I may thus admire him for what he does (I may admire him for his display of courage), but this doesn't show that I admire John for his own sake.

Love sometimes differs in this respect from admiration, though. If you ask me why I love Kath, I may reply that it's because of her quick wit and curvaceous figure. Am I thereby indicating that I love her having this wit and figure? Yes. Does this mean that the love I have for her is merely derivative? No. The *sort* of love I have for her is different from the sort of love I have for her wit and figure. The love I have for her is romantic; the love I have for her wit and figure is not. While I nonromantically love her having the wit and figure that she has for its own sake and thereby have a derivative nonromantic love for her, this leaves untouched the fact that I do indeed romantically love her for her own sake.

Still, this is not enough to establish that Kath has final value. What is the link between her wit and figure, on the one hand, and my romantic love for her, on the other? Perhaps it is merely causal. If so, this does nothing to show that my (romantic) love for her (for her own sake) is fitting or appropriate, and so we cannot conclude that she has final value.

But isn't my love for Kath, in light of her wit and figure, perfectly appropriate? Certainly, if all this means is that her having this wit and figure gives me *no* reason *not* to love her. But I take it that that is not all that's intended by the thesis at issue. Rather, the claim is that to say that something is valuable (for its own sake) is to say that one has reason *to* adopt a certain pro-attitude toward it (for its own sake, given that one is contemplating it in the first place). Thus, in the present context, the claim is that Kath's having the wit and figure that she has gives me reason to love her for her own sake. I think this is false.

Suppose that Kath has an identical twin, Kay, identical not only in terms of appearance but also in terms of personality, and so on. If Kath's wit and figure give me reason to love her for her own sake, then Kay's wit and figure give me equally good reason to love *her* for her own sake. But this is a disturbing thought.[15] It's disturbing because it seems incompatible with the attachment that I have to Kath in particular.[16] The fact is that neither Kath, nor Kay, nor I believe that reason somehow requires me to love Kay as I do Kath. Romantic love is simply not subject to duplication in this way. In this sense, it is not a rational attitude. For confirmation of this claim, compare romantic love with the sort of love that a stamp-collector may have for a certain stamp.[17] Suppose that it is the stamp's rarity (and nothing else – not its color, or shape, or whatever) that moves him. If his love for the stamp is to be rational, then surely he must love (or be prepared to love) any equally rare stamp (indeed, any equally rare object) just as much; otherwise, I cannot see how the emotion in question can be declared rational. This is important because it shows, I think, that it is *not* the stamp that is the immediate object of the collector's love. Nor, I should add, is it the stamp's *existence* that he immediately loves. Rather, it is the stamp's *being rare* that he immediately loves. It is its rarity that he immediately values, and that's why he values it in turn.

It might seem that, in saying this, I have overlooked the phenomenon of rational satiation. That I rationally want a piece of cheesecake doesn't imply that I will also want a second, qualitatively identical piece of cheesecake. Similarly, that I rationally love Kath doesn't imply that I will also love someone qualitatively identical. But, while this is so, it misses the point. If I rationally want just one piece of (a certain kind of) cheesecake, what I want is my having a single piece of cheesecake (of that kind). Which piece I have doesn't matter to me, if my desire is purely rational. Rationality doesn't require a special attachment to one piece rather than another; indeed, it requires that there be *no* such attachment. So too with Kath. If my love for her were rational, it might be based not just on her wit and figure but, more particularly, on being in the company of just one person with such a wit and figure; so that, while being in her company, I wouldn't welcome the company of a clone, should one walk by. But, again, in such a case it wouldn't matter who came first, Kath or the clone, whereas in fact this does matter very much to me.

In order to exploit the connection between value and the fittingness of pro-attitudes, the proponent of the view that individual objects can be the bearers of final value must find not only a pro-attitude that is directed toward individual objects, but one that is directed toward them for their own sakes and, moreover, one that there is a universalizable reason to direct toward them for their own sakes. I doubt that this can be done. Rabinowicz and Rønnow-Rasmussen might claim that this is exactly what they have done in the case of Diana's dress: its having belonged to Diana gives us good reason to treasure Diana's dress for its own sake, and this is duplicable in that Diana's shoes' having belonged to Diana gives us equally good reason to treasure them for their own sake. Here, though, I would once again point out that this just doesn't seem to be a case of treasuring the dress or the shoes nonderivatively, but rather to be a case where the value of the objects is being traced to some source (their having belonged to Diana or, more generally, their having a certain sort of connection to someone of a certain sort) which is itself the thing that is being treasured nonderivatively.

To this, though, Rabinowicz and Rønnow-Rasmussen might respond as follows.[18] Even if it were agreed that Diana's dress's having belonged to Diana is something that we value, it would be a mistake to say (as I have just done) that it is something that we treasure. But we do treasure the dress. Given that these attitudes are appropriate, this shows that the state and the object have different types of values, and thus that the latter's value cannot be derivative from the former after all.

This is tricky. I acknowledge that sometimes the attitude we have toward an object is different from the attitude we have toward some state of the object. (As I have noted, I have a romantic love for Kath but only a nonromantic love for her having the wit and figure that she has.) But it's not at all clear to me that we treasure only Diana's dress (on the assumption that we place any value on it at all) and not also its having belonged to Diana; on the contrary, I'm inclined to think that we do take the same attitude toward both object and state. Still, other cases could be cited. Rabinowicz and Rønnow-Rasmussen claim that we honor people but appreciate, rather than honor, their achievements, and that we respect people but appreciate, rather than respect, their courage.[19] Such cases could be multiplied. What do they show?

I don't think that they show that individual objects can have final value. First, it is again not at all clear to me that we do not in fact honor people's achievements or respect their courage. Perhaps it is sometimes somewhat stilted to apply the same verb to both state and individual object, but that may just be an accident of language.[20] More importantly, even if it sometimes is the case that the type of attitude we have (and which it is appropriate to have) toward a state is distinct from the type of attitude we have (and which it is appropriate to have) toward the individual object involved, I cannot see that this shows that the object has final value. This would at best seem to follow only if the final value of something depended on the *whole* nature of the attitude that is appropriate to it, which in fact is dubious. If the whole nature of the attitude were relevant, then the fact that many instances of virtue are admirable but many instances of pleasure, though valuable, are not admirable would appear to imply that such instances of virtue are incomparable in value with such instances of pleasure. But there is no reason to think that this is so. As long as the different attitudes have a common 'core,' a common 'denominator,' this may be all that's strictly relevant to the determination of value and hence all that's needed for the states at issue to be comparable in value. And so, even if it is the case that Diana's dress is to be treasured but its having belonged to Diana is not, as long as there is a common core to the attitudes that are appropriate to both object and state, there is no reason to think that the former's value does not derive from the latter's.

However, suppose it were denied that this common core is all that's strictly relevant to the determination of certain values. Even then the conclusion that individual objects have, or can have, final value can be resisted. What exactly is it about the idea that individual objects have a different sort of value from the value that states have that requires us to say that the former value is final? Why could it not be, for instance, that, even if Diana's dress is to be treasured but its having belonged to Diana is to be valued in some other way, still the dress is to be treasured, not for its own sake, but for the sake of the state in question? That one entity derives its value from another would not appear to require that the two have exactly the same type of value. We should not be beguiled by talk of 'source' and 'derivation' into thinking that some single item is somehow being transferred from one locus to another. Indeed, despite the fact that it is customary to talk, as I have done and will continue to do, in terms of derivative *versus* nonderivative value, it seems to me that, when it comes to the relation between nonfinal and final value, it would probably be better to think of the former, not as being derivative from the latter, but rather as being *reflective* or *revelatory* of the latter. When something is good not for its own sake but for the sake of something else to which it is in some way related, its value may be said to reflect or reveal the value in this something else. If we think in these terms, there is less temptation to suppose that nonfinal value must match final value in kind.

Fourth objection

If to admire John for his display of courage is no more than to admire his display of courage, and if to treasure Diana's dress for having belonged to Diana is no more than to treasure its having belonged to Diana, then one would expect us not only to rejoice in Peter's being pleased but to rejoice in Peter for being pleased. But we don't. This is an indication that to value Peter's being pleased is distinct from valuing Peter for being pleased, and thus that valuing John or Diana's dress is distinct from valuing the states involving them.[21]

Response

I concede the asymmetry. We admire John, we treasure Diana's dress, but we don't rejoice in Peter. I think this must have something to do with the particular pro-attitudes in question. I confess that I have no ready explanation either for why it is that we rejoice in Peter's being pleased but do not admire it or treasure it, or for why it is that the attitudes of admiration and treasuring can be directed toward both states and individual objects but the attitude of rejoicing-in apparently cannot. But even given the asymmetry, the objection is not persuasive. My claim is that it is John's display of courage that is worth admiring for its own sake, that it is Diana's dress having belonged to Diana that is worth treasuring for its own sake, and that it is Peter's being pleased that is worth rejoicing in for its own sake. If John can be admired and Diana's dress can be treasured but Peter cannot be rejoiced in, that does not alter the fact that it is the states that are worth valuing for their own sakes. If John is worth admiring, it is not for his own sake; if Diana's dress is worth treasuring, it is not for its own sake. In both cases the valuableness of the object is derivative from the valuableness of the relevant state. The fact that Peter isn't derivatively valuable doesn't somehow render the valuableness of John and of Diana's dress nonderivative. The thesis that, when an object has value, this value is parasitic on the value of some state, isn't undermined by the observation that some types of value don't sanction derivation of value from state to object.

Fifth objection

Even if the value of individual objects such as Diana's dress is derivative from the value of states such as the dress's having belonged to Diana, such an account simply cannot be accepted when the individual objects in question are persons. Kant has taught us that persons are uniquely valuable; they have a 'dignity' that requires that they be 'exalted above all price.'[22] It would be a gross distortion of his view to say that it is not persons that have such value but states involving persons that do. This would simply misidentify what Kant takes to be the locus of value.

Response

Whether persons are indeed to be 'exalted above all price' is a very difficult issue that I won't try to resolve here. The idea that they are to be so regarded is a powerful and welcome repudiation of the excesses of classical utilitarianism, which licenses the mistreatment of individual persons for the good of the many. But of course the Kantian view of persons faces difficulties of its own. There is no need to rehearse these difficulties here, however; for, even if Kant is right, this poses no problem for my view that it is states that are the bearers of final value.

The fact is that the sort of value that Kant attributes to persons is not the sort of value that I have called final value and have attributed to states. One indication of this is that, in saying that persons are to be 'exalted above all price,' Kant is evidently claiming that all persons have infinite worth. If this were understood as a thesis about final value, it would present at least two difficulties.

First, it would preclude the sorts of meaningful comparisons regarding final value that it is natural to make. Suppose, contrary to what I have said above, that John does have final value in virtue of his display of courage, and that Kath also has final value in virtue of her wit and figure. Wouldn't it be an extraordinary coincidence that they have precisely the same value? Suppose that Mary has none of the virtues of John and Kath and no other redeeming features, either; suppose, indeed, that all her personal qualities are reprehensible. Wouldn't it be absurd to say that she has a final value as great as John's and Kath's?[23]

Second, if the value that Kant attributes to persons were final value, it would seem to follow that all worlds in which a person exists are infinitely good (unless

Kant were to invoke some bizarre instance of the principle of organic unities according to which a 'whole' that contains persons can somehow be worse than its 'parts'). It is simply not credible that all such worlds are infinitely good, and I don't for a moment think that Kant would maintain that they were. In his discussion of dignity, Kant just isn't concerned with final value. He's concerned with the normative issue of how we are to treat persons, not the axiological issue of how good persons are.[24]

Sixth objection

Even if it is true that Diana's dress is valuable *only if* some state involving it is valuable, this doesn't show that the value of the dress is derivative from the value of the state. For it is equally plausible to say that the dress is valuable *if* the state is. We thus have an equivalence. No reason has been given to prefer reduction in one direction (from object to state) to reduction in the other (from state to object).

Response

Such reason has been given. Just as one attains a fuller understanding of what transpired once it is revealed that it is in particular the dress's being lavish that caused the sensation, so too one attains a fuller understanding of what is at issue once it is revealed that it is in particular the dress's having belonged to Diana that is valuable. This indicates that the state is more fundamental than the object, relative to the context in question.

There is a further important advantage to the view that I am advocating here. Almost everyone seems to agree that states (such as Peter's being pleased) can have final value.[25] If it is also admitted that *only* states can have final value, matters are simplified considerably. In particular, one can dare hope that an informative and helpful account of the *computation* of final value might eventually be provided. It is very hard to see how any such account could be given if the bearers of value were ontologically mixed. The prospects are much brighter if the bearers are ontologically uniform.[26]

Of course, even if the bearers of value are ontologically uniform, a useful account of the computation of value might still prove elusive. There is the possibility that the principle of organic unities is true, and this would pose a problem for any account of computation. There is also the fact that different attitudes seem appropriate to different states. As noted earlier, John's display of courage seems admirable whereas Peter's pleasure does not. This suggests that the values of these states may be incommensurable. I believe that both these problems are soluble, but this is not the place to address them.

4

If states are the bearers of final value, then the traditional talk of 'intrinsic value' rather than 'final value' is innocuous. For the final value of states supervenes on an intrinsic property that they have, namely, the property of having a certain constituent property. For example, the final value of Diana's dress having belonged to Diana supervenes on its having the property of having belonged to Diana as a constituent. This is part of the very nature of the state; as such, it is not only intrinsic to the state but essential to it.

Ingmar Persson has told me, in his distinctive manner, that he finds it rather peculiar to use the term 'intrinsic value' in this way. In his view, even if states are the bearers of final value, the term 'intrinsic value' should be restricted to those cases where the constituent property of the state is intrinsic to *its* bearer. Thus Peter's being pleased may be said to be not just finally but intrinsically good, since the property of being pleased is intrinsic to Peter. But Diana's dress having belonged to Diana may not be said to be intrinsically good, even if it is finally good, since the property of having belonged to Diana is not intrinsic to the dress.

This is not a matter of great moment. The dispute is merely terminological. However, I continue to think that 'intrinsic value' is properly used when used in the way that I have proposed. This is because it seems to me most natural to say that something has intrinsic value just in case the value in question supervenes on and only on one or more of *its* intrinsic properties. This is precisely the case with the final value of states.[27]

Notes

[1]   Sometimes it might be better to say that events, rather than states, are causes. (Perhaps Diana's dress ripped as she emerged from her limousine, and this is what caused the sensation.) For the sake of simplicity, however, I will continue to talk in terms of states only. Note that I do not wish to deny that there might be an exception to the claim that talk of object-causation is reducible to talk of state-causation; perhaps agents are sometimes causes in such a way that their causation is not to be explicated wholly in terms of state-causation. My claim is only that the reduction is correct in the case of inanimate objects such as Diana's dress.

[2]   Korsgaard (1983), pp. 169–70; (1996), p. 250.

[3]   The sort of value at issue is ethical. Just how and why this is so is a topic that I cannot tackle here, however.

[4]   Korsgaard uses the term 'source' differently and, to my mind, rather oddly. In her (1983), p. 170 and (1996), p. 250, she says that something that has extrinsic value 'gets [its value] from some other source,' which suggests that something that has intrinsic

value is the source of its own value. She thus thinks of 'source' in terms of the intrinsic-extrinsic distinction rather than the final-nonfinal distinction.

5   There is a complication. A distinction can be drawn between 'basic' and 'nonbasic' value. Suppose that Peter's being pleased is good for its own sake, and that Paul's being in pain is bad for its own sake. Presumably the compound situation of Peter's being pleased and Paul's being in pain may be assigned some value in light of the final values assigned to its components. What *kind* of value is it that this compound situation has? It seems natural to say that this, too, is final value. But it also seems to be derivative, in some way, from the values of its components. If so, then not all final value is nonderivative; only basic final value is.

It may be the idea that all final value is nonderivative that leads Moore to say that what is good for its own sake (or 'ultimately good,' as he sometimes puts it) contains no part that is not intrinsically good, whereas what is intrinsically good may contain such a part. (See Moore (1912), p. 31.) But this still doesn't quite capture the idea of something being nonderivatively good, since of course a compound may be comprised only of good components and thus apparently qualify as being good for its own sake, in Moore's sense.

6   Korsgaard (1983), p. 185; (1996), p. 264. She fails to distinguish adequately between something having value in the sense that it is valued and something having value in the sense that it is valuable. It is the latter that is at issue in this paper.

7   Kagan (1998), pp. 285–6.

8   Rabinowicz and Rønnow-Rasmussen (1999), p. 41.

9   Kagan advocates continuing to use the term 'intrinsic value' to refer to final value, but he insists on the distinction nonetheless.

10 One might doubt whether what I have called nonfinal value is really a type of value at all. Why say that something has a nonfinal value simply in virtue of being related to something else that has final value? (See the opening paragraph to Rønnow-Rasmussen (forthcoming).) It's a good question, having to do with the distinction between eliminativism and mere reductionism. If one is to embrace the latter, one must say something about the *kind* of relation in question, since certainly not everything that is related in some way to something that has final value can be said therefore to have a value of its own; for then *everything* would be valuable. I won't pursue the matter here, however.

11 In my view, properties, understood as Platonic entities capable of instantiation, are not the sort of thing that can have final value, being on the wrong side of the abstract-concrete divide.

12 Rabinowicz and Rønnow-Rasmussen (1999), p. 43.

13 Cf. Rabinowicz and Rønnow-Rasmussen (1999), pp. 46–7, and (forthcoming).

14 Proponents of this thesis include, among many others: Brentano (1969), p. 18; Broad (1930), p. 283; Ross (1939), pp. 275–6; Ewing (1948), p. 152; Lemos (1994), pp. 12 and 15.

15 At least, it disturbs me, and I think it would disturb Kath. It seems not to disturb Velleman in his (1999), p. 372. It does disturb Keller a little, but his discussion of it in his (2000), p. 171, is unsatisfactory. He seems simply to deny that two people will ever

be sufficiently similar in the relevant way; this ignores the deeper question of whether I should, counterfactually, love Kay as I do Kath.

[16] Cf. Frankfurt (1999), p. 166: 'Substituting some other object for the beloved is not an acceptable and perhaps not even an intelligible option. The significance to the lover of what he loves is not that of an exemplar; its importance to him is not generic, but ineluctably particular.'

[17] Cf. Beardsley (1965), pp. 1–2, for discussion of such a case.

[18] Cf. Rabinowicz and Rønnow-Rasmussen (forthcoming).

[19] Rabinowicz and Rønnow-Rasmussen (forthcoming).

[20] Consider the following. Suppose that someone tells us that Diana's dress shocked the public. We ask why. The answer is that it was especially lavish. And then we say: 'Ah, so it was the dress's being (so) lavish that shocked the public.' Now suppose that someone tells us that Diana's suitcase broke the scale. We ask why. The answer is that it was especially heavy. To my ears, it would sound decidedly odd if we were then to say: 'Ah, so it was the suitcase's being (so) heavy that broke the scale.' May we infer from this that, although both objects and states may be properly said to be able to shock people, only objects and not states may be properly said to be able to break things? I doubt it. But even if we may infer this, such a fact about language would seem to provide no reason to deny that object-causation is parasitic on state-causation.

[21] See Rabinowicz and Rønnow-Rasmussen (forthcoming).

[22] Kant (1964), p. 102 (Ak. 434–5).

[23] *Pace* Kant, people can surely differ in value in ethically relevant ways. For example, some people are morally better than others, and this is a value that attaches directly to them. In my opinion, this is not a matter of their having greater final value, however. Cf. Lemos (1994), p. 27.

[24] This interpretation is confirmed by the following passage in Kant (1997), p. 44:

> What does the highest good consist in? The most perfect world is the highest created good. But the most perfect world involves the happiness of rational creatures and the worthiness of these creatures for such happiness ... If the world were full of ... rational creatures, who were all well-behaved, and thus worthy of happiness, and they were in the neediest circumstances, surrounded with sorrow and trouble, they would then have no happiness, and there would thus be no highest good there.

[25] Anderson may be an exception. See her (1993), pp. 20 and 26.

[26] Note that, just as one must guard against overcounting causes, for fear of diagnosing overdetermination where there is none, so too one must guard against overcounting value, for fear of mistaking the world for being better or worse than it really is.

[27] I have enjoyed and profited from discussions with Ingmar Persson about the issues treated in this paper. Many thanks also to Ben Bradley, Krister Bykvist, Erik Carlson, Toni Rønnow-Rasmussen, and especially Wlodek Rabinowicz for their help.

References

Anderson, Elizabeth (1993), *Value in Ethics and Economics* (Cambridge, Mass.: Harvard University Press).

Beardsley, Monroe C. (1965), 'Intrinsic Value', *Philosophy and Phenomenological Research*, 26: 1–17.

Brentano, Franz (1969), *The Origin of Our Knowledge of Right and Wrong* (London: Routledge and Kegan Paul).

Broad, C. D. (1930), *Five Types of Ethical Theory* (London: Kegan Paul, Trench, Trubner).

Ewing, A. C. (1947), *The Definition of Good* (New York: Macmillan and Co).

Frankfurt, Harry G. (1999), *Necessity, Volition, and Love* (Cambridge: Cambridge University Press).

Kagan, Shelly (1998), 'Rethinking Intrinsic Value', *Journal of Ethics*, 2: 277–97.

Kant, Immanuel (1964), *Groundwork of the Metaphysic of Morals* (New York: Harper and Row).

Kant, Immanuel (1997), *Lectures on Ethics* (Cambridge: Cambridge University Press).

Keller, Simon (2000), 'How Do I Love Thee? Let Me Count the Properties', *American Philosophical Quarterly*, 37: 163–73.

Korsgaard, Christine M. (1983), 'Two Distinctions in Goodness', *Philosophical Review*, 92: 169–95.

Korsgaard, Christine M. (1996), *Creating the Kingdom of Ends* (Cambridge: Cambridge University Press).

Lemos, Noah M. (1994), *Intrinsic Value* (Cambridge: Cambridge University Press).

Moore, G. E. (1912), *Ethics* (Oxford: Oxford University Press).

Rabinowicz, Wlodek and Rønnow-Rasmussen, Toni (1999), 'A Distinction in Value: Intrinsic and For Its Own Sake', *Proceedings of the Aristotelian Society*, 100: 33–52.

Rabinowicz, Wlodek and Rønnow-Rasmussen, Toni (forthcoming). 'The Tropic of Value'. *Philosophy and Phenomenological Research*.

Ross, W. D. (1939), *Foundations of Ethics* (Oxford: Oxford University Press).

Rønnow-Rasmussen, Toni (forthcoming). 'Instrumental Values – Strong and Weak.'

Velleman, J. David (1999), 'Love as a Moral Emotion'. *Ethics*, 109: 338–74.

Prioritarianism and Uncertainty

On the Interpersonal Addition Theorem and the Priority View[1]

Wlodek Rabinowicz

This paper takes its point of departure from the *Interpersonal Addition Theorem*. The theorem, by John Broome (1991), is a re-formulation of the classical result by Harsanyi (1955). It implies that, given some seemingly mild assumptions, the overall utility of an uncertain prospect can be seen as the sum of its individual utilities. In the two sections that follow, I discuss the theorem's connection with utilitarianism and in particular the extent to which this theorem still leaves room for the *Priority View*. According to the latter, the utilitarian approach needs to be modified: Benefits to the worse off should count for more, overall, than the comparable benefits to the better off (cf. Parfit 1995 [1991]).

Broome (1991) and Jensen (1996) have argued that the Priority View cannot be seen as a plausible competitor to utilitarianism: Given the addition theorem, prioritarianism should be rejected for measurement-theoretical reasons. I suggest, in the third section, that this difficulty is spurious: The proponents of the Priority View would be well advised, on independent grounds, to reject one of the basic assumptions on which the addition theorem is based. I have in mind the *Principle of Personal Good* for uncertain prospects. If the theorem is disarmed in this way, then, as an added bonus, the Priority View disposes of the aforementioned problems with measurement.

According to the Principle of Personal Good, one prospect is better than another if it is better for everyone or at least better for some and worse for none. That the Priority View, as I read it, rejects this welfarist intuition may be surprising to the reader. Isn't welfarism a common ground for prioritarians and utilitarians? Still, as I will argue, the appearances are misleading: The welfarist common ground is better captured by a restricted Principle of Personal Good that is valid for *outcomes*, but not necessarily for uncertain prospects. As will become clear, we obtain this surprising result if we take the priority weights imposed by prioritarians to be relevant only to *moral*, but not to *prudential*, evaluations of prospects. This makes it possible for a prospect to be morally better (i.e. better overall), even though it is worse (prudentially) for everyone concerned. The proposed interpretation of the Priority View thus drives a sharp wedge between prudence and morality. In the fourth section, I will argue that this divergence between moral and prudential evaluations should be recognized by prioritarians even for Robinson-type cases, in which there is only one person to consider. In that section and in the preceding one, I will also contrast the prioritarian morality, on which each person's welfare makes a separable contribution to the overall good, with egalitarianism, which denies such separability.

Finally, in the last section, I will discuss some underlying conceptual commitments of my interpretation of the prioritarian view. Since this interpretation takes very seriously the distinction between uncertain prospects and uncertainty-free outcomes, it goes against the standard decision-theoretical view according to which the distinction in question is more or less provisional and motivated by practical convenience.

Interpersonal addition

Broome's Interpersonal Addition Theorem is inspired by a formally similar aggregation theorem, due to Harsanyi (1955). While Harsanyi was concerned with aggregation of individual *preferences*, Broome (1991) considers aggregation of individual *betterness* orderings.[2] To state his theorem, we need some preparations. Suppose we start from

- a finite set $\mathbf{I}$ of *individuals*, $\{i_1, ..., i_n\}$,
- a finite partition Σ of mutually exclusive and jointly exhaustive *states of nature*, $\{S_1, ..., S_m\}$, where it may be uncertain which state in fact obtains,
- a set $\mathbf{O}$ of possible *outcomes*, where an outcome, intuitively, is a specification of what happens to each individual, with respect to the factors that are relevant to his/her welfare.

An (uncertain) *prospect* is any assignment of outcomes to the states of nature. For each possible state in Σ, a prospect specifies an outcome in $\mathbf{O}$ that would be realized if that state were to obtain. A prospect may be seen as a kind of lottery in which outcomes are possible prizes and the actual prize depends on which state happens to obtain. We can represent a prospect x as a vector, $x = (o_1, ..., o_m)$, where o_1 is the outcome that results on this prospect if state S_1 obtains, o_2 is the outcome that results if S_2 obtains, etc.

We assume,

- for each individual i in $\mathbf{I}$, an ordering B_i of prospects that specifies, for any two prospects, which of them is better for i or whether they are equally good for that individual.

Suppose also, in addition, that prospects are comparable in an impersonal way. That is, there exists

- an ordering B of prospects that specifies, for all prospects, which of them is overall better or whether they are overall equally good.

Thus, apart from the set of *individual* (or *personal*) betterness relations on prospects, one for each individual, there is also an *impersonal*, or – to use another label – *overall* betterness relation on prospects. Note that these betterness relations on prospects indirectly order outcomes as well, since any outcome o may be associated with the 'safe' prospect $(o, ..., o)$, which assigns this outcome to each state of nature. The ordering of safe prospects induces the corresponding ordering of outcomes.

Suppose we make the following assumptions about the betterness relations on prospects:

(P1) Each *personal* betterness relation B_i satisfies the axioms of expected utility theory. Thus, B_i is representable by a utility function u_i on prospects and a probability distribution p_i on states of nature, where u_i is expectational with respect to p_i and as such represents i's betterness relation uniquely up to positive linear transformations.

Similarly,

(P2) The *overall* betterness relation B satisfies the axioms of expected utility theory. Thus, B is representable by a utility function u on prospects and a probability distribution p on states, where u is expectational with respect to p and as such represents the overall betterness relation uniquely up to positive linear transformations.

That a utility function *represents* an ordering of prospects means that it assigns higher utility values to better prospects. It is *expectational* if the utility value it assigns to a prospect is the weighted sum of the utilities it assigns to its possible outcomes under various states,[3] with the weights being the probabilities of the states in question. (Given appropriate axioms on the underlying ordering of prospects, the probabilities of the states are uniquely determinable from that ordering.) Finally, such an expectational utility representation is *unique up to positive linear transformations* if all expectational functions that represent the same betterness ordering are positive linear transformations of each other. As such, they differ at most by the choice of the zero point and of the unit of measurement.

As the last assumption for the theorem, suppose that the overall betterness ordering of prospects is positively dependent on the individual betterness orderings:

(P3) *Principle of Personal Good:*
(a) Prospects that are equally good for each individual are equally good overall;
(b) If a prospect x is at least as good for each individual as a prospect y and if it is better than y for some individual(s), then x is overall better than y.

The Principle of Personal Good is based on the intuition that overall good is a function of the personal good of the individuals, and of nothing else (clause (a)). In addition, this function is strictly increasing in each argument (clause (b)): Making a prospect better for some without making it worse for others always makes the prospect better overall.

We are now ready to state the theorem:

Interpersonal Addition Theorem:
P1, P2, P3 $\Rightarrow$
If an expected utility function u represents the overall betterness relation B, then there are expected utility functions $u_1, ..., u_n$ that represent the individual betterness relations $B_1, ..., B_n$, respectively, such that u is the *sum* of $u_1, ..., u_n$:
$$u(x) = u_1(x) + ... + u_n(x), \text{ for all prospects } x.$$

This looks very much like *utilitarianism*, according to which the overall goodness of a prospect is the sum of its goodness values (welfare values) for each individual. That we should arrive at utilitarianism in this way is quite astonishing since the assumptions of the theorem seem to be relatively innocuous while utilitarianism is a deeply controversial view. However, as Broome argues, the appearances are misleading. The theorem, as it stands, is not about goodness but about utility. To be sure, the utility function u_i represents the individual betterness ordering B_i, which means that it orders prospects according to how good they are for a given individual. But such a utility function may still not be a proper measure of the individual goodness of prospects. It may instead be a strictly increasing but *non-linear* transformation of the underlying goodness function:

$$\text{For all prospects } x, u_i(x) = w(g_i(x)).$$

In this equation, g_i is the goodness function for i and the transformation w of g_i is supposed to be increasing but non-linear: the curve for this transformation slopes upwards but not in a straight line. (For example, w may be a root function, provided that the g_i-values are all non-negative, or a logarithmic function.) That w is increasing, i.e., that

$$w(g_i(x)) > w(g_i(y)) \text{ if and only if } g_i(x) > g_i(y),$$

implies that u_i orders the prospects in the same way as g_i, so that both functions represent the personal betterness relation B_i:

$$u_i(x) > u_i(y) \text{ if and only if } g_i(x) > g_i(y) \text{ if and only if } xB_iy.$$

However, the non-linearity of the transformation w would entail that g_i, unlike u_i, is *not* an expectational function. Remember that u_i was supposed to be unique up to positive linear transformations. Which implies that u_i is a linear transformation of each *expectational* function that orders the prospects in the same way as u_i does.

This means that the derivation of utilitarianism from the Interpersonal Addition Theorem would require an extra assumption. We need to assume

Bernoulli's Hypothesis:
Individual goodness is an expectational function.

In other words, the individual goodness of a prospect is the probability-weighted sum of the individual goodness values of its possible outcomes. Given P1, Bernoulli's hypothesis is equivalent to the claim that each individual utility function u_i that appears in the equation $u(x) = u_1(x) + \ldots + u_n(x)$ is identical with the goodness function for i up to a linear transformation.

In the absence of Bernoulli's hypothesis, Broome argues, we have not yet established utilitarianism. Without that extra assumption, there is room for other theories of the good, such as the Priority View that has been put forward by Derek Parfit (1995 [1991]). The Priority View distinguishes between how good a situation is for an individual and the *contribution* that this individual goodness makes to the overall goodness of the situation. The contribution is positive but not linear according to prioritarians: increased individual benefits have a successively decreasing impact on the overall goodness of a situation. On Broome's interpretation, then, the Priority View accepts the three assumptions of the theorem but denies Bernoulli's hypothesis. On that view, the expectational function u_i measures the contribution made by individual goodness but not the individual goodness itself. The former is supposed to be a non-linear transform of the latter, which means that the latter must be non-expectational, given the addition theorem.

While Broome admits the Priority View as a theoretical option, he is quite skeptical about its viability (cf. Broome 1991, p. 217). Jensen (1996) develops this line of criticism. Roughly, the difficulty with the Priority View is that its defense would require providing an *independent* method of measuring individual goodness. We must be able to measure the latter in some other way than the one we use to measure individual utility. But the two measures would still have to coincide in their ordering of prospects! That an independent order-preserving measure of goodness can be found is doubtful, to say the least.

On the standard measurement-theoretic view, quantitative measures are nothing more than representations of the underlying qualitative orderings and the measures g_i and u_i are supposed to *coincide* in their ordering of prospects. Therefore, the claim that these two measures essentially differ from each other can be meaningful only if the difference between them can somehow be made good in qualitative terms when we turn our attention from simple prospect orderings to more comprehensive or more complex qualitative structures. Suppose two such distinct structures give rise to the same prospect ordering and the prospect measures g_i and u_i are each derived from some numerical representation of its corresponding structure, without being derivable from any numerical representation of the other structure. *Then, and only then*, the two measures may be said to be essentially different. But the difficulty is that it is unclear what the relevant qualitative structures might be.

To find them, we might consider some more complex ordering relations. In particular, we could distinguish between two 'difference orderings' of prospects:

(1) an ordering R_i of the individual welfare differences:
   the change from x to x' is better for i than the change from y to y';

(2) an ordering R'_i of the differences in contributions made by individual welfare:
   the change in i's welfare from x to x' contributes more to the overall goodness than the change in i's welfare from y to y'.

In other words, while R_i compares changes in i's welfare, R'_i compares the contributions these changes make to overall goodness. Suppose now that R_i and R'_i are non-equivalent orderings: for some prospects x, x', y and y', the change from x to x', as compared with the change from y to y', gives i a larger increment in welfare, but this larger increment makes a smaller contribution to overall goodness. Suppose, however, that R_i and R'_i still yield the *same* simple ordering of prospects: the two difference orderings coincide whenever $x' = y$ and $y' = x$.[4] That is, an increment in i's welfare always makes a positive contribution to the overall value of a prospect. Still, if the functions g_i and u_i come, respectively, from the difference measures G_i and U_i that represent these two distinct underlying difference orderings R_i and R'_i,[5] and if u_i is not just a linear transformation of g_i, then we could argue that individual goodness and its contribution to overall goodness are non-equivalent concepts. The trouble with this approach, however, is that the comparisons needed to determine both difference orderings are quite demanding. It is by no means clear that we could have access to such sophisticated comparisons to the extent that is needed to distinguish between individual goodness and its contribution to the overall value of a prospect.[6]

Interpersonal comparisons and probability agreement

Broome's own view is that we should accept Bernoulli's hypothesis. If we do so, we move from the Interpersonal Addition Theorem to a full-fledged utilitarianism.[7]

As a matter of fact, I do not think we can get full utilitarianism that easily, simply by accepting the three assumptions of the theorem together with Bernoulli's hypothesis. The Interpersonal Addition Theorem states that for each expectational representation u of B, there are *some* expectational representations $u_1, ..., u_n$ of $B_1, ...B_n$ that sum up to u. Now, even if each u_i in the sum $u = u_1 + ... + u_n$ is just a linear transform of the corresponding g_i, it is still possible that we need to use *different* linear transforms for different individual goodness functions in order to obtain such a simple additive formula. For example, suppose that the transformations in question are as follows:

$u_1 = 2g_1$, while for all $i \neq 1$, $u_i = g_i$.

Then we have:

$$u = 2g_1 + g_2 + ... + g_n.$$

In other words, in the calculation of the overall utility, individual 1 counts twice as much as anyone else. This is, of course, alien to the utilitarian way of counting, according to which each individual is to count as one.[8] Still, the assumptions of the theorem together with Bernoulli's hypothesis do not suffice to exclude this anti-utilitarian possibility. Something more is needed. What could it be? What additional assumption would do the job?

Well, we would be home if we could assume *interpersonal* betterness comparisons. Suppose there exists an interpersonal betterness ordering of prospects that specifies, for all prospects x and y and for all individuals i and j, whether x is better or worse for i than y is for j, or whether x is as good for i as y is for j. In terms of this underlying *extended* ordering, which really is an ordering of prospect-individual pairs,[9] the different individual orderings can be easily defined. We define i's betterness ordering from the interpersonal ordering as follows:

x is better for i than y iff x is better for i than y is for i.

The definition of 'equally good for i as' is analogous. We can now impose an impartiality condition on the relationship between overall betterness and interpersonal betterness, from which it follows that any two individuals i and j count equally from the overall point of view:

Impartiality: For all prospects x and y, and for any permutation π on the set **I** of individuals, if for all individuals i, x is as good for i as y is for $\pi(i)$, then x and y are equally good overall.

This excludes the possibility that some individuals count for more than others. But to formulate such an impartiality condition, we need to rely on interpersonal betterness comparisons, which Broome (1991) wanted to avoid. When he wrote *Weighing Goods*, he thought that Bernoulli's hypothesis gives us all we need. To fill in the remaining gap between the Interpersonal Additional Theorem and utilitarianism, we should simply deny that there can be any meaningful difference between how good a prospect is for an individual and how much its goodness for that individual *counts* for its overall goodness. Consequently, the interpersonal comparison is achieved as soon as we find the individual utility functions that add up to overall utility. These individual utilities give us interpersonal comparisons. (Cf. ibid., pp. 215–20.)[10]

However, Broome has recently changed his views on this issue:

> ... in *Weighing Goods* I offered the wrong account of the meaning of interpersonal comparisons of good. [I suggested that] the size of a benefit [i.e., the size of an increment in individual goodness] is nothing other than the amount the benefit counts in determining the general [= overall] goodness. [...] I now think this whole approach to interpersonal comparisons of good must be mistaken. My reason is that it makes good sense to say it is better for some given amount of good to come to one person than to another. [...] We can make a distinction, then, between an amount of good and how much that amount counts in general [i.e., overall] good. (Broome, 1999, section 3.3).

The distinction in question is thus possible to make, at least conceptually. In personal communication, Broome has made the same point as follows:

> I no longer think that line [from *Weighing Goods*] is successful, because there is a clear difference between a person's good and how much that person's good counts in overall evaluation (between internal and external value, as I now put it). So in my present book [Broome, 1999] I have a different account of interpersonal comparison, which means I need the impartiality assumption [for his formulation of this assumption, cf. Broome, 1999, section 7.1].

In what follows, I shall assume that the problem of interpersonal comparability has been dealt with in a satisfactory way. We may suppose that all personal betterness orderings come from the same underlying extended betterness ordering, which means that each person's goodness is measurable on a common scale. I shall also assume that some form of the impartiality condition is satisfied by overall betterness.[11] In what follows, however, I shall not dwell upon these issues anymore. But we should be aware of the problems that are thereby swept under the rug.

There is another problem I will sweep under the rug: the one concerning probabilities. Given the Principle of Personal Good, it can be shown that the personal probability distributions p_i on states cannot differ from each other: they must all coincide with the probability distribution p that can be elicited from the impersonal betterness relation on prospects (cf. Broome 1991, ch. 7). As Broome points out, this *probability agreement theorem* is a singularly welcome result. The individual *betterness* ordering of prospects, as opposed to an ordering that reflects that individual's *preferences*, should not depend on that person's subjective probability assignment. Instead, it should be a ranking that is based on a probability distribution that does not differ from one individual to another. Unlike individual preferences, individual betterness orderings of prospects do not depend on private and idiosyncratic probability assignments to states. Thus, the probability agreement theorem gives us just what we need. However, the theorem essentially depends on the Principle of Personal Good and the validity of this principle will be questioned in what follows. Therefore, we need some other way to make sure that the different personal betterness relations are based on a common probability distribution. One such way would be to derive them all from the underlying extended betterness ordering of prospect-individual pairs, as has been suggested above. All of them would then depend on the same probability distribution on states – the one that can be elicited from the extended ordering that underlies them all. Another way would be to use the classical von Neumann-Morgenstern axiomatization of expected utility theory, in which the objects of comparison are not uncertain prospects but objective lotteries, with explicitly specified probabilities of outcomes. But again, in what follows, we shall keep this problem under the rug.

The priority view – two interpretations

As stated in the introduction, I want to concentrate on the interpretation of the Priority View. To clarify the difference between that view and utilitarianism, it is best, I think, to begin with their respective ways of evaluating *outcomes*. Evaluation of uncertain prospects is a question to which we shall come back later. Forget now about the Interpersonal Addition Theorem for a moment and suppose we try to determine how good an outcome is, overall. Assume that we take the overall goodness of an outcome to be positively dependent on how good this outcome is for each individual. That is,

$$g(o) = f(g_1(o), \ldots, g_n(o)),$$

where f is increasing in each of its arguments.

When a utilitarian evaluates an outcome, he considers how good this outcome is for each particular person and then simply adds these individual values:

Utilitarianism for Outcomes: $g(o) = g_1(o) + \ldots + g_n(o)$

Thus, for a utilitarian, the function f is simple addition. It is different with the Priority View. According to a prioritarian, *in the determination of the overall good, the benefits to the worse off count for more than the benefits to those who are better off.* As a result, the welfare level of a worse off person is given a higher moral weight in the aggregation:[12]

Priority View for Outcomes: $g(o) = t(w(g_1(o)) + \ldots + w(g_n(o))),$

where t is some increasing transformation, and the moral weight function w is chosen in such a way that the marginal contribution of increments in individual goodness is always positive but *decreasing*, i.e., w is strictly increasing and strictly concave.[13] On some versions of the Priority View, it may also be assumed that the marginal contributions of such individual increments converge to zero as the individual's goodness level increases to infinity. As for the transformation t, the simplest solution is to let t be the multiplication with 1 (or, what amounts to the same, to remove t altogether). Then the overall goodness of an outcome will just be the sum of its morally weighted individual goodness values. However, as will be seen in the next section, the transformation t might also take a non-linear form. Still, we shall argue that the simplest solution is also the right one.

Unlike utilitarianism, the Priority View *hinders unrestricted interpersonal compensations*: It makes it more difficult, and sometimes outright impossible, to justify sacrificing the worse off for the benefit of the better off.[14] At the very least, the strict concavity of the weighting function w has this implication: If an amount of welfare is transferred from a worse-off person and distributed among the better off as additional increments, the result will always be worse overall, since the marginal contribution of such increments is decreasing.

What would a proponent of the Priority View say about the individual goodness of *prospects*? How good is a prospect $x = (o_1, \ldots, o_m)$ for an individual i? I would suggest that, for a prioritarian, the goodness of a prospect for i is simply its expected goodness for i:

Prioritarian Individual Goodness of Prospects:
$$g_i(x) = \Sigma_{k=1,\ldots,m} P(S_k)g_i(o_k).$$

Thus, my suggestion is that *for a proponent of the Priority View, individual goodness is expectational* – Bernoulli's hypothesis is satisfied.

The Priority View on *Broome's* interpretation would have a different formula for the evaluation of the individual goodness of prospects. The prioritarian connection between individual utility and individual goodness, for both prospects and outcomes, is according to Broome given by the formula: $u_i = w(g_i)$. Consequently, we get the following derivation:

$$u_i(x) = \Sigma_{k=1,...,m} P(S_k) u_i(o_k),$$

which means that

$$w(g_i(x)) = \Sigma_{k=1,...,m} P(S_k) w(g_i(o_k)).$$

Let m be the *inverse* of w, i.e., m is the function such that, for any real number r, $m(w(r)) = r$. If we now apply the transformation m to both sides of the equation above, we get the following result.

Prioritarian Individual Goodness of Prospects – Broome's version:
$$g_i(x) = m(\Sigma_{k=1,...,m} P(S_k) w(g_i(o_k))).$$

Note that this formula for the *individual* goodness of prospects relies on the function w, which is the same concave moral weighting function that the proponents of the Priority View use in their evaluation of the *overall* goodness of outcomes. Thus, on Broome's reading of prioritarianism, and contrary to my own proposal, moral weights have two roles: They are used not just in the determination of the overall value of an outcome from its individual values, but also in the determination of the individual value of an uncertain prospect from the individual values of its possible outcomes.

Who is right? In defense of my proposal, I would like to point out that, for the proponents of the Priority View, the decreasing weight of individual goodness is essentially an expression of a *moral* concern. The improvements for the worse off are given moral priority as compared with the improvements for the better off. Easy interpersonal compensations are thereby disallowed. I take this view to be a reaction to the well-known Rawlsian objection: The trouble with utilitarianism, says Rawls, is that it 'does not take seriously the distinction between persons' (Rawls 1971, p. 27). A utilitarian takes the view of an impartial spectator who sympathetically identifies with all persons and thereby fuses them all into one:

> For it is by the conception of the impartial spectator and the use of sympathetic identification that the principle [of rational choice] for one man is applied to society.

It is this spectator who is conceived as carrying on the required organization of the desires of all persons into one coherent systems of desire; it is by this construction that many persons are fused into one. (Ibid., p. 26.)

Just because 'many persons are fused into one', the principle of rational choice for one person can be applied to the society viewed as a unit. Thereby, for a utilitarian, *inter*personal compensations become as unproblematic as the *intra*personal compensations have always been according to rational choice theory: It may be rational for a person to sacrifice some of her objectives in order to realize other goals. But if this diagnosis is right, i.e., if prioritarianism is driven by a concern for the distinctness of persons, then the priority weights should only be used in an *inter*personal but not in *intra*personal balancing of benefits and losses. In particular, these weights should not be used when we ask whether, from an *ex ante* perspective, an individual's loss in one possible outcome is compensated, *for that same individual*, by his gain in another possible outcome. Consequently, we should not use priority weights when we calculate the individual goodness of an uncertain prospect.[15] The individual value of a prospect can be identified with the simple expectation of the individual value of the resulting outcome.

Now, given this purely expectational interpretation of individual goodness, it turns out that the Priority View must reject one of the central assumptions of the Interpersonal Addition Theorem – the Principle of Personal Good. Here is an illustration of this point, with two individuals, i and j, and two equiprobable states of nature, S_1 and S_2. Suppose we compare the following two prospects with each other:

	Prospect x		Prospect y		
	S_1	S_2	S_1	S_2	$P(S_1)=P(S_2)=^1/_2$
i	10	10	16	5	
j	10	10	5	16	

The values in the matrices specify how good the different outcomes are for each person, i and j, respectively. In prospect y, as compared with prospect x, i's welfare is increased by 6 units in S_1 and decreased by 5 units in S_2, while for j it is the other way round. In each case, the increase is larger than the decrease, but – if we use priority weights – we may suppose that the 5-unit loss for a person detracts more from the overall goodness of an outcome than the 6-unit gain. Thus, $w(10) - w(5) > w(16) - w(10)$. For each state, then, prospect x yields an outcome that is better overall than the corresponding outcome of prospect y. If we make a plausible assumption that overall betterness satisfies *dominance* (= 'a prospect that results in a better outcome given each state, is better'), it follows that

Prospect x is overall better than prospect y.

On the other hand, when it comes to individual betterness,

Prospect y is better for i than prospect x,

since its expected goodness for each individual is greater, and we have assumed that the individual goodness of a prospect is just its expected individual goodness. Analogously,

Prospect y is better for j than prospect x.

Thus, we get a counter-example to the Principle of Personal Good:

Prospect y is overall worse than prospect x, even though y is better than x for each individual.[16]

This is a counter-example to clause (b) of the Principle of Personal Good: Prospect y is overall worse than prospect x, even though it is better than x for each individual. Can we set up a counter-example to clause (a) as well? Certainly. Just change the example so as to equalise the gains and losses in individual goodness. (For example, replace in the matrix for prospect y both occurrences of 16 by 15.) Then prospect y is as good as x for each individual but x still is better than y overall: individual losses in each of y's outcomes detract more from the overall goodness of the outcome than the equal-sized individual gains.

Note that this prioritarian counter-example to the Principle of Personal Good only concerns the application of that principle to (uncertain) *prospects*. For *outcomes*, the principle is fully valid. If an outcome o is better than an outcome o' for some individuals and as good as o' for everyone else, the Priority View will imply that, overall, o is better than o'. Since the overall goodness of an outcome is an increasing function of its priority-weighted individual goodness values, the overall goodness of an outcome will increase when its individual goodness for some person increases. Similarly, if two outcomes are equally good for everyone, they are equally good overall. Thus, the Priority View can still be seen as a fundamentally welfarist position, at least as far as the evaluation of outcomes is concerned. It is only when the Principle of Personal Good is applied to uncertain prospects that the Priority View starts having problems with this principle.

This means that a proponent of the Priority View can escape Broome's and Jensen's criticisms. If individual goodness is expectational, it can be measured in the standard way – in the way we measure utility. There is no need for a measurement of individual goodness that would be independent from the measurement of individual utility. We can directly elicit individual goodness values from the betterness orderings on risky prospects. But the Interpersonal Additional Theorem no longer follows, since one of its principal assumptions, the Principle of Personal Good for prospects, has been rejected.

If we let the individual goodness of a prospect be its expected individual goodness, then it seems natural, if not mandatory, to do the same for overall goodness, i.e., to let the overall goodness of a prospect $x = (o_1, \ldots, o_m)$ be its expected overall goodness:

$$g(x) = \Sigma_{k=1,\ldots,m} P(S_k) g(o_k).$$

Thus, on this reading of prioritarianism, overall goodness will be just as expectational as individual goodness. Measuring overall goodness thus boils down to measuring overall utility. The latter can be identified with the former, up to a positive linear transformation.

Above, we have seen that prioritarians want to distinguish between a person's good in a prospect and the contribution that person's good makes to the overall goodness. The person's good is represented by function g_i. To represent its contribution, we need some preparations. As we have suggested above, the overall goodness of a prospect is the probability-weighted sum of the overall goodness values of its possible outcomes under various states. The overall goodness of an outcome is an increasing transform of the sum of its morally weighted individual goodness values. If we simplify for a moment and assume that the increasing transform t just consists in the multiplication with 1 (in the next section it will be argued that such a simplification is well-motivated), we obtain the following formula for the overall goodness of a prospect $x = (o_1, \ldots, o_m)$:

$$g(x) = \Sigma_k P(S_k) g(o_k) = \Sigma_k P(S_k) t(\Sigma_i w(g_i(o_k))) = \Sigma_k P(S_k) \Sigma_i w(g_i(o_k)) = \Sigma_i \Sigma_k P(S_k) w(g_i(o_k)).$$

This allows us to separate the contributions made by each individual's welfare to the overall value of a prospect:

$$c_i(x) = \Sigma_k P(S_k) w(g_i(o_k)).$$

This individual contribution to the overall value of x is the probability-weighted sum of the contributions made by i's welfare to the overall values of the possible outcomes of x, under various states. The overall value of x is the sum of such individual contributions:

$$g(x) = \Sigma_i c_i(x).$$

Note that the function c_i, which measures the individual contribution to overall value, is expectational, just like function $g_i(x) = \Sigma_k P(S_k) g_i(o_k)$, which measures individual goodness. The contribution of i's welfare to the overall value of a prospect equals its expected contribution to the overall value of the resulting outcome:

$$c_i(x) = \Sigma_k P(S_k) c_i(o_k).$$[17]

However, the two functions g_i and c_i are *not* just positive linear transformations of each other, since the two prospects orderings that are represented by these functions do not coincide. For a prioritarian who rejects the Principle of Personal Good, a larger increment in individual goodness of a prospect can make a smaller contribution to overall goodness. In our example above, a prospect y is better for i than a prospect x,

$$g_i(y) > g_i(x),$$

but the contribution made by i's welfare to the overall value of y is smaller than the corresponding contribution to the overall value of y,

$$c_i(y) < c_i(x).$$[18]

For the other individual, j, the case is analogous.

That's how my interpretation of the Priority View is supposed to work. But is such an interpretation plausible? I have been arguing that a prioritarian will not use moral weights in the *intra*personal balancing of benefits and losses in various possible outcomes. Moral weights have no role to play in the determination of the individual goodness of a prospect. But consider the following objection to my claim. On the Priority View, being worse off is morally bad. In this context, however, 'being worse off' is not meant to refer to a relation between one individual and another. Rather, it refers to a relation between how an individual is and how he might have been. In this respect, the view in question differs from *egalitarianism*.[19] As Parfit puts it:

> [...] on the Priority View, we do not believe in equality. We do not think it in itself bad, or unjust, that some people are worse off than others. [...] We do of course think it bad that some people are worse off. But what is bad is not that these people are worse off than *others*. It is rather that they are worse off than *they* might have been.[20] [...] on the Priority View, benefits to the worse off matter more, but that is only because these people are at a lower *absolute* level. It is irrelevant that these people are worse off than others. Benefits to them would matter just as much even if there *were* no others who were better off. (Parfit, 1991 [1995], p. 23.)

Now, this prioritarian emphasis on the comparisons of how an individual is with how he 'might have been', as opposed to the egalitarian comparisons of one individual with others, might suggest that Parfit would want us to use priority weights even in the determination of the individual goodness of a prospect. It might seem that the moral weights should apply not just to interpersonal balancing but also to those intrapersonal balancings that determine an individual's welfare in a prospect.

I disagree. What Parfit says certainly suggests that moral weights should be used in the determination of the individual contribution to the *overall* goodness (or badness) in all cases, even when there are no others who are better off than the individual under consideration. This need not imply that the moral weights should be used to determine how good a prospect is *for a given individual*.

Still, the above quote makes it clear that the function of the moral weights for Parfit cannot simply be to hinder unrestricted interpersonal compensations (gains for the better off at the expense of the worse off). If this were their only role, moral weights could be made dependent on the *relative* levels of individual goodness. Benefits and losses to a given person could be allowed to have varying moral impact depending on how that person fares in comparison with other people: *Ceteris paribus*, they would have larger impact if the others were better off.[21] Insofar as this relativization to others is disallowed, however, the function of moral weights must be more far-reaching. They must be taken to express a moral concern for the welfare of each individual taken separately – a concern that decreases with increases in that individual's welfare, without taking into account the welfare of others.

Prioritarianism and the overall goodness: one-person case

Probably, then, Parfit would maintain that the moral weighting function should be used to determine the overall goodness of an outcome not only when no others are better off (cf. the quote above) but also when there *are* no others, i.e., when the outcome only involves one person. On such a view, we can still distinguish between the *individual* goodness of a one-person outcome and that outcome's *overall* goodness. The same distinction should therefore be possible to make for prospects that involve just one person. It should be possible to distinguish between how good a prospect is for this person and how good it is morally (i.e., overall). It is only for this latter issue that moral weights are allowed to play a role.[22] To elaborate on this point, let us again consider the prioritarian formula for the overall goodness of outcomes:

Priority View for Outcomes: $g(o) = t(w(g_1(o)) + \ldots + w(g_n(o)))$

If we let t be idle (i.e. if we let t = the multiplication with 1), the overall goodness of an outcome will simply be the sum of its weighted individual goodness values. The moral weights will then play a role for overall goodness even in a one-person case (i.e., a case when $\mathbf{I} = \{i\}$, for some individual i). We shall have, for that case, the following formula:

Robinson Outcomes: $g(o) = t(w(g_i(o))) = w(g_i(o))$.

The overall goodness of a one-person outcome will thus differ from its individual goodness. This difference, however, will not show in the ordering of Robinson outcomes that involve one and the same person i. For any two such outcomes o and o', o is overall better than o' iff o is better for i than o'.

But what about *prospects*? If t is idle, then prioritarianism, on my interpretation, will lead to a quite striking divergence between prudence and the prioritarian morality. The two will diverge even in some of the cases in which the agent i is the only individual involved. Thus, suppose that there are just two possible states, S_1 and S_2, each of them equally probable, and let i have a choice between a risky prospect $y = (o', o'')$ and a safe prospect $x = (o, o)$ that yields the same outcome whatever happens. Assume that o' is better for i than o, which in turn is better for i than o''. In particular, suppose that i's goodness values for the different outcomes are related to each other as follows:

$g_i(o') - g_i(o) > g_i(o) - g_i(o'') > 0$.

Then, prudence dictates that i should choose the risky y: $g_i(x) > g_i(y)$ (given that individual goodness is expectational, as we have assumed). As compared with o, which is the guaranteed outcome of x, his gain in o' is larger than his loss in o'' and these two possible outcomes of y are equiprobable.

Suppose, however, that this larger gain weighs less than the smaller loss, in terms of w:

$w(g_i(o')) - w(g_i(o)) < w(g_i(o)) - w(g_i(o''))$.

Or, what amounts to the same,

$w(g_i(o)) > 1\,\frac{1}{2}w(g_i(o')) + \frac{1}{2}w(g_i(o''))$.

Then the prioritarian morality prescribes x, even though prudence dictates y. The safe prospect x is better overall:

$g(x) = g(o,o) = P(S_1)g(o) + P(S_2)g(o)$ [since overall goodness is expectational]

$\quad = \frac{1}{2}t(w(g_i(o))) + \frac{1}{2}t(w(g_i(o)))$ [by the Priority View for Outcomes]

$\quad = \frac{1}{2}w(g_i(o)) + \frac{1}{2}w(g_i(o))$ [given that t is idle]

$\quad = w(g_i(o))$

$\quad > \frac{1}{2}w(g_i(o')) + \frac{1}{2}w(g_i(o''))$ [by assumption]

$\quad = \frac{1}{2}t(w(g_i(o'))) + \frac{1}{2}t(w(g_i(o'')))$ [given that t is idle]

$\quad = P(S_1)g(o') + P(S_2)g(o'')$ [by the Priority View for Outcomes]

$\quad = g(o', o'') = g(y)$ [since overall goodness is expectational]

That prudence and morality can diverge in Robinson-type cases may seem counter-intuitive for some prioritarians. If, contrary to Parfit's suggestion, the only function of moral weights were to hinder unacceptable interpersonal compensations, then it would be natural to expect the coincidence of prudence and morality in Robinson cases.

To guarantee such coincidence, we could make the transform t depend on the weight function w, in such a way that the two functions cancel out in the one person-case. (I owe this suggestion to John Broome, but, as we shall see below, Broome no longer thinks it to be reasonable.) If we let t be the *inverse* of w, i.e., if we let $t = m$, the overall goodness of an outcome will reduce to its individual goodness in the Robinson-type cases:

$$g(o) = t(w(g_i(o))) = m(w(g_i(o))) = g_i(o).$$

In the same way, on this suggestion, the overall goodness of a *prospect* $x = (o_1, ..., o_m)$ that involves only one individual reduces to the individual goodness of that prospect:

$g(x)\ = \Sigma_k P(S_k)g(o_k)$ [since overall goodness is expectational]

$\quad = \Sigma_k P(S_k)t(w(g_i(o_k)))$ [by the Priority View for Outcomes]

$\quad = \Sigma_k P(S_k)mw(g_i(o_k))) = \Sigma_k P(S_k)g_i(o_k))$ [if t is the inverse of w]

$\quad = g_i(x)$ [since individual goodness is expectational]

Which view, then, should be taken by prioritarians? Depending on their choice of the transformation t, they can reach conflicting conclusions as to the relationship between prioritarianism and prudence. If t is idle, prudence and the prioritarian morality will diverge even when the agent is the only person involved. But letting t instead be the inverse of w removes this divergence.

In my view, the former alternative is the more reasonable one. According to the latter option, as long as he is alone on his island, the prioritarian morality gives

Robinson purely prudential recommendations: He should choose a risky prospect rather than a riskless one, if the former has for him a higher expected goodness value. But as soon as the man Friday comes into the picture, Robinson is no longer allowed to go for the risky prospect, even though – as we might suppose – his choice *would not affect Friday in any way*. If Robinson's larger gain in one state weighs less, morally, than his smaller loss in the other (equiprobable) state, and Friday's welfare given each state is the same whatever prospect Robinson chooses, then, with Friday present, the risky prospect is overall worse than the riskless one.[23] This extreme sensitivity to 'other persons being present' is counter-intuitive. Surely, if Robinson's choice cannot affect what happens to Friday, bringing Friday into the picture should not matter, morally, according to prioritarianism. The riskless prospect should be morally (i.e. overall) better in the absence of Friday if and only if it is morally better in his presence. We get this desirable result if we let t be idle. Therefore, prioritarians would be well advised to view the overall value of an outcome as the simple sum of its morally weighted individual values.

There is also another reason for this simplification. In section 9.3 of *Weighing Goods*, Broome considers a choice between the following two prospects, which involve two individuals and two equiprobable states:

	Prospect x		Prospect y		
	S_1	S_2	S_1	S_2	$P(S_1)=P(S_2)=\frac{1}{2}$
i	2	1	2	1	
j	2	1	1	2	
	o_1	o_2	$o_3\ldots$	$\ldots o_4$	

For an *egalitarian*, as Broome points out, prospect x should be preferable to prospect y: the former guarantees equality, in each outcome, while the latter guarantees inequality. For a *utilitarian*, on the other hand, the two prospects are equally good. Each of them gives each individual the same expectation of individual goodness: 2 with probability $\frac{1}{2}$ and 1 with probability $\frac{1}{2}$.

A natural question for us to ask is what a *prioritarian* should say about this case. (I am indebted to Marc Fleurbaey for raising this issue.) *If* we let t be idle, then the Priority View, just as utilitarianism, will imply that prospects x and y are equally good overall. The reason is simple: As we have seen in the preceding section, if t is idle, then the overall goodness of a prospect is the sum of the individual contributions to the overall goodness of this prospect:

$$g(x) = \Sigma_i \, c_i(x),$$

where $c_i(x) = \Sigma_k P(S_k) w(g_i(o_k))$. The contribution of each individual is counted *separately* and independently of the contribution of others, just as in utilitarianism (with the only difference being that, in utilitarianism, $c_i(x)$ is set to $\Sigma_k P(S_k) g_i(o_k)$). Now, since in our example the contribution of each individual to each of the prospects is the same,

$$c_i(x) = \tfrac{1}{2}w(2) + \tfrac{1}{2}w(1) = c_i(y) \text{ and } c_j(x) = \tfrac{1}{2}w(2) + \tfrac{1}{2}w(1) = c_j(y),$$

it follows that $g(x)$ must be equal to $g(y)$.

However, if t instead is some non-linear transformation, it becomes impossible to separate the individual contributions to the overall value of a prospect. In particular, if t is strictly convex, which it must be if it is the inverse of the strictly concave function w, x will be overall better than y:

$$
\begin{aligned}
g(x) = \tfrac{1}{2}g(o_1) + \tfrac{1}{2}g(o_2) &= \tfrac{1}{2}t(w(2) + w(2)) + \tfrac{1}{2}t(w(1) + w(1)) \\
&= \tfrac{1}{2}t(2w(2)) + \tfrac{1}{2}t(2w(1)) \\
&> t(w(2) + w(1)) \quad \text{[if } t \text{ is strictly convex}^{24}] \\
&= \tfrac{1}{2}t(w(2) + w(1)) + \tfrac{1}{2}t(w(1) + w(2)) = \tfrac{1}{2}g(o_3) + \tfrac{1}{2}g(o_4) = g(y)
\end{aligned}
$$

In other words, with a convex t, prioritarianism will be considerably closer to egalitarianism. Surely, this is *not* a desirable consequence. As we have seen, Parfit has been at pains to point out that the benefits to a person should count as much independently of how other people fare. Consequently, on the Priority View, and contrary to egalitarianism, the welfare of each individual in various outcomes should make a *separable* contribution to the overall goodness of a prospect, independent of the welfare of others, which could not be the case if t were a non-linear transform. This point has been forcefully made by Broome (2001).[25] Therefore, Broome now agrees with me that my interpretation of the Priority View will have to lead to the divorce of morality from prudence. The reconciliation between the two in one-person cases cannot be achieved by letting the transformations t and w cancel out. However, Broome still prefers his own interpretation of prioritarianism, which rejects Bernoulli's hypothesis and accepts the Principle of Personal Good. On that interpretation, of course, morality and prudence automatically coincide in all Robinson-type cases.

Uncertainty all the way down?

On my interpretation of prioritarianism, the distinction between prospects and outcomes is taken seriously. For an outcome, its overall value is the sum of its morally weighted individual values. But for a prospect, the relationship between its overall value and its value for various individuals is much less straightforward and indirect. In fact, there is no functional dependence in this case: two prospects may be equally good for each individual and still differ as far as their overall value is concerned. This means that, on my interpretation, a prioritarian must take seriously the distinction between prospects and outcomes. He cannot treat outcomes as 'small worlds' in Savage's sense (cf. Savage 1972 (1954), section 5.5), i.e., as situations that are assumed to be free from uncertainty only provisionally, for the problem at hand. He cannot adhere to the view, so popular among many decision theorists, that uncertainty really is present 'all the way down' and that it can always be discerned, in any outcome, if we only use a sufficiently strong magnifying glass. To illustrate this popular view, consider the famous example of *Savage's omelet* (ibid., section 2.5): I have broken five eggs into the bowl, to make an omelet. Should I do the same with the remaining sixth egg, or should I break it into a separate saucer? If I do the former and the last egg turns out to be rotten, I will have to throw out everything. For the purposes of my decision problem I can treat this as one possible outcome. From a more discerning perspective, however, the 'no omelet' outcome can be seen as shot with uncertainties: What will happen if I don't get my omelet? Will I miss my lunch altogether, and, if so, how will it affect my mood and behavior? Will I overeat in the evening, will I be irritable for the rest of the day, etc? And what might *this* lead to, in turn? Thus, if we wish, we could re-describe the outcome in question as an uncertain prospect which, depending on various factors, can result in different more specific outcomes. These can in their turn be re-described as uncertain prospects, and so on.

It is in this sense that Savage's outcomes are 'small' possible worlds, as he puts it, rather than 'grand worlds' without any residuum of potential uncertainty. The reason he adduces for the small-worlds approach is that of practicality: the decisions we make in real life are never made with a view to all the uncountable uncertainties that may arise in connection with our actions (cf. ibid., section 5.5). Behind this practical point, one might add (even though Savage himself might not be prepared to go as far as that), there is a more fundamental fact: Our preferences as regards various occurrences are preferences for these occurrences *under descriptions* (cf. Schick 1982). *Pace* behaviorism, preferring is an intentional attitude, which means that preference at least to some extent is *representation-dependent*. Since our representational capacities are limited, 'grand worlds' cannot be fully represented, in all their details. Therefore, if a decision theorist wanted to start from an agent's preferences over grand outcomes, he would have to allow for the possibility that one and the same grand outcome might be valued differently by the agent depending on how this outcome is represented. He would also have to accept that the agent's preference ranking would contain huge gaps, as the agent's ability to discern between different grand outcomes is severely limited: As ordinary agents, with finite powers of conceptual discrimination, we can only discern between *classes* of grand possible worlds, but not among individual worlds of this kind. [26] Restriction to small outcomes allows the decision-theorist to avoid these difficulties. As long as he keeps to small outcomes, the outcomes and their propositional representations need not be distinguished from each other.

Prioritarians who take seriously the distinction between prospects and outcomes must instead opt for the 'grand' interpretation of outcomes. The outcomes must be comprehensive possible worlds, which, in principle, contain a determinate answer to every question of fact. Otherwise, if an outcome might just as well be seen as a prospect, with larger magnification, it would be difficult to defend a theory that treats prospects and outcomes differently. Thus, the question arises: Can a prioritarian assume the existence of univocal (i.e. representation-independent) betterness orderings on *grand* outcomes? The answer, it seems, must in part depend on the connection between betterness and preference. It may be that this connection is quite close and that, in particular, an ordering of betterness is grounded in pro-attitudes of some kind, which are just as intentional as individual preferences (cf. Schick 1982). If these attitudes are supposed to be directly aimed at the relata of the betterness ordering, rather than at various general good-making features of the relata, the prospects for a univocal betterness ordering of grand outcomes look very bleak indeed. But the possibility remains that the relation between the ordering of betterness and our pro-attitudes is not as straightforward. It may well be that betterness orderings of comprehensive possible worlds should be seen as theoretical constructs. If at all, such constructs would only be indirectly based in our pro- and contra-attitudes of certain kinds. Rather than aiming directly at comprehensive possible worlds, the pro- and contra-attitudes that underlie the construction are immediately directed at various general features (in particular, various aspects of individual well-being) that such grand worlds may exhibit. Such indirectly constructed betterness orderings need not be fundamentally representation-sensitive. As long as this possibility remains, the interpretation of prioritarianism suggested in this paper does not make this view doomed from the start.

Notes

[1] For comments and discussion I am much indebted to Gustaf Arrhenius, John Broome, Johan Brännmark, Krister Bykvist, Erik Carlson, Roger Crisp, Sven Danielsson, Dan Egonsson, Marc Fleurbaey, Magnus Jiborn, Mats Johansson, Karsten Klint Jensen, Philippe Mongin, Erik Persson, Ingmar Persson, Toni Rønnow-Rasmussen and Derek Parfit. Apart from Broome and Parfit, who figure so prominently in what follows, I have special debts to Jensen and to Ingmar Persson. Pondering on the former's thought-provoking PhD-thesis led me to the idea of this paper, and the latter not only gave me some very good advice, but also made available a copy of Parfit's seminal paper on the Priority View, which by that time was still quite difficult to come by.

[2] In addition to this philosophical difference, there is a technical difference as well:

While Broome's betterness orderings range over uncertain prospects (= assignments of outcomes to states of nature), Harsanyi's preference orderings range over von Neumann-Morgenstern lotteries, i.e., over probability distributions on outcomes.

3   We let the utility of an outcome o be the same as the utility of the corresponding safe prospect $(o, ..., o)$.

4   Defining simple prospect orderings from the corresponding difference orderings is straightforward. Thus, a prospect x is better for i than a prospect y iff the change from x to y is better for i than the change from y to x. Analogously, i's welfare makes in x a larger contribution to overall goodness than in y iff, as far as i's welfare is concerned, the change from x to y contributes more to the overall goodness than the change from y to x.

5   Let G_i be any value assignment to pairs of prospects such that $G_i(x,x') > G_i(y, y')$ if and only if the change from x to x' ranks higher in R_i (i.e., this change is better for i) than the change from y to y'. Set $G_i(x, x)$ to 0, for any x. U_i is constructed in the same way, as a representation of R'_i. We define a prospect measure g_i from G_i as follows: Let x^* be an arbitrary prospect. Then, for every x, $g_i(x) = G_i(x^*, x)$. The definition of u_i from U_i is analogous.

6   Note, however, that Broome has recently become much more sympathetic to the possibility of drawing such fine distinctions. He now admits that it makes good sense, at least *conceptually*, to distinguish between a person's good and how much that person's good counts in the overall evaluation (cf. Broome, 1999).

7   At least for those cases in which the set of individuals can be assumed to be *fixed* as one moves from one prospect or outcome to another. If different individuals are allowed to exist in different outcomes that are being compared with each other, the situation becomes much more complicated. We shall ignore this complication in what follows. We shall also ignore a number of other complications:

(i) Utilitarianism, as usually understood, contains a normative component: Apart from the welfarist specification of the relationship between individual welfare and overall goodness, it also involves a consequentialist *injunction* to act so as to realise what is best overall.

(ii) Utilitarian theories often involve a list of one or more specific factors that are supposed to determine the orderings of individual betterness, i.e., such factors as happiness, preference satisfaction or, in a more objective vein, standard of living, capabilities, personal relationships, etc.

(iii) Some utilitarians decline to assign overall value to uncertain *prospects*, as opposed to outcomes. (On this view, the normative status of an action depends on the relative value of the outcome that the action would *actually* result in, as compared with the corresponding outcomes of its alternatives, rather than on the relative value of the prospect it is associated with.)

8   Objection: But if individual 1 is 'counted twice' in this way, then the resulting function u will not be right. It will not represent the correct utilitarian overall betterness ordering. We will be able to find two prospects x and y such that x is overall better than y, but the u-function ranks them in the reverse order. The Interpersonal Addition Theorem does not claim that *every* choice of utility representations for individual

betterness relations gives us utility functions the sum of which represents overall betterness, but only that some choice like this is possible. If utility representations for different individuals are chosen independently of each other, the sum of utility values will normally *not* represent overall betterness.

Answer: The point of the difficulty raised in the text is different, namely: What is there to guarantee that the overall betterness ordering, which u is supposed to represent, does *not* count some individuals 'twice'? The assumptions of the theorem, in conjunction with the Bernoulli hypothesis, do not exclude this anti-utilitarian betterness ordering.

9   Thus, in symbols, $(x, i) \geq (y, i)$ iff x is at least as good for i as y is for j.

10   For a useful discussion of the similar issue of interpersonal comparability in connection with Harsanyi's aggregation theorem, cf. Mongin (1994) and Mongin & d'Aspremont (1998).

11   This remark should be qualified. Note that the impartiality assumption, as formulated above, implies as a special case clause (a) of the Principle of Personal Good. (To derive this clause from Impartiality, just let the permutation π be the identity relation.) Since I will be arguing that the Priority View, if correctly interpreted, accepts the Principle of Personal Good only for outcomes and not for prospects, the impartiality assumption must also be restricted to outcomes, in order to be acceptable for prioritarians.

12   This describes what Parfit (1995 [1991]) calls the *moderate* (teleological) version of the Priority View. He suggests that the extreme form of prioritarianism is Rawls' difference principle, which gives *lexical* priority to the improvements for the worse off, and not just a greater weight. For reasons to be explained below, in note 20, I don't think this is quite right, but, in what follows, we shall concentrate on the moderate version. Also, we will not consider *deontological* versions of the Priority View, according to which giving priority to the worse off is a normative requirement on action, which need not have any direct connection with the overall value of the resulting outcome.

13   Due to the non-linearity of w, the Priority View for Outcomes might appear to presuppose that the individual goodness of an outcome is measured on a common *ratio* scale, rather than just on a mere interval scale. For it is easy to see that the comparisons between the sums of w-weighted individual goodness values are not invariant with respect to the changes in the zero point of the scale, if w is non-linear. Suppose, for example that $w = \sqrt{\ }$ and consider two outcomes, o *and* o', with just two individuals involved, i and j. Let $g_i(o) = 0$, $g_j(o) = 16$, while $g_i(o') = g_j(o') = 4$. With this representation of individual goodness, both outcomes are equally good overall from the prioritarian perspective: $\sqrt{0} + \sqrt{16} = \sqrt{4} + \sqrt{4}$. But if we move down the zero point of the goodness scale by one unit, i.e., if we add one unit to each g_i- and g_j-value, the Priority View for Outcomes implies that o is overall better than o'. Thus, it appears that a prioritarian cannot allow the choice of the zero point for individual goodness to be arbitrary.

However, this argument assumes, somewhat questionably, that the shape of the weight function w is fixed *independently* of our choice of the numerical representation for individual goodness. If the weight function instead is allowed to undergo appropriate compensatory adjustments as we move from one such representation to another, the need for an absolute zero for individual goodness is obviated. Thus, in our example, moving down the zero point of the individual goodness scale by one unit may be accompanied by an appropriate adjustment in the weight function: instead of $\sqrt{k}$, we might let $w(k) = \sqrt{(k-1)}$, for all values k. This adjustment in the weight function will cancel out the effect of the scale transformation. (I owe this observation to Magnus Jiborn.)

14   *If* the weighting function is such that the marginal contributions of all increments in personal goodness approach zero (or any other fixed value) when the goodness level increases, then the imposition of weights not only hinders impersonal compensations – it sometimes makes them impossible. If the worse off are much worse off than the better off, then, for a fixed number of individuals, we will not be able to compensate a considerable loss to the former by *any* gains to the latter, *however large*.

15   In personal communication, Derek Parfit has confirmed that this is how he himself would interpret the Priority View. The prioritarian weights are moral, not prudential. Therefore, they have no role to play for the individual goodness of prospects.

16   Roger Crisp has suggested an alternative treatment of this example (in private communication). Like myself, and unlike Broome, Crisp takes prospect y to be better for each individual than prospect x, from the prioritarian point of view, but he suggests that prioritarians should keep the Principle of Personal Good for prospects intact. Therefore, they must conclude that y is overall better than x, even though y yields a worse outcome than x, overall, under each state of nature. Which means that the prioritarians must reject *dominance*: A prospect is better even though its outcome is worse under each state. Needless to say, this is a very radical suggestion – too radical in my view.

17   Proof: For any outcome o, $c_i(o)$ equals i's contribution to the safe prospect, $c_i(o, ..., o)$. Since the latter equals $\sqrt{}_k P(S_k) w(g_i(o_k)) = w(g_i(o))$, it follows that, for any x, the expected contribution of i, $\sqrt{}_k P(S_k) c_i(o_k)$, equals $\sqrt{}_k P(S_k) w(g_i(o_k))$, which equals $c_i(x)$.

18   As we have assumed, $w(10) - w(5) > w(16) - w(10)$. This implies that contribution $c_i(y)$, which equals $1/2w(16) + 1/2w(5)$, must be smaller than $c_i(x)$, which equals $1/2w(10) + 1/2w(10)$.

19   This difference between the Priority View and egalitarianism is emphasised in Persson (1996).

20   This shows, by the way, that it is incorrect to interpret Rawls' difference principle as the extreme, lexical form of the Priority View. Rawl's principle gives absolute priority to those people who are worse off than all the *others*.

21   I am indebted to Ingmar Persson for this observation.

22   In personal communication, Derek Parfit has confirmed that this is how he himself would interpret the Priority View.

23   To see this, let us compare a prospect $y = (o', o'')$ with a prospect $x = (o_1, o_2)$, where both states of nature are supposed to be equiprobable. Prospect x is safe for Robinson: $g_r(o_1)$ $= g_r(o_2)$. Prospect y, on the other hand, is risky for him:

(i) $g_r(o') - g_r(o_1) > g_r(o_1) - g_r(o'') > 0$ (and similarly for o_2).

(i) implies that the risky prospect y is better for Robinson than the safe alternative x. If t is set to m (the inverse of w), this entails that, *in the absence of Friday, y is overall better than x*.

Let us now bring in Friday into the prospect and assume that Friday's goodness function g_f is such that, from his point of view, the choice between x and y does not matter, whatever the state happens to be the case. I.e., $g_f(o') = g_f(o_1) = k_1$ and $g_f(o'') = g_f(o_2) = k_2$. If $t = m$, the overall goodness of y now equals

(Gy) $\frac{1}{2}m(w(g_r(o') + w(k_1)) + \frac{1}{2}m(w(g_r(o'') + w(k_2))$,

which can be compared with the overall goodness of the safe prospect x:

(Gx) $\frac{1}{2}m(w(g_r(o) + w(k_1)) + \frac{1}{2}m(w(g_r(o) + w(k_2))$.

Now, (i) is fully compatible with:

(ii) $w(g_r(o')) - w(g_r(o_1)) < w(g_r(o_1)) - w(g_r(o''))$.

In view of (ii), Robinson's larger gain in o' (as compared with o_1) weighs less than his loss in o'' (as compared with o_2). Since function m is strictly increasing, it follows that the increase in the first term of (Gy), as compared with the first term of (Gx), is smaller than the corresponding decrease in the second term in (Gy), as compared with the second term of (Gx). Which means that, *in the presence of Friday, x is overall better than y*. But this change cannot be explained by reference to Friday's welfare, which is assumed to be the same under each prospect, whatever state happens to obtain.

[24] Explanation: For any strictly convex t and any real numbers k and l, it holds that $\frac{1}{2}t(2k) + \frac{1}{2}t(2l) > t(k + l)$. Therefore, $\frac{1}{2}t(2w(2)) + \frac{1}{2}t(2w(1)) > t(w(2) + w(1))$.

[25] See, however, Fleurbaey (2001) for an interesting criticism of the idea that the Priority View is fundamentally opposed to egalitarianism.

[26] Another worry in connection with 'grand' outcomes is whether the idea of such outcomes is conceptually coherent, to begin with. Here, I assume that the answer is yes, i.e., that it is meaningful to postulate such comprehensive possible ways for the world to be. But I am fully aware that this assumption itself is controversial.

References

Broome, John (1991), *Weighing Goods*, (Basil Blackwell: Oxford).

Broome, John (1999), *Valuing Lives*, book manuscript.

Broome, John (2001), 'Equality versus Priority: A Useful Distinction', http://aran.univ-pau.fr/ee/page3.html

Harsanyi, John (1955), 'Cardinal Welfare, Individualistic Ethics, an Interpersonal Comparisons of Utility', *Journal of Political Economy* 63: 309–21; reprinted in John Harsanyi, *Essays on Ethics, Social Behavior and Scientific Explanation*, (Reidel, Dordrecht 1976), pp. 6–23.

Fleurbaey, Marc (2001), 'Equality versus Priority: How Relevant is this Distinction?', http://aran.univ-pau.fr/ee/page3.html

Jensen, Karsten Klint (1996), 'Measuring the Size of the Benefit and Its Moral Weight', in Wlodek Rabinowicz (ed.), *Preference and Value – Preferentialism in Ethics*, Studies in Philosophy 1996:1, Dept. of Philosophy, Lund University, pp. 114–45.

Mongin, Philippe (1994), 'Harsanyi's Aggregation Theorem: multi-profile version and Unsettled Questions,' *Social Choice and Welfare* 11: 331–54.

Mongin, Philippe, and Claude d'Aspremont (1998), 'Utility Theory and Ethics', in Barbera,

S., Hammond, P. and C. Seidl, *Handbook of Utility Theory*, Vol.1, Kluwer, Dordrecht, pp. 371–481.

Parfit, Derek (1995) [1991], 'Equality or Priority?', The Lindley Lecture 1991, Department of Philosophy, The University of Kansas.

Persson, Ingmar (1996), 'Telic Egalitarianism vs. the Priority View', in Wlodek Rabinowicz (ed.), *Preference and Value – Preferentialism in Ethics*, Studies in Philosophy 1996:1, Dept. of Philosophy, Lund University, pp. 146–61.

Savage, Leonard J. (1972) (1954), *The Foundations of Statistics*, Dover Publications, New York, 2nd ed.

Schick, Frederic (1982), 'Under Which Descriptions', in Amartya Sen and Bernard Williams (eds.), *Utilitarianism and Beyond*, (Cambridge: Cambridge University Press), pp. 251–60.

Virtue Ethics[1]

Torbjörn Tännsjö

Introduction

Many thinkers have seen the turn to virtue ethics as a timely way out of the deadlock posed by the ongoing discussion between traditional moral stances such as Kantianism, theories of fundamental moral rights, and utilitarianism. This is how Elizabeth Anscombe saw the situation in her 1958 article 'Modern Moral Philosophy', which inaugurated the present revival of virtue ethics. The main thrust of the present article is different: Virtue ethics is no sound alternative to Kantianism, theories of fundamental moral rights, or utilitarianism. At most, virtue ethics is a complement to such views, and a complement of only marginal importance.

One point of departure is the idea that a fundamental problem of ethics is what we ought to do in particular situations. Ethics should help us solve such practical problems. In order to do this, I would claim that ethics must provide us with both criteria of right action and decision methods that can aid us in the application of these criteria. And the thrust of my argument is that virtue ethics does not provide us with any plausible criterion of right action, nor is it very helpful with regard to decision methods applicable in practical life.[2]

Some preliminaries

I take for granted in my discussion that there are true answers to practical moral questions, i.e., I take for granted that it is meaningful to say such things as that, in the circumstances, it was wrong when a certain person performed a certain particular action. He or she should have done something else instead. I also take for granted that, when a certain action is right or wrong, it is right or wrong *because* of something. Moral characteristics supervene upon empirical characteristics. I do not take for granted, however, that there are general moral truths of the kind presupposed by, for example, the utilitarian criterion of rightness, according to which all right actions are right because they exhibit the same characteristic (they are optimific) and wrong actions wrong because they exhibit another characteristic (they are not optimific). This means that I allow for the particularist idea that, while one characteristic in one situation may make an action right, the same characteristic may, in a different situation, be irrelevant to the normative status of the very same kind of action and even, in the circumstances, a wrong-making characteristic.[3]

The assumption that there are true answers to practical moral questions should not be taken to imply too much. I hold a minimalist view of 'truth' and my assumption should be understood in the light of this minimalism.[4] In particular, the belief in true answers to practical questions does not imply that these answers exist independently of our conceptualisation, our evidence, and so forth. As a matter of fact, I do believe they do,[5] but this assumption is not made in the present context. However, the assumption here made does imply that we can hold opinions about what to do in particular cases; it implies that we can argue for and against (the truth of) these opinions, referring to the right-making and wrong-making characteristics of these actions, and it implies that meaningfully we can acknowledge that our beliefs about moral rightness and wrongness in particular cases may be mistaken.

By practical questions I think of questions such as the following one, which I have discussed at length elsewhere, and which I will use as a point of reference in my present discussion.[6] This example is not special, however. It is easy to describe similar cases that health care professionals face on a daily basis, and the example can be generalised to other more mundane decisions we have to make in our everyday life.

A doctor finds that, according to some statistical evidence that is forthcoming, a new drug tested on HIV positive people in a randomised trial may be killing one patient out of two hundred; there is no other known significant difference with regard to side-effects between the traditional drug (received by the patients in the control group) and the new one (received by the patients in the test group), and the new one promises to be more effective than the standard drug (although, for all we know, it may be less effective). Should the trial be stopped, or can it be continued until it has been ascertained whether the new drug is more effective than the standard drug, and to the point when it can be ascertained whether the new drug does really kill some patients?

Typical of virtue ethics is that it focuses on very general traits of character. Virtue ethicists define certain character traits or dispositions and think of them as desirable. Virtually all virtue theorists provide us with *lists* of those traits of characters that *are* virtues.[7] And, as we shall see below, most virtue ethicists provide answers to the question of what makes a trait of character a virtue. They provide a *criterion* in virtue of which a certain trait of character belongs to the list of the virtues. However, many virtue ethicists are silent on the following normative questions: why ought I to be virtuous? How do the virtues connect to normative questions in general? It is a striking fact about *much* of the new literature in this field that no clear answer to this kind of question is provided. This is true of important, much discussed, and anthologised contributions such as Philippa Foot's 'Virtues and Vices',[8] Iris Murdoch's *The Sovereignty of Good*,[9] or Walter Schaller's 'Are Virtues No More than Dispositions to Obey Moral Rules?'.[10] But there are exceptions to this rule. Here I will concentrate on such exceptions, i.e., on defences of virtue ethics that do provide an answer to this question, and, in order to cover the entire field, I will also speculate about merely *possible* such answers.

Three main possibilities seem to be open here. First of all, virtue ethics may be considered to provide a criterion of right action.[11] So, if we develop these virtues and act on them we will as a matter of fact act rightly. And our actions will be right *because* we, who perform them, are virtuous agents. Or, perhaps, because these actions are such that they *would* be performed by a virtuous agent. Secondly, virtue ethics may be considered to provide us with an answer to what kind of characteristics we ought to develop in ourselves and to foster in our children, but to no other normative questions. So, by developing these virtues we do only what we ought to do, period. Thirdly, virtue ethics may be considered to provide us with a plausible method of moral decision-making, which helps us to solve difficult moral problems, or at least to steer clear of some kinds of immoral behaviour that we are otherwise prone to exhibit. All this means that if we develop these virtues, we become more *likely* to act rightly. But on this reading, the rightness of the actions we perform is independent of the character we exhibit when we perform them.

According to Justin Oakley, it is a defining characteristic of virtue ethics that it explains moral rightness in terms of virtues.[12] However, I do not think we have to accept this restricted use of the word 'virtue ethics'. There is no established terminology in the field. And it seems more fruitful to use the term 'virtue ethics' more inclusively, to cover all three kinds of views adumbrated above. However, even if we do, the prospects for a tenable and interesting virtue ethics are bleak. To see this, let us discuss the three kinds of virtue ethics in order.

Virtue ethics and criteria of right action

If a person faces a difficult practical question such as the one faced by the doctor in my example above, we should be able to conclude on this first interpretation of virtue ethics that a certain answer to the question (such as stop the trial!) must be right, because a virtuous person would stop the trial. Virtue ethics is often described in a manner that invites the interpretation that virtue ethics provides us with a statement of a criterion of rightness. Consider for example the following statement of one central tenet of virtue ethics by Rosalind Hursthouse:

> An action is right iff [if and only if] it is what a virtuous agent would do in the circumstances.[13]

When reading this, I must confess that I get the impression that the author thinks of virtue ethics as providing us with a statement of a criterion of rightness of actions.[14] And, as was noted above, it is taken by Justin Oakley to be a defining characteristic of virtue ethics that it explains moral rightness with reference to the virtues of the agent. However, this is not an interpretation of virtue ethics that makes the idea at all plausible.

To be sure, virtue ethics conceived of as an ethical theory providing a criterion of rightness has sometimes been set aside too quickly. It has sometimes been argued that, since a good character is a character that tends to lead to right actions, the rightness of the actions it leads to cannot be explained in terms of it. This would lead us into a vicious circle.[15] But this is not correct. The virtue ethicis need not argue that a good character is good because it tends to lead to right actions. This is pointed out by Justin Oakley who notes that there are, broadly speaking, two main kinds of approach taken by virtue ethicists in grounding the character of the good agent.[16] Some accept Aristotle's view that the content of virtuous character is determined by what we need, or what we are, qua *human* beings.[17] Others argue with Michael Slote that there is a plurality of traits that we commonly find admirable in human beings in certain circumstances;[18] these traits are characteristic of virtue.

All this may seem strange, for reasons explained below, but the argument is not circular. So the reason why virtue ethics does not provide us with plausible criteria of rightness is different.

First of all, *being such that it would be performed by a virtuous person* can hardly be a right-making characteristic of an action. We cannot explain the putative (moral) fact that a certain action should be performed with reference to the fact that it *would* be performed by a virtuous person, be this person a flourishing human being or such that we tend to admire him or her. Why not? Because the explanation of why the action is right, if it is, must minimally refer to *some* concrete aspect of the situation where the action is performed. It must refer to the *actual* motive of the person who performed it (in taking it, did the doctor care for his or her patients) or, more plausibly, to the *consequences* for those who are affected by it (in the trial, were the patients exposed to an unreasonable risk, say?).

But if the action would be performed by a virtuous person, must not this be the case because it has certain concrete characteristics in virtue of which it would be selected by a virtuous agent? And do these characteristics not explain its rightness?

This may very well be the case. However, in that case, these characteristics *themselves*, not the fact that the action would be chosen by a virtuous agent, are what make the action right. So the virtue of the agent does not enter into the moral explanation of why the action was right, after all.

But could we not then say that an action is right if and only if it is *actually* performed by a virtuous person, and otherwise wrong? In a recent article, Michael Slote has characterised this position as 'agent-based' virtue ethics.[19] This may seem more promising, but it seems to me we have to resist this idea as well. Let me first discuss the simple version of this idea, followed by a subtler version, defended by Slote himself. In the simple version an action is right if, and only if, it is performed by a virtuous person but otherwise wrong. And if it is right, it is right *because* it is performed by a virtuous person, and if it is wrong, it is wrong *because* it is performed by a vicious person. There are obvious problems with this suggestion.

In the first place, this *exclusive* focus on the agent is strange. Must not the reason for the action being right or wrong have *something* to do with what happens to those who are affected by it? Can it be right for one doctor to put a patient at a certain risk but wrong for another doctor in exact similar circumstances to do so just because these doctors have different characters? Secondly, it is strange if only virtuous persons can perform right actions – be they flourishing human beings or admirable persons. After all, morality should have something to inform even those of us who are seriously wanting in terms of virtue. But if the agent's possessing a virtuous character is a right-making characteristic, and lack of virtue, or the presence of vice a wrong-making characteristic, then there is no way that a vicious person can act rightly. If the doctor is vicious, he or she acts wrongly, whatever action he or she takes. We seem to have constructed a morality that cannot guide choices. And, finally, this version of virtue ethics has the strange implication that whatever action a virtuous person performs (even a horrendous action), would be right.

In order to meet this last objection, Slote has tried the following approach. In order for an action to be right, it is not sufficient that it is performed by a virtuous agent. And in order for an action to be wrong, it is not sufficient that it is performed by a vicious person. In both cases, something more is required. In Slote's own version of agent-based virtue ethics:

> Acts ... do not count as admirable or virtuous for an agent-based theory ... merely because they are or would be done by someone who in fact is admirable or possesses admirable motivation – they have to exhibit, express, or further such motivation or be such that they *would* exhibit, etc., such motivation if they occurred, in order to qualify as admirable or virtuous. [20]

A way of understanding this would be as follows. An act is right if and only if it *reflects* or *expresses* good motivation, and it is wrong if and only if it *reflects* bad motivation. This would mean that Slote had strengthened both the criteria of right action and the criteria of wrong action. Not only must an action, in order to be right, be performed by a virtuous agent, it must also 'reflect' the virtuous character of the person who performs it. And not only must an action, in order to be wrong, be performed by a vicious person, it must also express the vicious character of the person who performs it.

It may seem that if we strengthen both the criteria of right action and the criteria of wrong action, then this must leave many cases undecided. We will have a class of actions lacking normative status; they are neither right nor wrong. This seems to me to be counterintuitive and at variance with the claim that morality should guide our actions. However, to the extent that only *hypothetical* actions lack normative status, this defect may seem to be of little importance. And, to be sure, *some* of the actions lacking normative status, in Slote's view, are merely hypothetical. To see this, consider first of all horrendous actions that would be performed by a virtuous person. It may of course be doubted whether a truly virtuous person can perform horrendous actions. According to Slote he or she can, however:

> Of course, the really or perfectly benevolent person will not refuse to help, but the point is that she could, and such refusal and the actions it would give rise to do not count as admirable according to the simplified agent-based view that makes benevolence the touchstone of all moral evaluation.[21]

I am tempted to agree.[22] We ought not to conceive of characters as straightjackets. It is true that a virtuous person *can* perform evil actions. We may have recourse to the possible world metaphor to explain this. In the closest world where a virtuous person performs a horrendous action, this person is still virtuous. However, his or her action does not reflect his or her character. The horrendous action must rather be explained as a 'slip' of the virtuous person, or as an expression of *akrasia*. Nor does this action reflect a vicious character, of course (we have assumed that the agent has a virtuous character). So it follows that, in Slote's view, this action lacks normative status. However, a truly virtuous person never performs such actions. So it is perhaps not such a big problem that these merely hypothetical actions lack normative status.

However, the case is different and more troublesome with a vicious person. It is easy to imagine situations where such a person does perform generous actions. When he or she does, these actions do not reflect the agent's character, of course. We have to explain them differently. We have to say, for example, that the reason that this truly vicious person performs a certain generous action must be that he or she wants to promote his or her career, or that he or she fears being exposed and submitted to punishment. Such actions are very common indeed. And I must confess that I find it counter-intuitive (and even moralistic) to claim that they lack normative status. These actions are, in my opinion, right actions.

A way of avoiding the problem with actions lacking normative status would of course be to take an action to be wrong if and only if it is performed from a bad motive (simpliciter).[23] But it seems to me this would be to have virtue ethics collapse into the Kantian idea of the supreme importance of a good will. Another way of avoiding the problem with actions lacking normative status would be to introduce new normative categories. Perhaps we could with these three: (1) there are actions that are *right*, i.e., actions performed by virtuous persons and expressing their agent's virtuous character, (2) there are actions that are in a new category, let us call them *all right*, i.e., actions performed by vicious persons but not reflecting the vicious character of their agents, and, (3) there are actions that are wrong, i.e., actions performed by vicious persons and reflecting the vicious character of their agents.[24] However, it seems to me that this does not only mean normative complication but normative confusion as well. Suppose I have two options: Either I become a monk, develop a virtuous character and perform only right actions – but, alas, make little difference to the world as such. Or, I become a vicious person who, as a matter of fact, by mostly acting out of character and performing actions that are all right, make an enormous difference (for the better) to the world. Which option is 'preferable' (to use a neutral term) for me to adopt? The question boggles the mind. And be this as it may, my main objection to all kinds of agent-centred virtue ethics (as well as to the Kantian idea of the supreme importance of a good will) remains to be answered. It would be utterly strange if the rightness or wrongness of an action of an agent (the doctor in our example) should have nothing at all to do with what happens to the *patient*. To be in the least plausible, an ethic must be, not only 'agent-based', as Slote has it, but also, and more importantly, 'patient-based' as well.

We may think well of a virtuous person who does harm merely because of bad luck, and yet, for all that, we do consider such harmful actions (objectively) as being wrong. And no matter how carefully we consider a matter, and no matter how well intentioned we are when we act, if we take morality seriously, we must always nourish the uneasy suspicion that, for all our moral zeal and for all our moral goodness, our actions may still turn out to be wrong. This is a crucial part of moral phenomenology. Our moral situation *qua* moral agents gives no room for complacency. And the wrongness of our actions, if indeed they are wrong, must be explained with some reference at least to the harm they do to some *patients*. How else *could* it be explained?

Virtue to be chosen for its own sake?

We have seen that the virtues do not figure in any essential way in any plausible general criterion of rightness and wrongness of actions. But perhaps we have misconceived our problem altogether. We have tried to see whether virtue ethics provides a criterion of rightness and wrongness of actions that is superior to more traditional criteria such as utilitarianism or Kantianism, and we have found virtue ethics wanting. But perhaps the problem with the traditional approaches to ethics is not that they give the wrong answers to the right question in the final analysis, but that they are based on a false assumption: the very question they set out to answer is the wrong one. It has sometimes been argued by virtue ethicists that we should not be so obsessed with normative questions. We should focus instead on the virtues and try to find out what they are. Which traits of character are valuable? A very radical statement of this position can be found in Anscombe's previously mentioned article, which inaugurated the new interest in virtue ethics:

> ... the concepts of obligation, and duty, that is to say – *moral* obligation and *moral* duty,– and of what is *morally* right and wrong, and of the *moral* sense of 'ought', ought to be jettisoned if this is psychologically possible ... It would be a great improvement if, instead of 'morally wrong,' one always named a genus such as 'untruthful,' 'unchaste,' 'unjust'.[25]

But could a search for the virtues go on completely unperturbed by *any* normative considerations whatever? I think not. If it does, the result will be of little moral importance. However, the normative question we ought to focus on is perhaps not what makes right actions right (in general) but, more narrowly, on what traits of characters we ought to foster in ourselves (and in our children through education). And virtue ethics may provide an answer to this narrower class of normative questions, setting the rest of them to one side. Perhaps virtue ethics provides us with a criterion of rightness *applicable only in decisions relevant to moral development and education*. This is the move to be discussed in the present section.

There are two problems with this move in defence of virtue ethics. One is that it relegates the virtues to a very marginal role in ethics. And the other, and more important problem, is that it leads to inconsistency, or *ad hoc* solutions.

Take first the problem of marginality. It is strange if an ethical theory should only address the problem of rightness of actions in relation to a narrowly circumscribed class of actions (our choice of traits of character in our moral development and education). After all, our moral life consists of so much more than this. It is hard to believe that an adequate morality could be silent about this.

Moreover, if we hold that virtue ethics does provide us with a criterion of rightness, but a criterion only of rightness of some actions (to do with moral development and education), we run the risk that compliance with this criterion may mean that we act wrongly on some other, quite general criterion of rightness, such as the utilitarian or Kantian ones. This would happen if we were to develop a certain virtue in a situation where this would lead to bad consequences – or come to flout the demands of the categorical imperative.

In order to counter this possibility the virtue ethicist, who has narrowed his or her moral theory to state a criterion of rightness of actions to do with moral development and education only, would have to claim that all these competing claims are false. However, this move would leave the rest of morality covered by no criterion of rightness at all, which would not only be strange but a very sad fact indeed. Or, may the virtue ethicist hold that while utilitarianism or Kantianism or some other moral theory may be true in general, this otherwise true moral theory must be silent about problems to do with moral development and education. But this is utterly *ad hoc*. If what makes right actions right is that they are optimific, or conform to the categorical imperative, or whatever we may think of, why should this not *also* be true of our decisions regarding moral development and education?

Virtue ethics and methods of decision-making

If virtue ethics does not provide us with plausible criteria of rightness of particular actions, does it at least provide us with a sound method of moral decision-making? This is how Aristotle's own virtue ethics has often been interpreted (when he claimed that the virtuous person *perceives* what is the right thing to do he must have taken rightness to be independent of the character of the virtuous person), and this is how virtue ethics is often thought to be of help. This line of argument may then seem more promising than seeing virtue ethics as providing criteria of right action. One way of understanding this argument is to take it to show that virtue ethics may help us find solutions to difficult moral cases.

Allow me to distinguish between three possibilities here. I have noted that it is not clear how virtue ethics conceives of right-making characteristics of particular actions. One possibility is that virtue ethics accepts that there exist general moral truths and allows that utilitarianism, or Kantianism, or some other principled stance to morality, explains (in principle) the rightness and wrongness of particular actions. A second possibility is that virtue ethics adopts a view defended most famously by W.D. Ross. According to Ross there are true general *prima facie* moral principles and true particular moral judgements, but there are no true absolute moral principles, explaining (together with statements of empirical facts) the rightness or wrongness of particular actions. In a particular case, when a concrete action is both prima facie wrong and prima facie right, we must *judge* as to whether it is right or wrong.[26] A third possibility is that virtue ethics adopts a particularist view. According to this view there are some empirical aspects of a situation that explain the rightness or wrongness of a particular action, but in a different situation the very same characteristics may be morally irrelevant; there are no true moral generalisations, not even of a *prima facie* character. In relation to these three ideas, virtue ethics may be seen as a method of moral decision-making. The general idea will be that, in particular situations, when we want to find out what to do, we ought to rely on what, in the situation, we believe a virtuous agent would do. Ideally we ought to become virtuous agents ourselves and perform the right actions out of habit (something that may well also take a sort of practical *wisdom* on our part). I would have none of this.

Consider first the situation if utilitarianism or Kantianism gives the true explanation of rightness and wrongness of particular actions. It is certainly true that we now need a method of moral decision-making. For no plausible moral principle can be applied in any direct manner (we do not know all the relevant facts of any particular situation). Utilitarians and Kantians agree that in particular cases there is no way to decide with any certainty what to do. This concession is commonplace among utilitarians, while Kant himself seems to have been hard pressed to admit that it was problematic to apply his ethical theory. It is commonplace among his commentators to note this difficulty, however.[27] There is often no way of ascertaining whether a certain act means that the agent breaks a promise, whether the execution of a certain person means that an innocent life is being sacrificed, and so forth. Even Kant himself does note that it might be difficult to know whether a person is acting from the right motive:

> The real morality of actions, their merit or guilt, even that of our own conduct, thus remains entirely hidden from us. Our imputations can refer only to the empirical character. How much of this character is ascribable to the pure effect of freedom, how much to mere nature, that is, to faults of temperament for which there is no responsibility, or to its happy constitution, can never be determined.[28]

Now, where does this leave the virtue ethicist? Does virtue ethics provide us with the method of moral decision-making we need? The general idea would be, I suppose, that a virtuous person performs right actions out of habit and/or practical wisdom. And a not so virtuous person can think: how *would* a virtuous person act in the kind of situation that I am in? Or, if such a person can be identified, how would *he* or *she* act in my situation?

Is it at all plausible to claim that, if the agent is virtuous, then the agent will perform right actions out of habit and/or practical wisdom? Of course not. Consider the example with the clinical trial discussed at the beginning of this article. Would it be advisable to continue with the trial? This decision cannot be reached merely by habit and practical wisdom. For the facts relevant to the solution of the practical problem here raised are hard to come by. Even if we simplify (and unless we simplify there is no hope that we will reach any decision at all), we have to go into complicated calculations of probabilities, and it is far from clear what kind of risk aversion would be appropriate in the circumstances. Such things are not settled habitually, nor can they be sensed by a wise person. In particular, it is impossible even for a wise (and morally sensitive) person to *perceive* the moral characteristics of the options open to those in command of the trial. For, to be sure, these characteristics depend on the actual outcome of the trial of which we cannot know anything at all in advance. No one can perceive the future. It is not even possible for a wise person to perceive what would be, in the circumstances, a *reasonable* stance to take. For this depends on difficult probability assessments, which can only be reached through (inferential) reasoning. It is true that a virtuous person can be good at making relevant empirical assessments, and also at making inferences from more general moral principles, but this has little to do with virtue as such. Even a wicked person (who is wicked in general) can be good at doing this (in a particular situation or a professional setting).

If utilitarianism gives a true explanation of the rightness and wrongness of particular actions I suppose the following line of argument would present itself as reasonable to a person who wants to reach a decision. First of all, as a rule of thumb, we have to simplify. We have to abstract from things we do not know anything about at all, such as the possibility that, by killing one patient with the medicine, we avoid some future disaster (the person would have had a child who would have had a child who would have become a new Hitler). We focus our attention on what we have considered opinions about. Furthermore, let us say we restrict our attention to the patients and future patients and we try to maximise expected happiness among these. The rationale behind this kind of argument would be that, by conducting it, we do our best at arriving at a reasonable solution to the problem. We use a method of moral decision-making that, if consistently applied, has no rival with better odds at producing, on the whole, better outcomes.

However, it is hard to tell what makes different people happy. As a rough approximation, let us assume that all patients value life without symptoms of AIDS positively, and every increment of life equally positively. If this is so, would it be reasonable for an individual to enter the trial? If it would, it might seem reasonable to offer the trial to a patient; if not, it would not seem reasonable to do so. It takes explicit calculation to find this out.

Then consider the case from a Kantian point of view. If, as a general law, trials of this kind should be allowed, this must depend on what happens to the people who are in the trial. Remember that according to Kant, you ought to act only on that maxim through which you can at the same time will that it should become a universal law. In order to see what we can will that it should become a universal law, we need to know what happens to the people in the trial, what kinds of risk they are exposed to and so forth. And in order to see what kinds of risk they become exposed to when they are allowed to enter the trial, we must conduct an argument of the kind already adumbrated here. So in order to reach a solution, the Kantian would have to know roughly everything the utilitarian needs to know and, in addition to this, something about what would happen if the kind of action considered was generalised.

In order to be able to perform the kind of argument needed in the situation, we must have some acquaintance with probability calculus. We must be capable of identifying with other people. We must be able to assess what does and what does not matter to them, and so forth. Note that all these things can be done just as well by a vicious as by a virtuous person. And it is of little avail to a person that they have a good moral character when this kind of decision has to be made. After all, even a sociopath can assess how a certain action would affect other people and, for some reason or another, act upon this knowledge (this is why it may be difficult to expose the sociopath in some circumstances).

In the concrete case referred to, those doctors I found most sympathetic reached, in my opinion, the wrong conclusion. They were too squeamish. They did not want to include their patients in the trial despite the fact that, upon closer examination it transpired that a person who held reasonable hopes that the new drug would be only somewhat more efficient than the old one, should enter the trial provided he or she wanted to maximise their life expectancy. The reader is invited to make the relevant calculations to find out whether this claim of mine is true or not.

Does this mean that what these doctors did exhibit was not *true* virtue? I think not. Their general disposition to be cautious may have been quite in order. This disposition may have stopped them in other situations from making rash and even seriously wrong decisions. Those who accepted the trial may, even if they were not sociopaths, have had characters that, more often than not, lead to unwise decisions. I will return to this below. There is some (limited) room for virtue in ethics. However, their virtue did not help them to solve the difficult moral case facing them in this particular situation. In the situation, virtue proved neither necessary nor sufficient to the finding of a solution to the practical problem facing these doctors.

Suppose now that there are general moral truths but only *prima facie* general moral truths and that in particular cases we need to make a judgement about what is, in the circumstances, absolutely right and what is absolutely wrong moral conduct. Does this mean that there is room for virtue in our moral decision-making.

Note first that if there are general *prima facie* moral truths then we cannot find a solution to practical questions unless we possess knowledge of these general *prima facie* moral truths. Let us suppose that we face a particular action and we want to know about this action (such as our going on with the clinical trial in question) if it is absolutely right or absolutely wrong. In order to decide this we must know, first of all, in what respects it is *prima facie* right, and in what respects it is *prima facie* wrong to go on with the trial. No matter how good a *character* we have, if we want to solve difficult practical questions we cannot by-pass the learning of these general truths (in our moral education). And a vicious person can come to learn about these general truths just as well as a virtuous person as far as I can understand, and a vicious person may be prepared, in a professional setting, to act upon his or her knowledge.

This leads us to the conclusion that in order to solve the problem at hand the moral agent need not only have general moral knowledge (about what makes actions *prima facie* right and wrong) but also particular knowledge about the action under scrutiny. Once again the agent needs to have some knack for probability calculus and also needs to be able to identify the interests of the people involved, and so forth. This is no different from the case already discussed. Now enters a new problem, however, the problem of reaching, in the situation, a moral judgement. Does it behove the agent to be virtuous, when this judgement is to be reached?

This question could be answered in the affirmative by an act of fiat, of course. It could be argued that, by definition, a 'virtuous' person is *a person who is good at making this kind of judgement*. But there are several problems with this approach. First of all, it means that we take the flesh out of the virtues and make the characterisation of them abstract. *How* do we learn to become good at making correct moral judgements? This is what we want to know, not simply *that* we should be good at doing this. Secondly, this approach does not pay due respect to the ordinary meaning of words. The main problem with this definition is not that it includes a capacity for making good judgements (phronesis) in its definition of virtue, but that it does *not* include a general tendency to act habitually on one's moral judgements.

The general tendency to act habitually on one's moral judgements seems to be crucial in our ordinary language notion of a virtue. However, the *general* tendency to act habitually on one's moral judgements is not necessary in the present context. To see this we need only acknowledge the rather obvious fact that a person who is bent on doing ill may well have developed an eye for what *really* hurts, and so forth. He or she may also be good at probability calculus. Then this person can make good moral judgements. And, to the extent that this person is prepared to act professionally, he or she may well, for this reason alone, implement these good moral judgements in a health care setting (saving his or her ill behaviour for leisure time). We would and should have nothing to object to such a doctor, I submit.

My discussion of the third (particularist) possibility should come as no surprise to the reader. In this case, further complications are being added to the situation. Everything that is morally relevant according to the principled approaches to ethics *may* be relevant in a concrete situation, such as the one discussed here. This means that a kind of general moral knowledge is needed after all but cast in a somewhat different form, however: An action *may* be right because it is optimific, it *may* be wrong because it is a case of murder, and so forth. Furthermore, all the arguments referring to the need for a skill in probability calculus, the identification with and assessment of interests, and so forth, must be confronted once again.

Finally, in order to settle the practical question, a judgement must be reached. The moral agent must find out what to do and the moral agent must find a way of explaining this by pointing to salient aspects of the situation. Is this a place where Aristotle's (and later, John McDowell's[29]) analogy with perception is in place? Is it possible for the virtuous person simply to 'perceive' what ought to be done?

No, if I am right in my insistence that what we ought to do may have something to do with the actual consequences of our actions, as compared to the consequences of various different possible alternative actions, it is not open to inspection. In order to reach and answer the question of what we should do we must make inferences. And all sorts of very complex information *may* be relevant to these inferences. This is true in particular if particularism is true! So all the talents and skills, which I have elaborated on and which can be exhibited by virtuous and vicious persons alike, are required.

Virtue as a guard against immoral action

My findings so far have been negative. There is *some* room in our moral practice for the virtues, however. I have referred to this fact in passing. I will now explain in more detail how I think the virtues may be of some importance in our moral lives. The virtues do not specify criteria of right and wrong action and they are of no avail when we want to settle difficult moral cases. However, they may be of some assistance when we want to avoid certain kinds of nasty behaviour to which we human beings sometimes seem to be prone. This is an aspect of the virtues that has been stressed for example by Philippa Foot:

> I shall now turn to another thesis about the virtues, which I might express by saying that they are *corrective*, each one standing at a point at which there is some temptation to be resisted or deficiency of motivation to be made good. As Aristotle put it, virtues are about what is difficult for men ...[30]

In many situations we can do with less than virtue. In most professional settings, for example, we simply want people to reach morally reasonable answers to the question of what should be done, and to act on these answers as well. This presupposes for example that health care staff are prepared to do their job, but not that they have *in general* very good characters. Doing their job includes treating their patients as individual people with individual interests, and tending to these interests in a professional manner. Even an evil person can do this. The same could be said about other professions. Now, if we like, we may here speak of 'professional' virtues. If we do we must acknowledge, of course, that such virtues are of importance. However, the role of the professional virtues is derivative and not fundamental.

Their content must be determined by a critical examination of the corresponding institution (profession). If there is something morally wrong about the design of the institution (profession), it might be a good thing if I am *not* prepared to act professionally.

In our relations with those who are near and dear to us, there may seem to be more room for the virtues properly conceived of (as very general traits of character). If I am a virtuous person then I am kind (habitually) to my children. I treat them well spontaneously, or out of habit and practical wisdom. This is all right when it comes to those who are near and dear. If I am a nurse I should however not treat my patients well out of kindness. I should not treat them the way I do because of any personal relations I may have developed in relation to them. On the contrary, I ought to care for them *irrespective* of my personal feelings for them. I ought to be impartial and professional with respect to them. But the situation with those who are near and dear *is* different. So it may seem that there is some room for the virtues here. However, even in close relations it seems as though even people who are in general very nasty may be able to behave decently. Even Adolf Hitler seems to have treated Ewa Braun in a loving, caring and respectful manner. This may be a disturbing psychological fact, but it is still a fact. So perhaps we should rather speak here of certain familial virtues than of virtues in general. And even these familial virtues should be put under scrutiny. Our interest in the well-being of those who are near and dear to us may go too far; this interest may, if it goes to extremes, mean that we pay insufficient attention to the suffering of strangers.

But would it not at least be somewhat helpful, both in professional and in personal settings, if people were *generally* more virtuous? Would it not mean that they had received a kind of 'vaccination' against certain kinds of horrible actions? Even if tempted to do so, a virtuous person would not take advantage of the weakness of other people, depending on him or her. A virtuous person would not only function well in certain well-known professional or private settings, he or she would also resist temptation in new and unprecedented circumstances. A truly virtuous person would be able to sustain the institutions of a good society. This seems to be the idea put forward, with reference to Aristotle, by Philippa Foot above.

Well, all this would be fine if it were possible. However, it seems that the prospects for this kind of virtue are bleak. This general kind of virtue is always fragile. *How* fragile it is has been nicely pointed out recently by John M. Doris.[31] Experimental data indicate that we may come to lose our virtue when our need for it is most pressing (when being tempted). If the 'situationist' experimental tradition in social and personality psychology is on the right track, then it seems as though behavioural variation across a population owes more to situational differences than dispositional differences among people. There are no robust traits of character.

If this is true, then in our attempts to avoid patients and students being treated badly, we should invest more hope in public surveillance and more restricted professional virtues than in the possibility of instilling through education or training *general* (robust) traits of character in the staff. And if we want a good society, we should focus more on the institutions of this society as such, and less on the very general traits of character of its citizens. This seems, by the way, to be the moral to be drawn from Bertholt Brecht's admirably subtle play, *Der guter Mensch von Sezuan*.

I do concede, however, that all this means that some narrow scope is left for strictly *professional* virtues, for *familial* virtues and perhaps even for some *republican* virtues. We should only not suspect that if a person rates high on one of these scales, he or she will also rate high on the other scales. Moreover, when faced with a radically new situation it is not at all unlikely that even a person who habitually behaves well within the confines of his family, at his job, and *qua* citizen, will for all that come to behave in an immoral way.

Conclusion

I have argued that virtue ethics is of little importance in sound moral reasoning. Virtue ethics does not provide us with a criterion of right action. The fact that a certain action *would* be taken by a virtuous agent does not make it right. Nor is it a plausible requirement of right actions that they are performed by people who, *as a matter of fact*, are virtuous. Even a vicious person can act rightly. And, more importantly, the rightness and wrongness of our actions must have something to do with what happens to those who are affected by them (the patients). If a reference to the virtues alone could settle matters of rightness and wrongness of our actions we could, in principle, ascertain that in a certain situation we had done the right thing by examining our own character. But this is at variance with an obvious piece of moral phenomenology: we know that, no matter how strongly we *try* to do the right thing, we may very well go wrong.

Does virtue ethics at least provide us with a criterion of right action in relation to actions to do with moral development and education? It does not. Such a criterion would be vulnerable to the possibility that it be at variance with a plausible *general* criterion of rightness, such as the utilitarian or Kantian one, applying *also* to actions to do with moral development and education. For it is all too much *ad hoc* to believe that there is a special criterion of rightness exclusively valid for actions in this narrowly circumscribed field.

Does virtue ethics then provide us with a plausible method of moral decision-making? It does not, or so I have argued. In order to solve difficult practical problems we need not only to be good, we need to posses various different skills. If there are general right-making characteristics then we need to know these characteristics, even if they are only of a *prima facie* character. In a particular situation they may be relevant. Moreover, we need to have a knack for probability calculus, we need be able to identify with other people and to assess the strength of their interests. All these skills have little to do with being virtuous. And even more importantly, even a vicious person may possess all the necessary skills and, in a strictly professional setting, exercise them in a responsible manner.

This does not mean that there is absolutely no room for virtue in our moral lives. Being prepared to do one's job may be seen as *a* virtue, I submit. Various different professional virtues may be needed in various different professional settings. And familial virtues may be of importance in our relations to our close ones. There may even be some room for certain 'republican' virtues in our relation to society at large. But these narrow virtues seem to be possible for us to exhibit independently of each other. It is also very likely that they differ between times and places.

What then of *true* virtue? I concede that being *truly* virtuous (good) may perhaps in some rare cases be an obstacle to taking advantage of people who depend on you. And perhaps it may in some rare occasions stop us in a situation of social and political crisis from getting carried away by totalitarian ideologies. Being truly virtuous may keep one on the right track. However, where an opportunity surfaces or when normal social norms break down, even a truly virtuous person *may* be tempted to make an aberration from duty. So this (derivative) room for *true* virtue in our moral lives is severely circumscribed by our poor human nature, captured nicely by situationist psychology.

Notes

[1] I thank Helga Kuhse, Hans Mathlein, and Michael Slote for valuable comments on earlier drafts of this paper.
[2] Note that the thrust of my argument is negative. Even if I am right in my criticism of virtue ethics, this does not substantiate the validity of any traditional principled stance, such as Kantianism, a theory of rights, or utilitarianism, of course. However, I have defended a particular principled ethical stance elsewhere, mainly in my recent book, *Hedonistic Utilitarianism* (Edinburgh: Edinburgh University Press, 1998).
[3] It might be wondered whether a particularist has to reject supervenience. After all, if two actions are similar in all natural respects, must they not, according to the thesis of supervenience, have the same normative status? And does this not mean that we have a kind of moral principle, cast in terms of the totality of the empirical properties present in the cases? Well, there are several possible responses that the particularist can adopt to this claim. One would be to reject that the notion of a complete empirical description of a situation makes sense. Then the thesis of supervenience must be stated otherwise, most plausibly in the following negative way: if two actions differ in moral respect

there must be some empirical difference that explains the moral difference. From this no kind of generalism follows. Another possible answer would be to insist that, in reality, all actions differ, so the concession to generalism rendered necessary by the acceptance of supervenience in the positive form is of no practical importance. For all we know, it may be impossible for us ever to state a moral principle that can account for rightness and wrongness in all particular cases we may come to confront. I discuss this in my 'In Defence of Theory in Ethics', *Canadian Journal of Philosophy*, Vol. 25, 1995, pp. 571–594 and in Chapter 2 of my *Hedonistic Utilitarianism* (Edinburgh: Edinburgh University Press, 1998).

4   I defend minimalism about truth in 'The Expressivist Theory of Truth', *Theoria*, Vol. LXVI, 2000, pp. 256–272.

5   I defend this claim in Chapter 3 of my *Moral Realism* (Savage: Rowman and Littlefield, 1990).

6   Cf. my 'The Morality of Clinical Research. A Case Study', *The Journal of Medicine and Philosophy*, Vol. 19, 1994, pp. 7–21, reprinted in Helga Kuhse and Peter Singer (eds.), *Bioethics: An Anthology* (Oxford: Blackwell Philosophy Anthologies, Blackwell, 1999).

7   What are we to make of these conflicts among virtue ethicists? Does their disagreement show that there is no fact of the matter, or that the virtues are relative to time and place? Most famously, Alasdair Macintyre has argued (in his *After Virtue*, London: Duckworth, 1987) from disagreement to relativism, but his line of argument is not irresistible. In *my* attack on virtue ethics, I will not take advantage of any argument from disagreement. After all, disagreement is commonplace not only in moral matters, but within philosophy as such, and I think it would be rash to draw irrealist or relativist conclusions from this fact. There are other ways to explain disagreement, respecting our basic realist intuitions about both moral matters and philosophical questions in general. So, for all the conflicting ideas among virtue ethicists, there may well exist a definite list of the *true* virtues (perhaps yet to be found).

8   Printed in Philippa Foot, *Virtues and Vices and Other Essays in Moral Philosophy* (Oxford: Blackwell, 1978), pp. 1–18.

9   Iris Murdoch, *The Sovereignty of Good* (London: Ark, 1985).

10   *Philosophy*, Vol. 20, 1990.

11   The distinction has been drawn, first and foremost, by R.E. Bales, in 'Act-Utilitarianism; Account of Right-Making Characteristics or Decision-Making Procedure?', *American Philosophical Quarterly*, Vol. 8, 1971, pp. 257–265

12   Justin Oakley, 'Varieties of virtue ethics', *Ratio*, (New Series) IX, 1996, pp. 128–52.

13   'Virtue Theory and Abortion', *Philosophy and Public Affairs*, Vol. 20. 1991, p. 219.

14   This need not be the only possible interpretation, however. Does Hursthouse really mean, not only that the actions that a virtuous person would perform are right, but that they are right *because* they would be performed by a virtuous person? This question is left open by the author and this means that it is doubtful whether Hursthouse is open to the kind of critique I am here putting forward.

15   This is essentially the critique put forward by William K. Frankena against the idea that the virtues could be conceived of as 'basic' in our ethical theory. Cf. his *Ethics* (Englewood Cliffs, N.J.: Prentice-Hall, 1963), p. 50.

16 Justin Oakely, ibid., p. 133.
17 As one among many representatives of this brand of virtue ethics Oakeley refers to Thomas Hurka, 'Virtue as Loving the Good', in Ellen F. Paul, Fred D. Miller, and Jeffrey Paul (eds), *The Good Life and the Human Good* (Cambridge: Cambridge University Press, 1992).
18 Michael Slote puts forward his view in *From Morality to Virtue* (New York: Oxford University Press, 1992), Chapter 5.
19 'Agent-based virtue ethics', *Midwest Studies in Philosophy*, Vol. 20, 1995, pp. 83–101, reprinted in Roger Crisp and Michael Slote (eds), *Virtue Ethics* (Oxford: Oxford University Press, 1997). The quotations below are from the latter source.
20 'Agent-based virtue ethics', ibid., p. 244.
21 Ibid., pp. 243–4.
22 Cf. my 'Blameless Wrongdoing,' *Ethics*, Vol. 106, 1995, pp. 120–127, and Chapter 9 of my *Hedonistic Utilitarianism* (Edinburgh: Edinburgh University Press, 1998) about this.
23 Michael Slote has suggested this in correspondence. As a matter of fact, I am not quite sure which interpretation of his text is the correct one.
24 This has been suggested to me by Jonas Gren.
25 'Modern Moral Philosophy', p. 26, originally printed in *Philosophy*, Vol. 33, 1958; here quoted from Roger Crisp and Michael Slote (eds), *Virtue Ethics* (Oxford: Oxford University Press, 1997).
26 Cf. his *The Right and the Good* (Oxford: Clarendon, 1930)
27 Cf. for example Onora O'Neill, *Acting on Principle: An Essay on Kantian Ethics* (New York and London: Columbia University Press, 1975).
28 *Critique of Pure Reason*, A551/B579.
29 'Virtue and Reason', the *Monist*, Vol. 62, 1979, pp. 331–50.
30 Philippa Foot, 'Virtue and Vices', here quoted from Roger Crisp and Michael Slote (eds), *Virtue Ethics* (Oxford: Oxford University Press, 1997), p. 169.
31 J.M. Doris, 'Persons, Situations, and Virtue Ethics', *Nous*, Vol. 32, 1998, pp. 504–530.

Fractal and Fragile Beauty

Göran Hermerén

Introduction

In his illuminating discussion of Sircello's new theory of beauty, Ingmar Persson [13] makes a number of useful distinctions. In particular, he defines a weak sense in which sensational beauty can be phenomenologically objective – that is, roughly, experienced as being located outside the body of the perceiver. Sensational beauty can be objective in this sense without being objective in the stronger sense of being independent of the constitution or perceptual apparatus of any perceiving subject. Persson argues, in my view convincingly, for the view that sensational beauty is objective in this weak phenomenological sense.[1]

Fragile but objective beauty

The Pythagoreans argued for an objectivistic account of beauty, because, in the words of Tatarkiewicz, 'beauty is constituted by harmony, harmony derives from order, order from proportion, proportion from measure and measure from number' ([15], p. 200).

According to the classic account of beauty in terms of organic unity, heavily influenced by the Pythagoreans, beauty is thus objective in a stronger sense than the phenomenological one. The general idea of which echoes can also be found in Plato (Philebus 51 C-D, Phaedrus 264 C) and Aristotle (Metaphysics 1024 a) is that beauty is a supervenient property in the sense that it depends on the internal organisation of the parts of the art work. Ideally, nothing can be added and nothing can be taken away without ruining or mutilating the art work. This conception of beauty is, though objective in a strong sense, also fragile, though the fragility is not due to the objectivity. A small change of the internal organisation of the work may ruin its beauty.

In the visual arts, the concretists from van Doesburg and Mondrian to contemporary artists like Gert Marcus are in a way close to this tradition, though the theoretical thinking underlying their conception is more subtle and sophisticated than any simple mathematical calculus.

Fractals in vogue – and in art

'Fractals' has become a word much in fashion and its use is rapidly increasing. It is used, for instance, in mathematics, geometry, artificial intelligence, chaos theory, physics, physiology, economy, psychiatry, the earth sciences and musicology [2,5,8,9,10,14]. I will not discuss here if and to what extent it is used in the same sense in all these contexts. In this brief paper I will focus only on one particular use of 'fractal' and the application to painting of the theory associated with it.

Fractals are not fragile, since they can be described, determined and produced in an objective manner. By implication, the same holds for fractal beauty. Recently, the conceptual framework of the theory of fractals has been applied to the drip paintings by Jackson Pollock in several publications by Richard Taylor and others [16,17]. Considerable claims for this approach have been made. Some of them will be examined below.

What are fractals?

Perhaps the easiest way of explaining what fractals are is to consider fractals in geometry. Since I intend to focus on the visual arts, this is also a very relevant starting point. Fractals are geometrical figures, just like circles, triangles or rectangles, but have special properties that distinguish them from other geometrical figures: self-similarity, fractional dimension, formation by iteration.

The difference between fractals and other geometrical figures has been described in somewhat different ways. Fractals are shapes that show similar features at different sizes (Damien M. Jones). A fractal is any pattern that reveals greater complexity as it is enlarged (Alan Beck). To obtain a fractal, a particular geometrical shape may be copied in different sizes. By implication, this means that a fractal geometrical shape can be subdivided in parts, each of which is an approximate copy in reduced size of the whole. In that way, within a given world, you have several similar worlds. The mathematics analysing these geometrical patterns can be quite complex, but there is no need to go into such details in this context.

Thus, if a and b are fractals, it is not enough that both a and b are geometrical figures of the same kind, say, triangles (though this is a necessary condition). The proportions of the sides of a and b also need to be related in a certain way; they have to be similar in the relevant sense. Fractals are formed by iteration, that is, by repeating the same pattern or figure over and over again. For example, if we start with a Sierpinski triangle (fig. 1) of a one-inch side, new figures can be obtained by doubling the length of the sides as many times (iteration) as you like.

Figure 1. The Sierpinski triangle

Fractals often look like objects in nature. For instance, they sometimes resemble parts of rocks or rugged and jagged coastlines, etc. In that sense many fractals, or objects that look like fractals, can be found in nature.

Fractals in Pollock

The basic contention in Richard Taylor's 1999 article [16] describing the fractals in Pollock's paintings, is that experimental observations of the paintings of Jackson Pollock reveal 'that the artist was exploring ideas in fractals and chaos before these topics entered the scientific mainstream' (p. 425).

Taylor goes on to ask whether science can be used to further our understanding of art. He argues that for the abstract paintings produced by Jackson Pollock in the 1940s and 1950s, 'scientific objectivity proves to be an essential tool for determining their fundamental content'. In his paper he attempts to analyse Pollock's patterns and show that they are fractal. In other words, they display 'the fingerprint of nature' according to Taylor.

Later, he qualifies this point somewhat by recalling that Pollock died in 1956, before the theory of chaos and fractals was described ([16], p. 428). He adds:

> It is highly unlikely, therefore, that Pollock consciously understood the fractals he was painting. Nevertheless, his introduction of fractals was deliberate. For example, the colour of the anchor layer was chosen to produce the sharpest contrast against the canvas background ... Furthermore, after the paintings were complete he would remove regions near the edge of the canvas where the pattern density was less uniform.

In Taylor's view, his analysis also has several interesting and important practical applications. For example, he writes:

> This increase in both the canvas size and the density of the trajectories was accompanied by a rise in the fractal dimension of the patterns from close to 1 to 1.72. Indeed, because the fractal dimension follows such a distinct evolution with time, fractal analysis could be employed as a quantitative, objective technique to both validate and date Pollock's drip paintings.

Pollock described nature directly, according to Taylor. 'Rather than mimicking it, he adopted the language of nature – fractals – to build his own patterns.' Taylor demonstrates this by comparing a photo of a detail of one of Pollock's paintings to 'chaotic and non-chaotic drip trajectories generated by a pendulum'. The question is what conclusions could be drawn from this, given also the problems of selection and context. We are reminded of the urgency to consider the latter by a statement quoted above from Taylor: '... after the paintings were complete he would remove regions near the edge of the canvas where the pattern density was less uniform'. Anyway, Taylor concludes, 'In doing so he [Pollock] was, in many ways, ahead of his contemporaries in art and science'.

Above I suggested that, according to Taylor, Pollock described nature in terms of fractals, 'rather than mimicking it'. But other interpretations may be possible as well. Perhaps all that Taylor wants to say or suggest is that Pollock intuitively picked up a formal relation which tends to be the result of random processes in nature, and that this relation is therefore manifested in his work. I agree that this is a possibility. But in that case, Taylor seems to have already given up his main idea that physics and science can contribute in a valuable and objective way to our understanding of the nature of Pollock's contribution to the history of art. Because, with this interpretation, he describes Pollock's works as intensional (and hence intentional) objects. This is a point I will return to.

Some theses: discussion

Even in a cursory comment on these ideas by Taylor, it is important to separate a number of different theses and discuss them separately. Suppose an event can be described in terms of a conceptual framework drawn from a certain theory. Even so, it does not follow that this theory can be used to interpret, explain or evaluate that event.

Thesis 1. (Certain formal patterns in) Pollock's paintings can be described in terms of fractals.

Let us begin at the beginning. This thesis is certainly empirically testable. The theory of fractals would then have to be applied to some of Pollock's paintings in order to see whether this theory provides a useful conceptual framework for the description of these paintings.

But it should also be remembered that a description of something in terms of concepts from a particular theory is not innocent. These concepts are theory-laden. So we must ask: How much of the theory is then more or less implicitly transferred to the domain of art and in this case to Pollock's paintings? This is an important issue. An analogy could be when concepts from one particular theory in psychoanalysis are applied to everyday human behaviour. What theoretical assumptions are then smuggled into the descriptions?

A second consideration is, of course: What conclusions can be drawn from thesis 1, if we disregard these difficulties and assume that it is correct? For example, does the following thesis follow?

Thesis 2. The artist explored the ideas associated with fractals or rather with the theory of fractals in his paintings.

In what sense did he explore these ideas, when he did not understand what he was doing, as Taylor writes in one of the passages quoted above. Perhaps Taylor means to suggest that Pollock explored these ideas without being aware of the implications, subconsciously, in a Freudian (or similar) sense?

Clearly, thesis 2 does not follow from thesis 1. The description is likely to be anachronistic. Since 'explore' refers to intentional actions, it is misleading to say that Pollock 'was exploring ideas in fractals and chaos before these topics entered the scientific mainstream'. But to avoid jumping to conclusions some alternative readings of Taylor's thesis above should be distinguished:

(A) To say that Pollock explored the ideas in fractals is to say that in his paintings he explored ideas about fractals.

(B) To say that Pollock explored the ideas in fractals is to say that in his paintings he explored ideas by means of fractals.

(C) To say that Pollock explored the ideas in fractals is to say that in his paintings he created patterns which *post factum* can be described in terms of fractals.

Interpretation (A) is hardly tenable, but what about (B)? Which ideas did he explore? The problem is that according to what Taylor admits elsewhere Pollock at this time could not have had any idea of fractals or the theory about fractals, since this theory had not been formulated at the time. After all, the most reasonable interpretation seems to be (C). It is the interpretation that is most easily defended – but also the least sensational one.

Thesis 3. The fractals allegedly found in Pollock's paintings determine the fundamental contents of the paintings.

Several questions are raised by this thesis: 'determine' in what sense? 'fundamental contents' in what sense? What view of artistic creativity is underlying this thesis? One of the reasons that this thesis is problematic is also that the authors say that it '… is highly unlikely, therefore, that Pollock consciously understood the fractals he was painting. Nevertheless, his introduction of fractals was deliberate'.

Two problems then suggest themselves at this point. The first is that it is said that Pollock introduced the fractals deliberately, but he did not understand what he was doing. In what sense is 'deliberate' used here? The second problem is raised by the statement that Pollock did not understand what he was doing, yet the fractals he painted 'determine the fundamental contents of his paintings'. The assumptions behind this conceptual framework need to be made explicit, especially the distinction between 'fundamental' and other contents.

To see the deeper problem raised by some of Taylor's claims, we have to consider some ontological questions. What is a work of art? In particular, what is the relation between artworks and real things? Suppose A and B are two identical physical objects or visual shapes, can one of them be a work of art, the other not? If so, how is the difference between them to be explained?

In re-entering this old battleground, to which Danto, Wollheim, Margolis, Jerry Levinson, Gregory Currie, and many others have contributed [3, 11,12,18] recently, we can easily get lost. If artworks are intentional objects, action types or anyway something distinct from physical objects, we need only focus on the relevance of this to the various descriptive, interpretative and evaluative theses singled out above.

Suppose physical objects and artworks ontologically speaking are quite distinct, and that fractals are (parts of) physical objects, or the theory of fractals offers one out of several possible ways of describing physical (but not intentional) objects. Then it would seem that fractals are quite irrelevant to anything that can be said about art works.

But suppose physical objects are parts of art works (or that works of art are embodied in physical objects, as Margolis has argued [12]). Then a description of the physical objects in terms of fractals would be relevant to partial description of the work of art. But what follows concerning the relevance of such a description to the determination of the contents, fundamental, symbolic or other, of an art work? Very little, if anything at all.

If art works are intentional objects, or if art works are like persons or like the utterances of persons, such a description is as irrelevant as any description of the physical script (like the size of dots, the length of lines, the shapes of curves, etc.) to anyone trying to capture the intention or meaning, open or latent, by what is said, or is trying to understand the illocutionary or perlocutionary acts performed by uttering certain words, to use Austin's terminology.

Thus, there are many well-established senses of the key terms above such that thesis 3 follows neither from thesis 2, nor from thesis 1, nor from theses 1 and 2 combined.

Thesis 4. The occurrences or uses of fractals explain why we like Pollock's paintings, why Pollock became a star of the art scene (as if critics like Clement Greenberg, galleries, curators, art collectors, and skilful marketing had nothing to do with it, nor friendship with influential people in the art world).

Is there any empirical evidence to back up this claim? Not in the article, but can it be found elsewhere – and what would it look like? At most it could be argued that the presence of what we now may describe as fractals in Pollock's works can help to explain – along with many other things – why we like Pollock's paintings and why he became a star on the art scene. Fractals certainly by themselves are not good-making properties, especially not if they are everywhere, as has been recently claimed [1].

Since originality is an important value in our art culture, drip paintings would not be met with much enthusiasm by art critics today, and drip paintings 50 years ago would not be comprehensible. The physical shape of the fractals alone, beautiful though they may be, does not explain why Pollock's paintings made such an impact on the art scene; other contemporary painters, like Barnett Newman, who also became stars, painted quite differently. To understand what happened, we also have to consider which norms Pollock broke deliberately, what he wanted to achieve by doing that, and so forth.

Thesis 5. The occurrences of fractals in a painting can be used to validate Pollock's paintings.

The first reaction to this contention by Taylor is perhaps: as if they were not valid without his ideas about fractals? But thesis 5 can be interpreted in several ways. First, 'validate' may be taken to have nothing to do with artistic quality at all but simply means 'date and test the genuineness of'. In view of many forgeries and the high prices for a Pollock drip painting this is a genuine concern. But is the thesis true when interpreted in this way?

It depends on whether it is understood in a strong or in a weaker way. Taken in the strong sense, the thesis above claims that this technique (analysis of fractals) can be used to date and test the genuineness of any Pollock painting alone. This is hardly likely to be true. This claim presupposes that the artist never returned to older ways of painting, but it seems many painters do this occasionally. So how do we know, without begging the issue at stake, that a particular undated painting fits into the pattern established by analysing already dated paintings with certainty?

The gist of the matter is simply this. If the fractal dimension in Pollock's work changes over time, suspected forgeries can be tested against this information. The problem is only that to test a suspected forgery x against the fractal dimension in the series a, b, c, d, ..., of paintings by Pollock, we must first have established the chronological order of these *other* paintings beyond reasonable doubt. If this could be done, and if the series includes all or nearly all of Pollock's works except the contested x, thesis 5 is reasonable; if not, there is a problem.[2]

A weaker and more reasonable position is to say that this technique can, if combined with others, be used to date and test the genuineness of any Pollock painting.

> *Thesis 6.* The fact – if it is a fact – that Pollock's paintings can be described as containing fractals – shows that he was ahead of his contemporaries in art and science and increases the artistic value of his paintings, makes them more interesting aesthetically, artistically and/or economically.

What is meant by 'ahead of his contemporaries in science'? As already mentioned, Taylor has written that it 'is highly unlikely, therefore, that Pollock consciously understood the fractals he was painting'. It is then not easy to understand what is meant by saying that Pollock was ahead of his contemporaries in science.

The tacit implication of 'ahead of his contemporaries in art' is that Pollock's painting have greater artistic or aesthetic value than many, or most, paintings of his contemporary colleagues.[3] To be ahead of one's contemporaries is to be laudable, particularly in view of the high value attached to originality in our culture since the late eighteenth century [6, chapter 2]. He was in one sense obviously ahead of his contemporaries in art. But the precise relations between the notions of fractals and artistic and aesthetic value are not even touched upon by Taylor.

Thus, even if fractals were relevant to understand the meaning and significance of art works, which they are not in my view, they are not relevant to a discussion of the artistic or economic value of art works.

Further problems

There are fractal patterns of different types. Some of the best-known ones include the Peano curve, the Sierpinski triangle, the Koch edge, the Lorence attractor

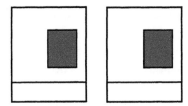

*Figure 2. Could one of these identical patterns be a work of art,
and the other not? If so, how is the difference to be explained?*

and the dragon curve. Pollock's drip patterns look different from all of these.[4] But I will not here question the empirical assumption that these patterns really are fractal – that is, that they satisfy the requirements any fractal pattern has to satisfy. Thus I shall assume that thesis 1 above is essentially correct. However, apart from the problem that most of the theses discussed above maintained by Taylor do not follow from his starting point (thesis 1), that there may be some doubt also about this thesis, and that the empirical evidence for the other theses is rather thin, there are other problems.

Some other objections could be stated as follows, if I may be allowed to digress for a moment to consider other art forms. Fractal music is sometimes characterised as a result of a recursive process where an algorithm is applied multiple times to process its previous output. In a wider perspective all musical forms, both at micro and macro level can be modelled with this process. It is not obvious that this mechanic repetition can be found in Pollock's paintings. Perhaps they are fractal-like rather than containing fractals in the strict sense?

Even if in a certain sense it may be said that the patterns in Pollock's drip paintings are produced at random, which could be debated, the artist afterwards decides whether to use the result or throw it away, whether to exhibit it or destroy it. Moreover, even if the patterns are produced at random, the artist chooses the colours, the order in which they are applied, and the areas of the canvas onto which they are applied – and this choice is not explained by the theory of fractals. To defend Taylor's theory it has to be made explicit that his theory about Pollock's painting certainly does not say everything that is worth saying about these paintings. In fact, is adds very little to that which is worth saying about Pollock's art.[5]

That this is so can be seen by the obvious fact that the theory of fractals can be applied equally well (or equally poorly) to pictures in black and white and to pictures in colours. In other words, it makes no difference to the theory when a fractal analysis of a painting is to be made, if it is a black-and-white picture or a picture in full colours. Another limitation is that this approach disregards the aesthetic and other qualities of the colours used.

Moreover, a random procedure for dripping paint on a canvas or a painting machine does not choose when to stop. But Pollock did. In other words, art is also – though not exclusively – intentional action. What is the point of describing a painting by Pollock – or by anyone else – in terms of the 'language' of nature, whatever that means? In what sense is this a 'language'? What can be asserted or denied by this language? What has been added to our understanding of Pollock's distinct contribution to art? Perhaps the physical structure of Pollock's paintings can be described in this way. But so what?

The originality and attraction of Pollock's paintings can be, and has been, described in many ways. Arthur Danto, for example, underlines 'the urgency, energy, spontaneity that Pollock got into his painting' [4]. This is very different from the metaphor 'the language of nature'. Danto's choice of words suggests that in his view what Pollock did was at least to some extent intentional actions, not just something produced at random.

This assumption is in line with a distinction Danto makes later in his book between manifestations and expressions [4]. He writes: 'each of us, in seeking to define the contours of the Other, must learn to discriminate in this way between what anyone might call "expressions" from what I shall infelicitously call "manifestations"' (p. 55).

One of the problems with the fractal analysis of Pollock's paintings is that it adds very little to these central questions about Pollock's art: What did he want to say or suggest by departing from his predecessors in the way he did?

Concluding remarks

If fractals are everywhere, as Bamsley has claimed [1], then the statement that they are to be found in art is not very informative. If anything is art, it is true that something is art. But if anything is art, there is nothing particular about art. In that sense it can also be said that if anything is art, nothing is art. If the notion of fractals is to have any significant application in art, we need to be able to contrast it with something.

Notes

[1] I want to thank my friend and former student Dr. Björn Petersson for helpful comments on an earlier version of this paper.

[2] Cf. the analogous problem of dating the Platonic dialogues on the basis of stylistic features or on the relation between Socrates and the narrator in these dialogues.

[3] There are many kinds of values that can be exemplified in works of art, such as antiquarian, personal, political – in addition to the obvious candidates economic, aesthetic and artistic values. In the literature, the distinctions between these different kinds of value have been drawn in several ways.

4   The theory of fractals is currently a hot topic, and my references represent just a small sample of the literature available. Much information on fractals, including fractal art galleries, is currently available on the Internet.

5   Even if the tone of this paper is critical, Taylor and his collaborators deserve credit for the ingenuous experiments set up to study the similarities and differences between chaotic and non-chaotic drip trajectories generated by a pendulum.

References

[1]   Bamsley, MF. *Fractals Everywhere* (New York: M Kaufmann, 2000).

[2]   Briggs, J. *Fractals: the Patterns of Chaos* (New York: Simon & Schuster, 1992).

[3]   Danto, A. *The Transfiguration of the Commonplace* (Cambridge: Harvard University press, 1981).

[4]   Danto, A. *Beyond the Brillo Box* (Berkeley and Los Angeles: University of California Press, 1992).

[5]   Gouyet, J. *Physics and Fractal Structures* (New York: Springer, 1996).

[6]   Hermerén, G. *Aspects of Aesthetics* (Lund: Gleeerup, 1983 (Acta LXXVII. Royal Society of Letters at Lund).

[7]   Hermerén, G. *The Nature of Aesthetic Qualities* (Lund: Lund University Press, 1988).

[8]   Lapidus, ML. *Fractal Geometry and Number theory* (Boston: Birkhäuser, 2000).

[9]   Korvin, G. *Fractal Models in the Earth Sciences* (Amsterdam: Elsevier, 1992).

[10] Mandelbrot, BB. *The Fractal Geometry of Nature* (New York: W H Freeman, (1977) 1984).

[11] Margolis, J. *Art and Philosophy. Conceptual Issues in Aesthetics* (Atlantic Highlands, N.J.: Humanities Press, 1980).

[12] Margolis, J. *Culture and Cultural Entities* (Boston: Reidel, 1984).

[13] Persson, I. *Sensational Beauty. In: Understanding the Arts*, edited by J. Emt and G. Hermerén (Lund: Lund University Press, 1992): 47–61.

[14] Solomon, L. *The Fractal Nature of Music* (Tuczon: Solomon, 1998).

[15] Tatarkiewicz, W. *A History of Six Ideas. An Essay in Aesthetics* (Warszawa: PWN & The Hague, Boston, London: Martinus Nijhoff, 1980).

[16] Taylor, RP, Micolich, AP and Jonas, D. 1999, 'Fractal analysis of Pollock's drip paintings', *Nature* 399:422.

[17] Taylor, RP. 'Splashdown', *New Scientist* 25 July 1998:30–31.

[18] Wollheim, R. *Art and Its Objects*. Second edition (Cambridge: Cambridge University Press, 1980).